GOD-MADE MILLIONAIRE

GOD-MADE MILLIONAIRE

Creating Wealth as an Emerging Entrepreneur

LETITIA HARRIS

CHRISTIAN-PRENEUR QUICK START GUIDE

TRUE DIRECTIONS
AN AFFILIATE OF TARCHER BOOKS

iUniverse®

GOD-MADE MILLIONAIRE
CREATING WEALTH AS AN EMERGING ENTREPRENEUR

All Scripture quotations, unless otherwise indicated, are taken from the MSG, *The Message*, Copyright © 1993, 1994, 1995, 1996, 2000, 2001, 2002. Used by permission of NavPress Publishing Group.

Holy Bible: King James Version. Public Domain, 1987. *BibleGateway.com.* The Zondervan Corporation, L.L.C.

Scripture quotations marked (NLT) are taken from the Holy Bible, *New Living Translation*, copyright © 1996, 2004, 2007 by Tyndale House Foundation. Used by permission of Tyndale House Publishers, Inc., Carol Stream, Illinois 60188. All rights reserved.

"Scripture quotations taken from the New American Standard Bible®, Copyright © 1960, 1962, 1963, 1968, 1971, 1972, 1973, 1975, 1977, 1995 by The Lockman Foundation. Used by permission." (www.Lockman.org)

iUniverse books may be ordered through booksellers or by contacting:
iUniverse
1663 Liberty Drive
Bloomington, IN 47403
www.iuniverse.com
1-800-Authors (1-800-288-4677)

Because of the dynamic nature of the Internet, any web addresses or links contained in this book may have changed since publication and may no longer be valid. The views expressed in this work are solely those of the author and do not necessarily reflect the views of the publisher, and the publisher hereby disclaims any responsibility for them.

Any people depicted in stock imagery provided by Thinkstock are models, and such images are being used for illustrative purposes only. Certain stock imagery © Thinkstock.

ISBN: 978-1-4917-6510-4 (sc)
ISBN: 978-1-4917-6509-8 (e)

Print information available on the last page.

iUniverse rev. date: 10/20/2015

Contents

Preface vii

Acknowledgments xi

Introduction xv

Chapter 1   Mind, Money & Spirit 1

Chapter 2   Preparation to Receive Wealth from God 9

Chapter 3   Who Am I *Really*? 33

Chapter 4   The Unfolding of Divine Vision 59

Chapter 5   Why Most Businesses Fail 81

Chapter 6   Taking Your Rightful Place 101

Chapter 7   Your Million-Dollar Idea Starts Now! 115

Chapter 8   Creating Your Million-Dollar Plan 137

Chapter 9   Your Business Breakthrough 153

Chapter 10   God-made Millionaire Money Mindset 163

Chapter 11 Getting Supernatural and Personal Mentorship 191

Chapter 12 Organization– A Key to Wealth. 205

Chapter 13 Building Your Online Global Presence. 219

Chapter 14 Social Networking – Creating Relationships 245

Chapter 15 Sharing Your Wealth – The Great Responsibility 281

Appendix A – Funding For Women 299

Appendix B – SEO Tools Resources 300

Appendix C – Did you know the following are Christian
              businesses?. 301

Appendix D – Business Affirmations. .302

References 305

About the Author 309

Preface *(My Story)*

I have always been fascinated with being in control of my own finances. I grew up being the poster child for what not to do when it came to money. I struggled for years to understand why anyone would want to live paycheck to paycheck like I had been for so long. I always wanted to have enough money and freedom to go, be and do whatever I felt like doing. I, also, understood, though, I had to work for it. I was never afraid of working but it was often unfulfilling. I jumped from one job to another looking for the next big check. I set out to find an occupation that would make me happy and pay me well. I had often admired my father for leaving his 9 to 5 to pursue his entrepreneurial dream. God had given me a dream of success, too, earlier in my life but it never seemed to be something I knew how to make happen. Yet I would soon find out. This feeling is what lead me to my entrepreneurial journey and this book called "God-made Millionaire – Creating Wealth as an Emerging Entrepreneur.

One day I was hit with the entrepreneurial bug and off I went. I started several business ventures, but for some reason success kept escaping me. I often failed my way through life, vacillating between corporate America and the entrepreneurial dream. At times, I didn't have access to money, relationships, or the knowledge to know how to get my business off the ground. But like I said, I was never afraid to work. I would pick a business, find wholesalers, and get started, not realizing there were pockets of missing information that would soon cause me to fail. Regardless, I still managed to start several businesses that earned me good money. I owned two retail stores, a boutique for women and a kid's clothing and accessory store. I ran an online eBay kid's shoe store in which I learned the true meaning of customer service. I loved it! I ran a very successful real estate investment company for years and was also a realtor. Even with these ventures, I had my share of failures that made me want to quit at times, but I never gave up.

One of these business ventures ended up being more successful than any of the others, and that was my real estate investment company where I bought and sold real estate, enjoying its lucrative returns. I had finally found my financial place of bliss. I was earning tens of thousands of dollars on many transactions. I was in heaven ... so I thought. It wasn't until the bottom fell out of the real estate market that I realized that earning a six-figure income with no money-management skills and a limited sense of business would lead me to my ruins. What I was headed for was the biggest financial disaster in my life. I lost it all! Our family faced foreclosure and homelessness, my car was repossessed, and our checking accounts were being seized by bill collectors to get their money. I was forced to seek help in a hurry, and this is where I gave my life back to Christ. I had given my life to Christ in high school but not to the extent where I depended on Him for guidance.

It was the weirdest thing because since I had started these various businesses and had accumulated these material possessions that represented success, I started attracting people who wanted to start a business. They didn't know about the devastating events that had just occurred, and I was able to help them. Friends and acquaintances would call me, I would offer advice and strategies to try, and they would work. So I began studying as much as I could about starting and building a business. I started following people that were doing what I wanted to do and applying the principles through study, attending events and practice. And don't forget—I was filled with knowledge of what "not" to do to avoid failure. Little did I know that God had taken over my life to show me what the true meaning of having wealth was all about.

I eventually started my own little coaching practice to put my experience and knowledge to work on a grander scale. I enjoyed it, and my students were seeing changes in themselves, which carried over into their businesses. They would say that God's voice was louder now than it ever was before with clearer directions on steps they should take. Who would have thought that my failures would be the catalyst for my clients' and students' successes? I knew I had found my purpose in the heartfelt passion of being an entrepreneurial coach, trainer, and mentor to emerging entrepreneurs, which I hope to spread worldwide. This chain of events is what led to the contents of this book.

Acknowledgments

I thank God for not letting me go while I strived to understand who I was and why I was created. Through my fight to find out the truth about purpose and the Kingdom of God, I found a loving God that always has His children at the forefront of His mind.

I want to thank my wonderful and insanely committed husband, Drew, who never gave up on me. You allowed me to experiment with life and finances until I found my rightful path. Thanks for the sacrifices you made to allow this book to be completed amongst my many other endeavors. I want to thank my children, Deja and Christian, who unknowingly allowed their mom years to sit at the feet of Jesus to learn all I could. It's to make a better life for you all, my loves.

I thank my loving parents, Joe and Carolyn, who always thought I was different but could never really put their finger on it. I always went left when you thought I should have gone right. Mom, thanks for leading me back to God and having God's heart and mercy toward anyone you meet. Dad, thanks for paving the way for my entrepreneurial desires because I am following in your footsteps. You set the example of what will and determination can do for a person who desires to succeed to leave a legacy. Without you both, I would not be here today to make a difference in the lives of others. I love you!

I want to thank my Auntie June for being my personal banker, at times, for some of my failed and most promising ventures whenever I knew *this* was the one. Auntie, you gave me the ability to go into my virtual lab to research and come out with so many "lessons learned" in business. You never asked me too many questions but instead agreed to help me. Every emerging entrepreneur needs someone like you in their corner. You don't know how much that meant to me and still does today because you are now a major contributor to the lessons learned that I can now pass on to others. Much love to you!

I want to thank my sister in Christ, Beverly. God dropped you in my path and made you my friend for life! You have been my anchor through my turbulent and "why me" moments in time. I have called you on many, many, many occasions to ask you to pray for me and rejoice with me, and you indeed loved and labored in the spirit with me. Everyone needs an intercessor, and I'm glad your gifting is being shared with me. Praise God for you!

I want to say thank you to family members—you know who you are—that helped me along the way by checking on me during times I couldn't explain my life. You continued to love me in spite of my insecurities and faults, and to you I say thank you!

To Pastor Charles E Nesbitt Jr. who put the beautiful songs of praise and worship into my life. Thank you. Under your auspice is where God started my reunion with Him and His word. Those anointed songs still ring free in my heart today. Whenever I feel discouraged, disappointed, or just want to show God how much I love Him, those songs break out in me.

To Pastors Dr. Creflo A. Dollar and Taffi Dollar who taught me how to walk in the spirit! When I first found out about your church, I knew it was for me. So many opinions tried to persuade me otherwise. When I walked in your church, there was a feeling that I had never felt before, and I will never forget it. I couldn't explain it, but I knew I had to be a part of whatever it was that was going on there. I spent three years under your guidance, and I have never looked back. You were a launching pad to even greater things that lay ahead for me. I found the "essence" of who I was in Christ. Thank you so much!

To my loving pastor, TD Jakes and First Lady Serita Jakes, thank you so much for your dedication to being mighty vessels of God. Under your parish, I have been elevated to new levels through the mind of Christ. Your masterful gifts have given new meaning to the existence of God and His Kingdom business. I continue to be amazed at how God speaks such divine instructions through you, which have been my shining light on my journey to purpose.

God Bless You All!

Introduction

This book is my effort to help Christian believers start a business using biblical and intellectual principles that God revealed to me on my journey. *God-made Millionaire* stemmed from my coaching private clients and volunteering as a facilitator for the YW of Dallas, a national non-profit organization that helps women with financial literacy. I realized that aspiring entrepreneurs had different backgrounds, resources, and experiences that gave them the confidence to start a business. But what made the coaching and teaching sometimes difficult for me, and possibly for the students, is the fact that there wasn't one particular guide I could use as a prerequisite to our sessions. It would have been easier to refer them to a particular chapter or page if I felt prework should be completed first.

This resource would be a quick-start training guide that could help new entrepreneurs see results in a shorter period of time, whether on their own or coupled with our sessions. Most people, Christian or not, start a business without considering the cost or knowing what it really takes to make it.

I believed that if they each were exposed to the foundational principles of starting a business, there wouldn't be so many failures—there would be more successes. This resource book would gauge if the desire to run a business was coming from a true place of passion or a place of selfishness for monetary gain.

More people in the world than you and I could ever imagine grow up with the dream of running their own company. But most never achieve this noble act because either they don't know how to overcome the obstacles set before them or they misinterpret the fact that they need more resources. Emerging entrepreneurs have been led to believe that as long as they have a good idea it will work. This is true, but only to a certain extent. An idea is one way to get started, but is it the most effective for forging full speed ahead? The vast majority of start-up entrepreneurs quit without knowing that if they had only taken the time to put their ideas down on paper and measured their progress, there would have been a higher chance of success.

"There's really no difference between biblical principles and business principles," Cathy Truett said at one of his Chick-fil-A restaurant openings, according to Business Insider.

Whatever practices you set up for your business should be in alignment with biblical principles. Throughout the Bible you will see how God operates in perfect timing, wisdom, and stature in everything He does. He dispenses only the best to His people. Therefore, we should practice the principles and disciplines that He has taught over the ages in order to get the calculated results that we want to achieve today. To become a well-known company or brand, one has to deliver excellence along with business practices that create a system that keeps your customers coming back.

Now, I am not telling you that there is an *exact* science for building a business because this would be far from the truth. As you'll soon find out, *you are the business* and *your business will be a reflection of you.* More so than you know, you have been created to do something that only you can do. With the right foundation, your journey to a profitable company, as with anything you put your hands to do, will prosper.

There are only two reasons why you don't have wealth today. Either you don't know the principles of wealth or you are not operating wisely within them. In this book, I will delve into some business principles that can help to move you along. The Bible mentions that if any person lacks wisdom and you want it, then just ask God for it. Oftentimes, we go through life not knowing what we *don't know* until our eyes are opened to new perspectives.

There are so many get-rich quick offerings for people who desire to get out of the rat race of life. We all long for ways to do more, to be more, and to have more. We want the freedom that money can afford us. But it doesn't start with finding out *how* to get more money. It starts with how to build wealth within so that you can enjoy the benefits of it in the world. Once you learn to build wealth within you, you will never be without.

You have a responsibility to create jobs, to teach and train others to be leaders, to give to charities and causes that can make this world a better place. You don't have to try to cure all the problems of the world, but you can take on one corner that brings about a necessary change.

This book is a merging of two worlds, the spiritual and the natural (reality). In order to have long-lasting wealth, you must understand how to utilize resources from both worlds. The promises of God for your business are too big to not involve Him in the process. Some people feel that God and business don't mix, but this is far from the truth! Many Christians struggle with loving God and believing He can give them a far greater life than they ever imagined for themselves. But in order to receive all God has for you, you must believe that He is who He says He is … and that He can help you get there! FAITH plays a major part in the grand scheme of your success. But there is still work to be done, which is to combine intellect, instinct, gifts, skills, and talent with the spiritual gifts and power of God.

There will be references to several scriptures because I want to show where I am getting the information I am sharing with you. I want you to become accustomed to *trusting* in what He says and *experiencing* what

He wants to do for you. The only way to know anyone is to spend time with them. This includes God. Eventually, you will come to experience the inner workings of God through His biblical principles and mostly His love. If you believe that actions truly do speak louder than words, then get ready because God's actions in your life will definitely get you moving. I can't stress this point enough: you must believe there is a better life beyond where you stand today, and in order to receive it, you must change the way you think.

I believe The Father, The Son, and The Holy Spirit form what is called The Trinity—God's presence in three separate beings that details Christianity. The Holy Spirit of God comes to us as a result of Jesus' dying for our sins, rising on the third day, and sitting now at the right hand of God. I use various interpretations of the scripture, but mostly The Message Bible (unless otherwise noted) throughout this book to explain in everyday language the scriptures for better clarification.

Now, to move forward with ease, you must believe that God wants you to be wealthy! It's often hard for a Christian to believe that having wealth (which could include millions) and being spiritual are still considered *blessed to be a blessing*. Some people think of financial prosperity and spirituality as rivals, like mixing oil and water. God loves you and will teach and train you to have and hold onto whatever He has for you. He wants you to be a co-creator of your life and business with Him.

There are many Christian business books out there, but none have explained HOW to build a relationship with God, to hear His voice and gain calculated moves in business along with technical guidance. This is all broken down into its simplest form so that you can come back to any chapter at any time for that specialized understanding. This book contains resources, tips, strategies, and God-moments that will empower you, inspire you, and motivate you to be all you can be.

There are techie strategies that can be implemented immediately for quick social media results. If you apply any of the information in this book, you will be better equipped than before you started reading it. Now, go get your blessings!

How to use this book

Chapters 1-3: Use these chapters to examine your life to make sure your actions and mindset are in alignment with Christ. If they are not, you may want to spend a little time dealing with those things that can prohibit your progress. The easiest way is to commit them to God so that He can help you conquer particular areas. These chapters can be used when you're not feeling your strongest. *Please don't skip.*

Chapters 4-5: These chapters check the stability of your vision. If you are struggling with it, you can find ideas here that can help bring clarity. *Please don't skip.*

Chapters 6-15: Since every emerging entrepreneur begins their journey at a different place in time due to their past experiences, knowledge, money, and relationships, these chapters are necessary to acquaint the starting business owner with resources and information that can cut one's learning curve for quicker results.

Note: I would suggest revisiting any chapter that you feel is necessary at any point during your business-building process. You may not need everything in these chapters now, but the information can be priceless later as well.

Mind, Money & Spirit

Beloved, I wish above all things that thou would prosper (the mind) and be in health (the body) even as thy soul prospers (spirit). ~3 Jn 1:2

Wealth in the hands of a fool can only make one a bigger fool. Wealth in the hands of a person that seeks to make the world a better place is the answer to many of man's problems. This is why God does not mind you being prosperous. He doesn't even mind you being a millionaire or a billionaire. He wants you to have peace while gaining the mindset to prosper at whatever you put your hands to do. God knows that money can change one person, a group, a nation, or the world if used to spread wisdom, love, and empowerment to others.

So what does a God-made millionaire look like? You don't hear that term being tossed around much, do you? There are more God-made millionaires in the world than you will ever know, partially because some of them don't think it makes much of a difference to broadcast it. They just want to do what is right, in the sight of God, and run a successful company. Now, there are God-made millionaires and self-made millionaires operating on the same plane but existing in two different worlds, mentally. Let me explain.

The difference between a *God-made* millionaire and a *self-made* millionaire is that God is your source rather than your own intellect (mind) being your total source. Self-made millionaires tend to lean more toward fulfilling their egos than anything else. There is no real sustenance behind the glory they receive for their wealth. People believe that you have to be exceptionally smart to build a thriving, successful company. If their wealth is attributed to all the things they have accomplished through all their hard work and intellect, then this would mean that you would have to have a very high IQ. As we all know, everyone is not born with the same size brain to become an Einstein, Freud, or even Bill Gates or Warren Buffet. But God can give you one idea that can take you straight to the top of the financial and influential charts, and this is what levels the playing field.

In life and business, to depend on God is to find the highest form of you and to gain exponential wealth—emotionally, spiritually, financially, and physically—to serve your highest good. In my opinion, a God-made millionaire is one who lives a *whole* life. They are fulfilled in mind, body, and spirit along with their finances. When trouble comes, they know where to find their strength, their power, and their wisdom to overcome any situation. They live and lack nothing because they find everything they need in living through a God-conscious life.

There are wealthy people who live an internally unhealthy and unhappy life. You hear of movie stars, musicians, athletes, and even politicians who have secret, dark lives, and no one ever suspects it. They have all the external glories but no internal glory to give them the fulfilled life they want. They are always feeling that something is missing and not quite right. Some are constantly wondering if they are being loved for their money or for them as a person. The missing part is finding out *who* they really are and not the person everyone else wants or thinks them to be. This makes for a life of continual performances.

In the Book of Matthew, Jesus spoke of the young, rich ruler who had everything and wanted to know what he could do to have eternal life. Jesus told of commandments such as, *"Don't murder, don't commit adultery, don't steal, don't lie, honor your father and mother, and love your neighbor as you do yourself."* The rich, young ruler said, "I have done all that, so now what?" Jesus told him to go and sell everything he had and give it to the poor and then to follow Him. Of course this depressed him. (*Hint*: Never get attached to anything that can be here today and gone tomorrow.) This is the last thing that the young, rich ruler wanted to hear because he knew he couldn't bear life without his material possessions. Jesus looked at him as he walked away in despair and said to His disciples around Him, *"Do you have any idea how difficult it is for the rich to enter God's kingdom? Let me tell you, it's easier to gallop a camel through a needle's eye than for the rich to enter God's kingdom."*

Now, before you start to think negatively about being rich, just know that the only reason it will be hard is that some who are rich do not know Jesus (The Divine) and will find themselves living a life of sporadic success in happiness, health, finances, peace, relationships, and even power. Nothing is guaranteed if there is nothing there with sustenance to maintain it. Their kingdom is built on faulty ground (material possessions) with no indication or guarantee on how to prevent it from crumbling one day. Because of this, there is room for things such as depression, loneliness, and a lack of trust in others, which can cause them to feel like their lives are not worth living. They may even be driven to chemical derivatives for relief instead of Jesus, who gives life. But those who have gone through tough times and lack have had a much better opportunity to experience God in the highest form because of their faith. I am not bashing rich or wealthy people because I consider myself one, in the highest sense. Just know that wealthy people with the right heart are doing magnificent things in the world—just as you will too!

Let me ask this: Have you ever heard someone say, "I am a self-made millionaire"? Check out what the word **self-made** means according to the dictionary. Random House Dictionary says *self-made* means **"having succeeded in life unaided; made by oneself."** The World Dictionary says it means, **"having achieved wealth, status, etc., by one's own efforts."**

Nowhere do these definitions mention the word "God." For those who declare to the world that they are *self-made millionaires*, I want to show you why this is not completely the truth. This is not to condemn those who have made this proclamation because they may not know what they are saying because they have not experienced Christ.

For those who have given their lives to Christ, however, here are two scriptures from The Message Bible that say otherwise about their proclamation as follows:

If you start thinking to yourselves, "I did all this. And all by myself. I'm rich. It's all mine!"—well, think again. Remember that GOD, your God, gave you the strength to produce all this wealth so as to confirm the covenant that he promised to your ancestors—as it is today. ~Dt 8:17-18

In the greatest book ever written, you are told that it is God who has given you the power to get wealth. So this tells me that all those who have accumulated wealth derived it from God, whether one chooses to acknowledge Him or not.

God claims Earth and everything in it, God claims World and all who live in it, He build on Ocean foundations, laid it out on River girders. ~Ps 24:1-2

Some people were given this gift or natural talent and instinct for accumulating wealth from birth. Some have been given this knowledge through training, skills, and from experience. Either way, it originated from God, The Source, because He owns it all! Just know God wants you to have wealth and to enjoy every bit of your life, as you'll find throughout the chapters.

Becoming a God-made millionaire is the practice of allowing God to direct your steps through the power of His Holy Spirit, to accumulate the true, long-lasting wealth you desire. *Anyone* can become rich with calculated steps and risks, whether with good or bad motives. But the challenge is being able to keep money or channel money to its highest and best use without becoming attached to it. Money in the hands of the ill-intentioned or financially inept person will lead to someone's destruction.

For example, you've seen people who lost money on Wall Street and committed suicide because they couldn't handle the loss. What about the woman who marries a wealthy man, but he decides he wants a divorce and she doesn't? He hires a hit man to kill her because he doesn't want to share his wealth with her. What about the lottery winner who was never taught how to handle money or invest it for continuous growth? They eventually lose it all, including their relationships with family or friends, plus that which they had *before* they won the money.

God loves you so much that He does not want wealth to destroy you. He knows that money will only magnify the good or bad qualities you already possess. In order to bring out the better qualities, you must learn the basis for accumulating wealth. You've heard people say, "It feels like I have holes in my pocket when it comes to having money." This is because they have not been taught *how* to handle money. One key thing you need to know about money is that if you do not put it to work, it will flow from you and into the hands of someone who will. And if you love your money so much that you hold onto it and hesitate to let it go, you will cut off the flow of it into your life.

Here's what the Bible says about the *love* of money, which is the *wrong* relationship with money. The *love of money* is to have it rule over you with wrong motives. Instead, you should be ruling over it with good motives to impact not just your life but the lives of others. God's Kingdom operates with unselfish motives.

But those who crave to be rich fall into temptation and a snare and into many foolish (useless, godless) and hurtful desires that plunge men into ruin and destruction and miserable perishing.

For the love of money is a root of all evils; it is through this craving that some have been led astray and have wandered from the faith and pierced themselves through with many acute [mental] pangs. ~1 Tim 6:9-10

If you have not yet thought of ways that you can impact the world with your God-made millions, I suggest you make a list. This will prove that your motives are not selfish. Your list doesn't have to be enormous, but deciding to give to one cause can make all the difference in the world. Because of your goodness, a legacy is born, one that can be passed down from generation to generation. How would that make you feel? If you proceed with the desire to build a multimillion-dollar business with wrong or undefined monetary motives, you are setting yourself up for disappointments and even some uncalled-for failures.

It all really boils down to the idea that the wealth you seek should be used for the good of the Kingdom of God. He is in the business of enhancing lives, through you! He understands that you have needs and that you have a big vision. Money is to be accumulated in order that you might enlighten others to the Love of God, through your financial efforts. Keep in mind, God will show you how to have more than enough to spend on yourself and enough to spread amongst those He places in your heart to serve.

If you are not a part of the Kingdom of God or if you are just an observer, this may be turning you off because you just wanted to know how this God can get you millions. But I do want you to know that everything that is written in this book is available to you. As you continue to read through, you will experience the opportunity to get to know more about the Kingdom of God *and* your business. This is a sample of what is available to you, right now, from God, if you want it.

"I know what I'm doing. I have it all planned out—plans to take care of you, not abandon you, plans to give you the future you hope for." ~Jer 29:11

God has been waiting to pour out His Spirit on you so that you can have a life that is more fulfilling, hopeful, and directive. You won't have to fumble around in life trying to figure out how to do this or get out or around that. He created you; therefore He knows how to care for you.

So, if you are thinking about starting a business or are struggling in your business, then help is here. God not only can help you achieve monetary wealth, but He can also help you achieve whatever you need in your life where fulfilment is not complete. It is often said that if the mind, body, and soul are not in divine unison with the spirit, there is always an unbalanced life to follow. I pray that God will open your spiritual eyes of understanding so that you can see the vastness of riches that He is waiting to pour out upon your life.

Chapter 1 – God-made Millionaire Exercise

1. Write down *why* you want to be a God-made millionaire. List at least three reasons.

2. Examine whether your reasons benefit you or other people. Make changes if needed.

Preparation to Receive Wealth from God

"If God gives such attention to the appearance of wildflowers— most of which are never even seen—don't you think he'll attend to you, take pride in you, do his best for you? What I'm trying to do here is to get you to relax, to not be so preoccupied with getting, so you can respond to God's giving. People who don't know God and the way he works fuss over these things, but you know both God and how he works. Steep (saturate) your life in God-reality, God-initiative, God-provisions. Don't worry about missing out. You'll find all your everyday human concerns will be met. –Mt 6:30-35

For any changes to take place in your life, you must acknowledge that you are *open to receive*. A person with a closed mind will never see the ways or the creations of God. No man has ever obtained spiritual consciousness without seeking it. Don't just accept your old ways of thinking and what you may have been taught in the past. In Matthew, Jesus talks about coming to Him as a child comes to a parent. A child seeks the protection and provision of an adult because they are not able to care for all their own needs. This is the belief and trust that God wants you to have in Him.

A child can hold a dream, a thought, and a memory until it has not been cancelled out by life's limited beliefs or truths given by those they trust. Life is so much more fun when you are open to possibilities. I really think this is why people don't live the lives they so desperately seek to live—they won't let go. A child's mind is fertile ground for the planting of any seeds (thoughts) put there. And those seeds grow by watering them with words of wisdom and loving on them until the right values of life bring forth the proper perceptions to help them find their way. What I am suggesting is to open your mind to receive a new seed that will bring forth a harvest that even the greatest farmer could never have imagined!

God has made it possible for people all over the world to communicate with Him. He has sent forth His will, His Love, and His Son so that we can all come to Him with any concerns that we possess. According to the scripture above, God says to relax, to rest and let Him provide for you. He says that all those things of life that you need and want can be met by Him. Now who do you know that can actually say something like that and *mean it*? Let alone *do it*? And it does not mean that you just sit back and do nothing. You must put your beliefs into actionable steps.

To obtain these benefits, you must first become part of God's family, if you are not already. You might be asking, "How do I know if I am part of God's family?" or "How do I become part of His family?" I am glad you asked.

I am going to give you the shorter version of how you can become part of God's family. Allow me to tell you about some of the benefits of entering into The Kingdom of God. We all want benefits, don't we? I will share here only a few, but believe me—there are far more than I could ever know or give you.

Being part of God's family is like none other. It's a family in which words can be exchanged and they will never become lies, with Him. It's a family where provisions will be given before you even speak a word, such as just having a thought. It's a family in which you are accepted just as you are with your faults and imperfections. You will not be judged by your past failures and erroneous acts that you think can never be erased. It is a family and world in which impossibilities become possibilities. It's where your most exciting life can become even greater! God does exceedingly and abundantly above all you could ever ask or think. He knows exactly what would make you happy. He takes you on a journey from being a caterpillar that emerges from its cocoon to becoming the most beautiful butterfly of its kind. The successful kind. There is only *one* you. And God created *you* for something great!

You will be taught and molded to become the best YOU that you could ever be. You will be prepared to understand how to be victorious over the situations and circumstances that enter your personal and business life, even the ones you think you can't handle. God says, ***"The person who wins out over the world's ways is simply the one who believes Jesus is the Son of God," according to 1Jn 5:4.***

You might ask, "What does all this have to do with me being a God-made millionaire?" As you may already know, starting and running a successful business is not easy. By gosh, if you are like me, it's sometimes a challenge just to run your own life! It's hard to step outside yourself and see where you are missing the boat or what to do next to bring about the financial success you desire. It's hard to see the big picture when you're in the frame. But there is a way to bring about the changes you desire. You don't have to depend on your own intellect or inferiorities to make things happen.

The Holy Spirit – God's Wealth Transfer

Since giving my life to Christ and acknowledging The Holy Spirit as my helper, whenever I run into stumbling blocks in my life and business, I ask for help. If I can't figure something out because I don't have enough experience, knowledge, connections, or even finances, I seek God's wisdom. Let me prove that God will help you, too. Take a quick look at the word of God for proof.

⁵ If any of you is deficient in wisdom, let him ask of the giving God [Who gives] to everyone liberally and ungrudgingly, without reproaching or faultfinding, and it will be given him.

⁶ Only it must be in faith that he asks with no wavering (no hesitating, no doubting). For the one who wavers (hesitates, doubts) is like the billowing surge out at sea that is blown hither and thither and tossed by the wind.

⁷ For truly, let not such a person imagine that he will receive anything [he asks for] from the Lord,

⁸ [For being as he is] a man of two minds (hesitating, dubious, irresolute), [he is] unstable and unreliable and uncertain about everything [he thinks, feels, decides]. –Jas1:5-8

God is literally saying that whatever you lack in knowledge in any area of your life, feel free to ask it of Him. But you cannot *doubt* that He is God and can do the things you have asked Him to help you accomplish. If you doubt, you are like a ship that any wind can blow back and forth all over the sea with no control. Or you are like a person that takes on the doubtful thoughts of others and believe, above Him, that you were not meant to do any great thing. God cannot work under those conditions in your life. I know that if you ask God to show you how to start your own business—even though you may not have an idea—things will be set in motion to deliver an idea to you. I believe that if you have the thought of wanting to go into business for yourself, then there is already provision, within you, to accomplish the task. Once you believe He can do this for you and are resilient in your efforts, then you will *receive* it from Him. God's answer will come through any means that He deems necessary to move you forward. So keep your eyes open!

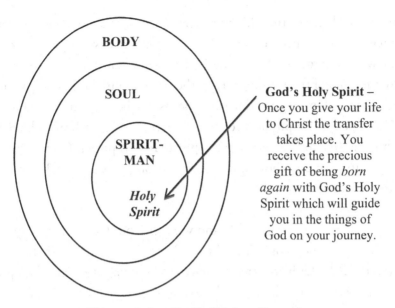

Figure 2.1 – God's Divine Transfer

Here's a wonderful concept that God revealed to me about the birth and divine transfer of His Holy Spirit. As you may know, you are a tri-part being according to Thessalonians, *"… put you together— spirit, soul, and body—and keep you fit…."²* God can only dwell in a designated place within you that is pure, holy, and sacred. When you were being conceived, God left a place in you for Himself to one day dwell with you, if you ever *said* you believed. See **Figure 2.1** as I prepare to explain the process in visual form for a better understanding. This is the beginning of the great things to come!

When you give your life to Christ, God penetrates to your spirit-man, which is that part of you that lies dormant, waiting for the day of awakening. *All human beings contain an essence of God* whether one believes it or not. God impregnates you with His Holy Spirit, therefore giving birth to the new you, which is your God-consciousness. Now, when you say *yes* to Jesus as your Lord and Savior, everything will still seem the same, but yet you are about to become different through a divine metamorphosis.

God reminded me that Mary's experience is the same; He is still impregnating His people today. Mary's experience was a precursor for what was to come to all who desired to know God in a greater way. Take the story of the Virgin Mary in the Book of Luke 1:26-38 in which God came and impregnated her with Jesus. He became the Holy Guide of God's people, in physical form, on Earth. God sent Jesus, His Son, to show us *how* to live and *how* to operate in His power. God wrapped Himself in flesh and showed the world, through Jesus, exactly what to do to achieve success in life.

Everyone is born dead to the life and ways of God. I know this may not sit well with some people, but those who call themselves atheists and Believers of the Universe and its deliverance have yet to embark upon the fullness of God. They are all missing their true existence! It is not until God's process happens in one's life that one will *truly* begin to live a purposeful and meaningful life.

After giving your life to Christ, just like a newborn baby, it is time to learn how to speak the language of God. This is done by ingesting the word of God as often as possible, just like an infant ingests baby food. Your feeding is to take place on a daily basis until you been satisfied in spirit. You start saying a few of the scriptures and start recognizing what the various words mean. Your Christian environment encourages you, and you celebrate this victory with joy, just as a baby gets happy at a parent's praise of progress. A baby speaks in gurgling sounds as they are trying to formulate words through the process of mind with what they are hearing in order to have the power, soon, with their own words, to manifest what they wish to have.

At this stage, you, too, are trying to mimic the words you hear your Christian parents, teachers, and preachers speak through your formation of the spirit-filled words, to manifest the life you want to live. Your words are not very powerful at this stage because you are testing the waters, so to speak. If you are serious, you are transitioning to God's system of living. As you are ingesting and digesting the written word, they are empowering you to go from crawling to taking your very first steps in the Lord. These steps are preparing you for what I call your "trust walk" with God. As you grow in the Lord, you should be eliminating those negative words, relationships, and surroundings for a more positive and powerful environment. Now, you are learning to stand in an upright position in order to represent the Lord in a more dominant and glorifying way. You will have times when you fall down, but with continued encouragement and manifestation, you will become the spiritual being God created you to be!

Figure 2.1 shows that we are birthed in the image of our Maker, God. In the beginning, from birth, our soul is the ruler of our being. Each of us is born with a clean, uncontaminated soul. As we get older, our soul gets thicker and denser, filled with all our life experiences that include our emotions, our will, our intellect, and our habits, both good and bad. Over time, this can cause our instincts (our God-given ability to do things naturally) to go unnoticed and to be drowned out by life. Eventually, this is what causes us to, initially, do what feels good and therefore live a *soulish* or *devilish* life. That old saying that "the devil made me do it" is not always so true. When you were living with no regard for God, your spirit was not enlivened until you decided to connect your life with Christ Jesus.

When we give our life to Christ, we are just as a man and a woman who join themselves together as one during intercourse to create new life. The only difference is that God produces His Holy Spirit within you instead of as an external being, such as a baby. Before you think that I am off my rocker and stop reading the book, just listen to me for a moment.

God makes it easier for us to navigate in life through the power of His Holy Spirit. The Holy Spirit was given to us through the death, burial, and resurrection of Jesus, The Christ—The Son of The Living God. As we *believe* Jesus is the Son of God, The Holy Spirit will then dwell within us. Stay with me now as I show you what I mean. I know this may be a bit heavy for some who do not understand, but it is essential that you get the foundational basics of what makes you powerful through Jesus' death and resurrection. Listen to what Jesus is saying to his disciples as he prepares them for his departure to the cross and His special gift to mankind.

"If you love me, show it by doing what I've told you. I will talk to the Father, and he'll provide you another Friend so that you will always have someone with you. This Friend is the Spirit of Truth. The godless world can't take him in because it doesn't have eyes to see him, doesn't know what to look for. But you know him already because he has been staying with you, and will even be in you! ~Jn 14:15-17 [4]

I have come to know and understand the ways of God because I have been walking the life of a Christian long enough to *experience* God. I have lived my life through the help of the indwelling of The Spirit of Truth, from the day I said *yes* to Jesus as my Lord and Savior. Now, I have not been perfect in my walk, but this is the great thing about God—He understands. He makes accommodations through His Grace until He can help you perfect your ways. We are all still works in progress!

There is one great benefit that needs to be emphasized and that's the protection you receive from your "I made a mess moments" in life. I just mentioned God's accommodations for us through His grace. God's grace is simply God's extension of His kindness, His unmerited favor, to those who don't deserve it. Everyone has experienced a moment when they did something that they knew they should *not* have done and they should have been reprimanded for it. For example, you may have been speeding; you knew you had broken the law but the officer let you go. That was the Grace of God because you know you deserved that ticket. Maybe you have been taking supplies from work and using them at home because no one ever said you couldn't. But you know it's wrong. Although you never got reprimanded for your actions, God's grace was at work on your behalf.

Now, not all wrongdoings are overlooked, by society or God, due to the laws that have been put in place. These misfortunes are for one's good. Everyone has a *free will* to make their own choices. (We'll talk

Figure 2.2 – Renewing Your Mind

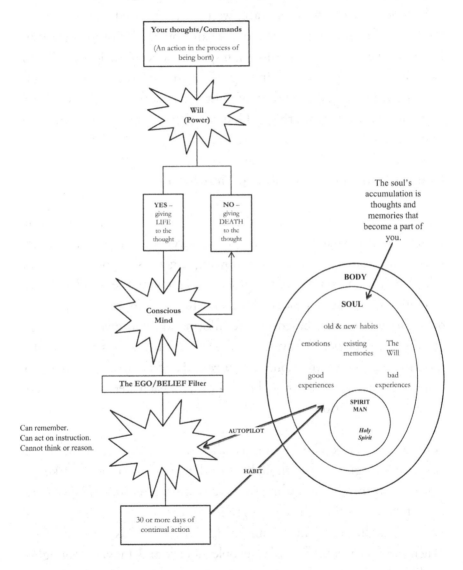

more about free will in a moment.) If one obeys the law, then one is protected by the law, and if one obeys the spiritual instructions of God, then one is protected by the Hand of God. Now grace in such cases can be seen in the instance of a person being given a lighter sentence when they should have gotten a harsher sentence for a specific deed or crime committed. Through grace, we have been saved because of our faith (belief in Jesus), and therefore we are covered for our mistakes in life while we get life right. Although grace has been made available to us, this is not a "get out of sinning free card" nor the chance for you to disregard your responsibility for your actions. That would be taking God for granted. Connecting to God can keep your actions on track so that you can become the person you've only dreamed of being.

Control Your Thoughts – Renew Your Mind

Successful people have come to realize that taking control of your thought life is what makes you a truly successful person. You must learn to be aware of what you are allowing to get inside your head. Let's take a look at an example of the process of renewing the mind and also at how your thought process flows and how it can generate positive or negative outcomes based on the information you give it. God has given you the power to have control over your life, so it's time to take it back. Focus your attention on *Figure 2.2* and think about ways you can better manage your thoughts as I explain each step of the process for better clarification.

Your Thoughts & Commands is where it all begins. It stems from our own thoughts or the thoughts of others that we allow to take up space in our minds. According to the 2 Corinthians 10:5, God advises us to take every thought into captivity by casting down the negative ones. Thoughts can enter your mind through books, newspapers, magazines, television, everyday people, songs, and movies. Thoughts are like the many sperm cells that are vying for new life by entering into our incubation portal (conscious mind) until they can find life in our consciousness in hopes that they will be birthed into its physical form. Your thoughts are waiting to be pushed into a physical action that your body will carry out in obedience. I remember reading somewhere about how we entertain anywhere from 50,000 to 70,000 thoughts per day of which 70–80 percent are mostly negative. As you know, negative thoughts can come from worry, doubt, fantasy, and the world's view without God. Every minute of our lives, we are being impressed upon to take on the ways of others, which may not be our path in life. Through the series of thoughts that you allow into your mind, you are building the world you see and live in today. Understand this process takes practice!

Your Free Will – Next on the chart is your *will*, which is conducive to your *will power* and is connected to the *control of your impulses and actions,* your self-control. If you don't have willpower, then you are out of control and need guidance. God gave you the will to decide what you will and won't do in your life. This can mean the difference between a mature and an immature decision based off an internal or external belief. You can decide to give your life to Christ and serve Him, wholly and fully, or you can decide to never believe there is a God. Although He gave us *free will,* it is not without its imperfections when the humanistic ways are involved in the equation. Remember in the Lord's Prayer where it says, *"Let **thine will** be done on earth as it is in heaven"?* God knew that we would need His power to make the *right* decisions to fulfill our purpose. He gave us the very words to pray for as often as we would need it. In order to have strong decisions that bring about the right actions, you must take on the *willpower* of God to combat any erroneous decisions or thoughts that could delay your progress. Until you readily surrender your will to God, will you see the change that will lead you to victory. God allows you to carry on in life, controlled by your ego, until you get tired of living a defeated life. Now, take a look back at Figure 2.2 to see how your decisions can affect your life.

> **Answering YES to the thought** – If you decide *yes*, the body
> will prepare to move forward to do a task as the thought is being

passed down into your conscious mind to gather the necessary information to act upon this decision.

➤ **Answering NO to the thought** - If you decide *no*, that you do not want to move forward with the thought whether it is because of your morals, lack of willpower, your character, or not enough information, then the thought can die here, for now. The reason I say *for now* is that you can revisit it, from memory, if someone or some situation reintroduces the thought to you. This is why you have to be careful with outside influences. But this is where you can continue in God's divine willpower to cast down the thought if it is not good for where you're headed in life. The more you say *no* to a negative thought or act, the easier it will become to resist it. Resist evil (thoughts that oppose your purpose/vision in God), and it will flee from you.

Conscious Mind – Once the thought reaches this point through your sight, hearing, taste, touch, or smell, it sits here for processing purposes. At this point, you start to bring up internally stored information and possible external sources to help you make a conscious effort to learn or commit to the thought. Your commitment can come through the views and results that you have witnessed throughout life. As human beings, we tend to naturally *not* take on the things that have not been proven by us or someone else. But if you have a strong willpower to succeed, then your thought may not sit here long. In the mind, this is a place of reasoning and finding support to validate the thought and its reason to live.

For example, you've decided you want to learn how to start a business and one day soon quit your job. You buy your first book on entrepreneurship or attend a seminar in order to validate your decision. As you read the information listed in the book or hear the instructor, you reason between the failures and successes of that which goes along with this decision. Your mind flows through your life and current surroundings to see if you have the stamina, resources, or support system to accomplish this new venture. Based off your beliefs or the beliefs of others around you, this thought can live or die at this stage. This is why it is so important to keep positive thoughts flowing through your mind as often as possible. You can abort any positive thought by saying *no* because of fear, anxiety, or a support system that reminds you why you can't do a thing, therefore aborting or delaying your destiny.

In this part of the mind, it can become a war zone, where your thoughts wear boxing gloves and fight in an unconscious manner. Thoughts battle to become a priority as your body awaits the final outcome to carry out the right or wrong decision. The longer you meditate, or say *yes* to any gathered information, the thought will take on a visual form in your imagination and become a picture that can lead you to a perfect or imperfect place in time. This is where the renewing of the mind (*filling it with positive or scriptural words*) is most important to overcome the voices that may ring negatively all around you.

Your EGO depicts your individuality in life, the person you have become today. Your ego is built up of the things you have been told and researched, and the things you have decided to believe about you and the world you live in. The dictionary defines the ego as *the part of the mind that mediates between the conscious and the unconscious and is responsible for reality testing and a sense of personal identity*. That's why it is very important that you understand WHO you TRULY are before any thoughts get to this point! If you have not identified yourself correctly, throughout life and at the conscious level where all the reasoning and research has taken place, then you will live a life with a distorted perception. In this state of mind, your reality is tested.

For example, if you grew up with parents who believed that rich people were not good for humanity and were crooks and swindlers, then you may be questioning your desire to become a God-made millionaire. Your parents' thoughts created this negative self-image that continues to play out in your mind that financial success is not good for you and not an identity with which you should associate. So you go through life believing you should be pleased with being mediocre and never earning more than $35,000 a year in your lifetime. Your attitude with yourself, which affects others around you, has been skewed by the perceptions of those you trust, although it was formed during your spiritual immaturity. Our ego was meant to take on the nature of God's "I AM" identity. It is meant to show ourselves and others around us that we are the success we seek to be. Every person, experience, or piece of information you are exposed to adds or subtracts to the validation and identity of who you are and who you are becoming.

Your Subconscious Mind is filled with habits you believe are the truth that have been passed down through the thoughts from consciousness. This area of your mind cannot think or reason. It can remember and can act only on your instructions or suggestions. It is regulated and controlled by your thoughts, impressions, and suggestions from your conscious mind. Your subconscious mind does not know the difference between what's real and what is only coming from your imagination. So the negative or positive thoughts you have created, through consciousness and your ego over time, will now be carried out. That's why it is most important to change the channel of your mind if your thoughts are not those of success, fearlessness, and power to accomplish great things. If you do not think these types of thoughts, then it is necessary to go back to the conscious mind and enter new information until it reaches your subconscious—renewing the mind.

Remember, your conscious mind is very impressionable with the habitual things of the world, so you must renew it often. The more positive information you regularly bring from the conscious to the subconscious, the faster and easier it will become to accomplish the things you want to create. It's funny how the subconscious mind will come to your rescue without your even asking. For example, my husband was diagnosed with Muscular Sclerosis years ago. When going into the grocery store, he says that he often finds himself walking near the cool beverage aisle or freezer sections, even if that is not the place to find the item on his list. He says that his body automatically finds the coolest places in the store to give him relief. For anyone that has MS, you understand that heat is *not* your friend. He says that he does not have to make a conscious effort. The subconscious mind was created to carry out our routines through automation for a more productive life. When it comes to the automated routines, you must feed it positive data in order to get positive results.

This is why, if you want to become a God-made millionaire and do great things, you have to guard whose voice you allow to speak into your life. If you don't, you will find yourself validating those negative things that are being said about you. The greatest way that I have found to program my subconscious mind is to meditate for an extended period of time on such things as scriptures from the Bible, videos, movies, affirmations, successful habits of others, and even a vision board that is in alignment with my goals. Pick and choose any one of these resources and watch how your life will change for the better as well!

Body, Soul, Spirit – All the information that is fed to your mind comes from your soul where it is all stored in what I call an "expandable container." Your soul becomes the world you live in today. Those who have had outer body experiences recognize that the spirit does not need the body to survive. All consciousness of the world you live in still exists long after the body is gone but without the frailties of life.

> ➤ The Body – This is the part of you that enjoys the things of the world when given the chance. It loves to do what *feels* good in a selfish manner. It loves to do what it wants to do, when it wants to do it—no matter the cost. It definitely responds to the five senses of taste, touch, smell, sight, and what it hears it can do. If operating from a worldly ego, then it can take you to places that you never should go.
> ➤ The Soul – This is a collection of everything that you have learned and gone through in life. Your soul grows over time, from the day you were born until the day you leave this Earth. It is a great big data storehouse from which the subconscious mind draws for its actions and instructions on how to carry

out your will. Maybe you may have been deeply hurt by an event or circumstance involving a good friend or loved one. This is how you can forgive someone but never forget because it is stored here and can come back at any unforeseen time through a triggered moment. This is why you need God's Holy Spirit to release you from these devastating memories. Another example is performing a task that you have mastered. Because you have done it thirty days or more, your subconscious mind can take that instructive behavior and have your body carry it out without your conscious effort. I believe this is how one is able to multitask. Some people call this going into "autopilot."

➢ The Spirit-man – Whether you know it or not, this is the REAL you. You are powerful beyond belief and wiser than you ever imagined because of this awakening by God's Holy Spirit. The REAL you is waiting to be discovered. So when you get tired of living a defeated or not-so-rewarding life, you will start to search for a higher version of you, which is within you already. God gave you His wonderful Spirit so that you can operate in power, love, and a sound mind and not in fear. This is the holy place within your soul where He can dwell and be with you always while leading you into your life's truths.

The Holy Spirit – We have discussed the essence of the Holy Spirit previously. He basically connects us to God and His storehouse of knowledge that is beyond our physical body. He is a powerful energy source! He is what empowers us to partake in the "I AM" consciousness of God through good thoughts and abilities to create. He is God's direct connect to our heart and motives in life. This is how God tailor-makes our lives and covers the stumbling blocks within our soul.

If you are allowing wrong thoughts to flow from within, then your thoughts are going to move your body to take an action that is most likely erroneous. Without the mind of God, the tendency can be an unwanted action. Now, if your God-consciousness pulls from the soul those things that are good, then it is going to reflect off the spirit-man and therefore cause you to bring about actions that are positive. Your spirit-man can expand or contract depending on whether you are working in conjunction with your flesh or the Holy Spirit. Take a look at *Figure 2.2* again, and you will see your spirit-man and the Holy Spirit. The longer you've been depending on and walking with God, the greater the expansion of your Spirit-man. Spending time with God can help you overcome much easier all those negative emotions, bad habits, and negative experiences that you had in your past. Gaining the wisdom of God, I believe, can clothe the soul area like an invisible shield with the outstretching of your spirit-man. This is how you radiate the presence and anointing of God for others to see and experience when in your presence.

Also know that if you decide to move away from the goodness of God, then your spirit-man will decrease from its growth, and your soul can be in control through past experiences and intellect, once again. Your spirit-man has to continually be fed with spiritual food in God's word. If you ignore it, it will not be strengthened in its efforts to guide your life. The Holy Spirit is still there, but He will not offer his services if they are not wanted. A great thing to remember here is that the Grace of God is covering you until you get your spiritual hearing in tune with His divine instructions.

Manifesting the Promises of God

"But the seed in the good earth—these are the good-hearts who seize the Word and hold on no matter what, sticking with it until there's a harvest." -Lk 8:14

Faith is the *only* way to receive *anything* from God! The Bible says that "without faith, it's impossible to please the Lord." I've learned over the years that if you don't believe God for *who* He says He is and *what* He says He can do, then you will never experience the blessings of God. Not having faith is like baking brownies without adding the salt—and anyone who bakes from scratch knows how important salt can be to a deliciously prepared pan of brownies! Your dish will lose all of what could have been a magnificent dessert. Like salt, faith is the missing ingredient in the manifestation of your dreams and your purpose. This is why so many are not living a more rewarding lifestyle. I remember hearing pastors and other men and women of God, in my beginnings, talking about just believing in the word of God, doing your part, and trusting God to bring it to pass. As a result, one would experience the harvest. So many times we can *think* we are in faith, *but* we are not. Faith comes from the heart and not the thought that never makes it out of the mind.

Let me explain how what you sometimes call faith is actually something you don't really believe. For example, God's word says we are to bring the whole tithe into his storehouse so that there will be sufficiency, and He will pour you out a blessing that you will not have room enough to receive. So you take on this scripture and declare that once you bring your tithe, your blessings are on their way. As months go by with no big blessing, you start to repeat the scripture over and over again but with some frustration. Deep within, you don't believe this anymore and want to quit tithing because you see no results. But you continue, when reminded of the scripture, to say it is true for you. Your heart is where it matters, and it is not in agreement with your mind; therefore, you are *not* in faith any longer.

So ultimately you let a thought enter the conscious mind, where your reasoning takes place. When a thought enters your mind and you have nothing in your memory to reference or validate it, it turns into doubt. You have not seen any proof yet; therefore, it must not be true. This is where so many Christians fail to see the hand of God operating in their lives. You must persevere and not let go of the promises of God until they have happened in your life. This is the ultimate prize of any true believer—to see the fruit of one's labor of faith in material form. If you run into any disappointments, frustrations, or a loss of strength and willpower to hold on, then pray when you need help and divine resources will be dispatched to you. And praise Him to abolish any guilt, shame, or condemnation of thoughts of failure to bring the joy back into your life so that you can continue to move forward and be restored.

So the process is, with a God-nature, to simply take in the thought or word of God and feed it continuously with good things so that it gets into the heart, and then you will eventually and automatically start to speak the thought into existence, as God did in the beginning. Then your body will move in obedience to your words, and because you now are able to stick it out and not quit, you get to enjoy that blessed promise of God.

Sealing Your Destiny through God

I want to give you an opportunity to connect with God to start or renew your life with Him. If any of these apply to you, by all means take some time here to reflect on them. The greatest investment in yourself that you could ever make is to acknowledge and dedicate yourself to your creator.

For the Truth Seeker – If you don't already walk with God and would like to, I will help you join the family right now. Prepare to receive from God by welcoming Jesus into your heart. Just say the following words, and you will be a "born again" Christian. You will be dedicating your life to God for continual guidance and love. He welcomes you just as you. There is no need to wait until you clean up your life. So open your heart and pray these words according to Romans 10:9-10.

"Lord Jesus, I repent of my sins. Come into my heart. I believe God raised you up on the third day to give me new life. I make you my Lord and Savior. Amen."

If you said this simple prayer for the first time, then congratulations and welcome to the family of God! All you need to do now is get into a good Bible-based church, surround yourself with like-minded people, and let the Lord transform you from the inside out. The Holy Spirit will now help you by protecting you and teaching you the ways of the Kingdom of God.

For the Backslider – If you have not been faithful in your walk with God, then this is the moment for you to ask Him for forgiveness. Because of

God's grace and mercy, you can come boldly before Him and confess of your sins and be forgiven. You can pick yourself up from any guilt or condemnation and continue in your pursuit of happiness with God.

If we [freely] admit that we have sinned and confess our sins, He is faithful and just (true to His own nature and promises) and will forgive our sins [dismiss our lawlessness] and [continuously] cleanse us from all unrighteousness [everything not in conformity to His will in purpose, thought, and action]. ~ I John 1:9

<u>For the Non-Believer</u> – If you decided not to say the prayer, then I understand because it takes time to know and trust what you may hear for the first time. I will invite you to read more about God's great love through His Son, Jesus, and his journey, to give you more understanding. You can start with the Gospels of Genesis, of course, and read of Jesus' journey through the New Testament, in the Amplified Bible or Message Bible. Of course, these Bible versions are suggestions because they are written in a more everyday language without the "thees" and "thous," if that matters.

I do want you to know that if you have decided not to accept Jesus as your Lord and Savior, then your success will not reach its *full* potential because you will always feel as though something is missing. God is the creator and the fulfiller of life.

You may be thinking, "I know people who are very successful, and they don't know Jesus or acknowledge Him." I am not saying that you won't be successful because many people are that don't know Jesus, but they are not living life in its highest meaning. They don't realize the exponential growth their company and personal life can achieve through knowing Jesus and The Holy Spirit.

Let me let you in on a quick secret about the lack of business success of Christians compared to those of the successful non-believers. Of course, this does not apply to every Christian. If you examine any wealthy person that does not operate or believe in the power of Jesus, they have something that is most valuable to *any* successful person. Wealthy people have an enormous belief in their abilities and unfailing courage to see this process through to its success! Most Christians fall short on their belief in their abilities and use fear instead of courage to move blindly into the future. But the process is quite the opposite. A Christian should have faith in the power within them and the divine knowledge that God has made available to them. Christians are at a better advantage than those who do not know God. Christians can avoid the pitfalls and setbacks of life far greater than the non-believer and therefore move farther faster. If the Christian combined divine faith and divine knowledge with the gifts, skills, and talents given by God, this would make for unstoppable and infinite capabilities!

Now, non-believers are actually operating out of any one or more of the "laws of the universe," which are available to anyone who puts them into action, believer or non-believer. All of these laws were derived from what God put in place for the Earth to operate as one, scientifically, before the foundation of the Earth. Whether you realize it or not, God and science are one. Listen to what God said to Job: ***"Do you know the laws of the universe and how the heavens influence the earth?"*** -Jb 38:33 [The Living Bible]

Here are some of the well-known and time-tested universal laws accepted by various religions throughout history. I have listed twelve of them to demonstrate the reciprocal of one's actions, but I am not insinuating that these are all the universal laws God speaks of in the preceding verse. As you can see, if you perform any one of these actions, you are activating any one of these laws as shown in **Figure 2.3. – Universal Laws.** These laws can be found floating around repeatedly on the Internet and validated by many. These are just a few as there are more actively going on daily throughout the universe.

For example, let's look at the *Law of Compensation.* How many times have you experienced a gift, money, a new relationship, or a right-on-time blessing? You are often compensated in unexpected and expected ways for something you did in the past for someone else. It is often said that one should not look for the reciprocation to always come from the vessel into which you sowed the goodness, such as a friend, charitable organization, or unknown person. Life always sends it back in a multiplied manner than when you presented itself. A charitable heart will always see tangible goodness.

Now take the *Law of Attraction*. This one has been widely used in countless movies, books, audios, and seminars over years. The reason it works is simply because whatever you put out in energy and effort, you get back. If you keep attracting people that are painful to be around, then you have pain that needs to be rectified within yourself. If you always seem to have such great friends, it's because you, first, are a great friend to someone else.

To know God is to communicate with Him as you would a friend in the good and bad times of your life. He just wants you to communicate with Him so that He can show you how to live a more abundant life. He can help you discover your gift and hone your skill to be used to prosper you. I got so excited when I read Proverbs 16:1 because it states basically that God must give you the ability to articulate and accomplish the plans He has for you! He has prepared a path just for you, as long as you keep Him involved. He has obligated Himself to guide you to your purpose like a scud missile locked on its target.

Figure 2.3 – Universal Laws

1. The Law of Divine Oneness
The first out of the 12 universal Laws helps us to understand that we live in a world where everything is connected to everything else. Everything we do, say, think and believe affects others and the universe around us.

2. The Law of Vibration
This Law states that everything in the Universe moves, vibrates, and travels in circular patterns. The same principles of vibration in the physical world apply to our thoughts, feelings, desires, and wills in the Etheric world. Each sound, thing, and even thought has its own vibrational frequency, unique unto itself.

3. The Law of Action
The Law of Action must be applied in order for us to manifest things on earth. Therefore, we must engage in actions that support our thoughts, dreams, emotions and words.

4. The Law of Correspondence
This Law states that the principles or laws of physics that explain the physical world - energy, Light, vibration, and motion - have their corresponding principles in the etheric or universe. "As above, so below"

5. The Law of Cause and Effect
This Universal Law states that nothing happens by chance or outside the Universal Laws. Every action has a reaction or consequence and we "reap what we have sown."

6. The Law of Compensation
This Law is the Law of Cause and Effect applied to blessings and abundance that are provided for us. The visible effects of our deeds are given to us in gifts, money, inheritances, friendships, and blessings.

7. The Law of Attraction
This Law demonstrates how we create the things, events, andpeople that come into our lives. Our thoughts, feelings, words, and actions produce energies which, in turn, attract like energies. Negative energies attract negative energies and positive energies attract positive energies.

8. The Law of Perpetual Transmutation of Energy
This 8 out of the 12 universal Laws is a powerful one. It states that all persons have within them the power to change the conditions in their lives. Higher vibrations consume and transform lower ones; thus, each of us can change the energies in our lives by understanding the Universal Laws and applying the principles in such a way as to effect change.

9. The Law of Relativity
This Law states that each person will receive a series of problems (Tests of Initiation) for the purpose of strengthening the Light within. We must consider each of these tests to be a challenge and remain connected to our hearts when proceeding to solve the problems. This law also teaches us to compare our problems to others' problems and put everything into its proper perspective. No matter how bad we perceive our situation to be, there is always someone who is in a worse position. It is all relative.

10. The Law of Polarity
This Law states that everything is on a continuum and has anopposite. We can suppress and transform undesirable thoughts by concentrating on the opposite pole. It is the law of mental vibrations.

11. The Law of Rhythm
This Law states that everything vibrates and moves to certain rhythms. These rhythms establish seasons, cycles, stages of development, and patterns. Each cycle reflects the regularity of God's universe.Masters know how to rise above negative parts of a cycle by never getting too excited or allowingnegative things to penetrate theirconsciousness.

12. Yin & Yang
This last out of the 12 universal Laws states that everything has its masculine (yang) and feminine (yin) principles, and that these are the basis for all creation. The spiritual Initiate must balance the masculine and feminine energies within herself or himself to become a Master and a true co-creator with God

Chapter 2 – God-made Millionaire Exercise

1. Examine the words you are speaking about yourself and your life on a daily basis because they are driving your body to action. Use positive words throughout your day and take note of any differences.

2. If you are not in an environment that is positively affecting you, then bring in new relationships, books, mp3's, or a church that can see you through.

3. Find room in your schedule to spend time with God. Get to know Him by asking questions.

Chapter 3

Who Am I *Really*?

The first thing I want you to know is you are *not* who you think you are. "Whoa! I'm not who I *think* I am?" No, because you are far more than you could ever imagine about yourself. Just think for a moment about the biggest thing you have accomplished so far in your life. Maybe you are accomplishing it now. God will help you do "exceedingly and abundantly more than you could ever could ask or think" about yourself.

In life, you are basically only what you accept yourself to be. Are you the negative things people say about you, or are you all the positive things God says about you? No one can *ever* make you happy, so stop looking to others to validate your existence. Other people are still trying to figure out who they are, so how can they tell you *who you really are*? Only God can describe what He created. He has the instruction manual for you and your life.

Once you accept Jesus as your Lord and Savior, you become an unstoppable being. You have the *power* of God and the *love* of God operating inside you, so there's nothing impossible for you, nothing that can't be accomplished with God's help. God uses His Holy Spirit to display His power and love throughout the Bible and throughout mankind.

Did you know that your identity is one of the greatest factors in becoming purposeful? Knowing who God created you to be is finding your uniqueness and passion that help evolve the world in and around you. Even though the negative voices will always tell you who you aren't and what you can't do, there is nothing like feeling you can take on the world and knowing you have the provision and power to do so. *"If you don't know who you are, then you will become who others say you are."* The best advice I can ever offer you to find out who you really are is to ask God *why* He created you. That's what I did. Then stand back and watch Him take you on a journey through life. Hang on tight because it's an adventure!

Listen to what God's word says about you—even before you were born.

"Oh yes, you shaped me first inside,
   then out; you formed me in my mother's womb.
I thank you, High God—you're breathtaking!
   Body and soul, I am marvelously made!
   I worship in adoration—what a creation!
You know me inside and out,
   you know every bone in my body;
You know exactly how I was made, bit by bit,
   how I was sculpted from nothing into something.
Like an open book, you watched me grow from conception to birth;
   all the stages of my life were spread out before you,
The days of my life all prepared
   before I'd even lived one day."
~Ps 139:13-16

God says, "Your body and soul are marvelously made," so whoever told you that you were too fat, too thin, or not attractive or smart enough is just not telling you the truth. He even said, "The days of your life were all prepared, even before you lived one day." As a believer, God, as the Maker of your life, is the author and finisher of it! He gets the last laugh or the last word over anything else that has *ever* been negatively said about you. Everything about you is how He knew you would be and how you would act out your life. Everything you have ever done or will do is already been known by God, so he will see you through. Don't let anyone or anything keep you from God's best.

Let me show you just how powerful you are ....

God spoke: "Let us make human beings in our image, make them
reflecting our nature
So they can be responsible for the fish in the sea,
the birds in the air, the cattle,
And, yes, Earth itself,
and every animal that moves on the face of Earth."
God created human beings;
he created them godlike,
Reflecting God's nature.
He created them male and female.
God blessed them:
"Prosper! Reproduce! Fill Earth! Take charge!
~Gen 1:26-27

This scripture always gets me because God created us *godlike; with his nature.* God created you to operate like Him, in His image to dominate and rule on the Earth. *You are to prosper, reproduce, fill the earth and take charge of your life!* That says a whole lot about you. You are blessed and empowered to increase, in case you didn't know it.

I have strength for all things in Christ Who empowers me [I am ready for anything and equal to anything through Him Who infuses inner strength into me; I am self-sufficient in Christ's sufficiency]
~ Phil 4:13

At the sound of Jesus' voice, Peter was ready for anything, even the act of doing what seemed impossible like walking on water. Jesus asked Peter to come to him. Peter kept his mind on Jesus and began doing the impossible, but as soon as he started to think himself average and just a mere man, he began to fail. But Jesus was there to keep him from failing to show Peter that he had been empowered to do what he perceived as impossible. No man had been known to be able to do such a thing, so why should he be able to do it? It is *only* in our finite mind that we struggle to see and understand all that God has equipped and enabled us to accomplish in our lifetime. Everyone has a superpower that is a God-enabled power to do the impossible. No matter what you or anyone else thinks, there is something that only *you* have been empowered to do, in your lifetime, that is attached to someone else's future. And without you, they will never make it to their destiny.

Ye Are Gods

What I am about to share with you is not for the faint at heart. It is not for those who are content with being an average person in the crowd. It's also not for the person that feels they are in complete control of their own lives. According to the Book of John, Jesus says that "you are gods." Now, that's with a little "g" and with the plural meaning of "everyone." And this is specifically talking about *you*. This means that you have the ability to do the powerful and miraculous things Jesus did throughout the Bible and more.

Now wait a minute! You're saying that I can turn water into wine, seriously? Many of us won't have the need to do all the things Jesus did, but the power to do them is available to you, if you believe. Just as God spoke the world into existence, you too spoke the world you live in today into existence, through your words. So if you don't like the life you have created, then you must change your words, at once, and take on words that will steer your life in the direction that you desire. We just discussed that God made mankind in His image; therefore, you were born to live your life discovering who you truly are and what you were created to do with His power to impact a certain part of the world. As a result of your willingness, you get to live the life you have always dreamed of because God will give you the ability and the heartfelt desire to accomplish it!

Let me be clear that with or without God in your life, you are able to create your world. You can wake up today and decide you don't like the way someone is treating you and to give them a piece of your mind, therefore removing them from your life ... your world.

You can decide you would rather work for someone else than put up with the headaches of being the boss. This means you would rather help another person build their dreams by using your work and wisdom. You can decide that the only way to have the things you want in life is to marry a wealthy person. This could leave your life in ruins and emptiness if the marriage ever ends. Whether you know it or not, you are building your world, or a culture, through your thoughts and beliefs that have gathered over time.

But by accepting the power of God, you can learn to handle an unpleasant situation with careful words to build your character. You can earn the kind of money you really want instead of convincing yourself that you must marry a person that figured out how to do it. The real underlying problem is that you don't know *how* to increase your own finances.

As an employee, you can be led to gain knowledge and become experienced enough to run your own company and to create jobs for others. Which feels better, knowing you have someone in your corner that can show and tell you how to operate in the untapped electrifying power within you, or operating in a power that is mediocre? Hands down, walking out your life without god-like abilities can make or break your career choices, finances, relationships, and even your happiness.

Consider for a moment, for example, you are like a country that exists amongst other countries in the world. Each human being is a country within themselves. Whenever you meet another person, you expose them to your culture through your words, beliefs, and actions. They can decide if they ever want to visit the world you live in ever again because of the *experience* they had with you. Just as with any tourist spot in the world, they can decide to not come back because they thought you were not friendly, the price of being with you was too expensive, your outlook on life was too negative, or you didn't possess enough intellect to arouse their attention. This is how people feel the first time they meet you at work, out in public, or even after getting to know you for an extended period of time. Although you do not have control over how other people act and respond to you, you do have control over whether they leave your world better than when they first met you. You possess a power to directly or indirectly impress upon others your beliefs and judgments, good or bad, and adapt your ways to their world only to end up passing it along to others. Your God-given power is not to be spent all on you but to selflessly grow and empower others as you grow in God.

Each and every day of your life, you are using your power to impact your children or others seeking answers to whatever they need or want. They are impressed by your ability to talk, act, and accomplish great things in your life that they would love to do as well. They ask questions to get the answers they seek because they value, trust, or admire you. Due to a possible disconnect from God, you can instill others with possible prejudices and values that can be harmful in the long run. Of course, this can be attributed to the fact that you may not consciously know that you are doing these things. But not connecting with the power source of God can leave you and others living beneath your birthright.

Having the God-consciousness and walking in His power with whatsoever things are pure, just, and honest will guarantee that the others around you will experience nothing but the highest form of you. This is what allows the world to be a better place because the power of God is now operating and directing your interactions with others. This is how the word gets spread about you, just like a tourist attraction, that you are one of the greatest persons they have ever met because of the impact you had on their life. Whether it is in front of a large audience or the people that you meet in your everyday activities, you have the power to change the world one person at a time, including yourself. So are you accepting and using the power that has been made available to you from God?

You Are Your Transformation

"But to each one is given the manifestation of the [Holy] Spirit [the evidence, the spiritual illumination of the Spirit] for good and profit." – 1 Cor 12:7

Purpose is a subject matter in which most people tend to get confused or find difficulty discovering. The surest way I have found is to ask God and He will illuminate your understanding through His Holy Spirit. How can you have a successful business that is designed to bring you fulfillment of life, if you don't know which business you are supposed to be operating in? Is everyone destined to become a businessperson? No, because not everyone has the desire to become an entrepreneur. I believe if God designed you to start and build a business, you would have the desire already and know it. Plus, you wouldn't be reading this book. On your path to find purpose, you will discover whether there is a business within you, waiting to be born. I can't tell you how many people are searching for purpose by defining it through the lives of other people. If not careful, you can take on the purpose of others you admire, instead of finding your own.

Blessed (happy, fortunate, prosperous, and enviable) is the man who walks and lives not in the counsel of the ungodly [following their advice, their plans and purposes], nor stands [submissive and inactive] in the path where sinners walk, nor sits down [to relax and rest] where the scornful [and the mockers] gather. –Ps 1:1

Sometimes as a believer, you have to shut out the voices that are speaking to you. People mean well, but their words can have no profit for your life. Most people walking around today are not sure *who they are, whose they are,* or *why they are* here on Earth. If you are a true seeker of purpose, it is necessary to distance yourself from others so that you can hear the voice of God. And if you don't know how to do this properly, which we will talk about in a moment, God will set the stage for you. God has placed me in isolation on several occasions where I could hear only His voice. When I say *isolation* or *separation,*

I mean those moments when you have a problem where it seems no one can help you except God. Don't fight these moments but cherish them because God has carved time out especially for you to teach you His ways of success. The Holy Spirit is your guiding light and the intercessor between you and God for any questions or instructions on your life journey. God will never allow you to fail at *anything* He entrusts you to accomplish.

As you begin to seek God's voice and lessen the voices of others around you, there will be a heightened awareness of your surroundings, in the spirit. Now, some people discover purpose a lot sooner than others. But the sooner you decide to immerse yourself in the things of God, the quicker you will begin to be guided toward destiny. You will discover things that were once hidden to you because you would not have been able to understand them otherwise. There are gifts unknown to you that only Jesus as the key can unlock and unleash in your world and the world around you!

As you begin to move closer to God, you will start to feel you are not being fulfilled by the conversations and presence of unprofitable people and things. Your interests in what you watch, hear, and even the places you go will change. These are indications that you are submitting yourself to the will of God. He is moving you closer so that He can tell you the secret things about Him and even you. You will start to see yourself in a new light with possibilities you never dreamed of. Once you start to believe what He says about you and what He wants to give you, your life will never be the same. This is when the journey can truly begin! Everything in life becomes more profitable as you follow the promptings of His Holy Spirit.

Let me share with you a short story as an example. When I became serious about finding purpose, I sat down and asked God to show me how to manifest the things I needed to be successful in the Earth. I had owned two businesses before and was very successful at one of them, but because I was not skilled in the area of finance, I lost it all during the real estate downturn. I was also not skilled at managing my own personal finances, so it's no wonder I didn't have a backup plan that could have saved me. I had not ever saved nor invested *any* of the money I made for future needs except the 401(k) money from a past job loss. I ended up having to use all of it when I was without work. With so much pain in my heart and tears in my eyes, I knew that if God didn't help me, I wouldn't make it. Our family was headed for bankruptcy although I knew I was still supposed to be successful in business one day. After looking back over my life, I know that deep-hearted prayer set me on a course that would teach me about me, life, *and* about business God's way. It has been one roller-coaster ride after another with much knowledge gained from it. I must say, I've learned some very valuable and interesting things about me. God showed me my vision was not big enough. This is one of the things about God: His thoughts are not our thoughts, and neither are His ways our ways; they are much bigger!

Lean on, trust in, and be confident in the Lord with all your heart and mind and do not rely on your own insight or understanding. -Prv 3:5

God wants all people to allow Him to teach and guide them. Don't rely on just what you know and have learned over time, but listen to what He has to say. God has placed the roadmap for your life within you, so let your life unfold before your eyes. There are so many things in life that we have come to trust—our job, our friends, our education, our money, our accolades or rewards received from our experience. If you gained all of these without ever seeking God, then you may have built this on a foundation that is not solid. You have built your life based on what the world says equals success and your ego can build up mightily because of it. Take a look at *Figure 3.1*. This is actually a process that we all can go through when turning our lives over to God to rid our soul of worldly ways that would hinder our walk with Him. This is actually a depiction of my life, your life, or someone you know before and after trusting God.

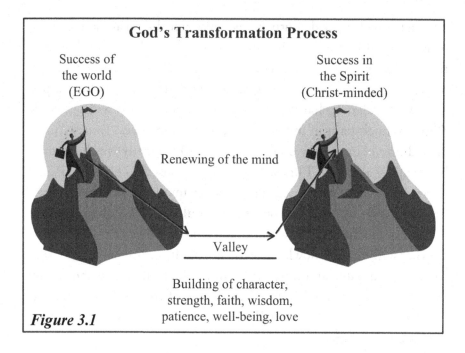

God's Transformation Process

Success of
the world
(EGO)

Success in
the Spirit
(Christ-minded)

Renewing of the mind

Valley

Building of character,
strength, faith, wisdom,
patience, well-being, love

Figure 3.1

Let me explain what this figure is actually all about. When you build your life on your own merits, as the world defines success, you will never be safe or satisfied with where you fit on its scale. You can feel threatened or even jealous of anyone that seems to defy the possibilities of what you have accomplished thus far. You can be knocked off the top of the mountain at any time, so your success can bring fear, anger, jealousy, and hatred because you will fight to stay on top. You will always scramble and become stressed to keep your status quo with no guarantee that you will always remain there. You may even resort to manipulation against anyone or anything that tries to defy your self-earned success. As a result of going through God's transformation process, you will no longer take on the mindset that you are the author and finisher of any and all successes in your life. God will remove the selfishness and give you one-ness with Him for an even greater fulfillment of *true* success. This includes the fact that there is a place on a mountain meant just for you to succeed with a confidence that brings others to the mountaintop with you.

Now, back to my story. I greatly enjoyed the fruits of my labor, but because I didn't have a spiritual foundation of learning, I was not prepared for the unknown in my surroundings or my financial affairs. I met with a circumstance that would turn my world upside down to what seemed like the point of no return. I sought God because no one could help me or our family to stop what was about to happen to us. The momentum had already begun for the unfortunate events that awaited us because of our financial inadequacies. We were headed for foreclosure, bankruptcy, embarrassment, and fear! I fell to my knees and asked God to help me because I had heard He was the God of the Harvest, of covenant wealth. Money was what I needed at that time, but what I actually needed was wisdom from God. I asked God to teach me how to be a better financial steward.

I remember that things had gotten so bad that as I prayed, God asked me to give Him all the money I had in my possession. We were behind in nearly everything. I thought, "Wow, I don't have that much, and I need every little bit I have." As I continued to pray, I kept hearing, "Give me all the money you have in the bank." I am being totally transparent with you here. I got up off my knees and headed to my computer to check my balance. The whole time I was hoping I didn't have that much so that I wouldn't have to give any of it away. How crazy was that kind of thinking! I got to the computer, checked my balance, and it said I had about (-$10.35). I sighed with relief. Now, how selfish was that! There I was, asking for financial blessings, and I didn't want to give God what was already His. He was showing me that I needed work on my stinking thinking first. Thank God for His grace, mercy, and love! I downright had serious issues back them. Obviously, I didn't know who He *really* was to me, even to the point of not knowing He was my saving grace.

I continued in my everyday life with my financial status not getting any better. I would cry often and hoped and prayed things would change. But little did I know that the *change* had to come from within me. One day things had gotten so bad with my lack of payment on bills that I broke down in my car. I often contemplated driving off a cliff because things had gotten so bad! I had to pull over and surrender to God. I had a money order that I had just picked up from one of my tenants, which still wasn't enough to pay toward my debts. I pulled over on the side of the road, and I knew I had to give myself and all my monies to Him. I took everything that I had in my possession and in the bank and gave it to Him in church offering the next day. I didn't care about how many bills I had or who I owed. I just surrendered because I had heard about tithing but never thought I could afford it. This is when my husband and I realized we were headed into a dark and gloomy place in our lives. Little did we know this would be our *valley*, or as it's better known, our *wilderness* season. We were right where God wanted us to be to begin our transformational process.

Your valley could be your health, your relationships, your job, or your finances. This is a place that you invited God to help you remove your old ways of thinking that have hindered your success in life. Let me explain it this way. The valley is a place in your life (mind) that appears dark, scary, and sometimes overwhelming to your outer world. But it is quite the opposite in the intentions of God. Your "valley" is a place where God has decided to answer your prayer, spend time with you, and give you His attention, for your teaching. It is a place in your inner world that is for your spiritual illumination and His showered love for your end results. It is almost like being reborn again because He has to take you out of the world and raise you up in a world where you have power and greatness to be who He created you to be. Without this process, you will never learn *who you are* and *what God's true love* is all about.

During this process, there may be godly people and godly resources sent to help you as you stay connected to God. Keep your heart *open* to receive from God during these times. Don't harden your heart in bitterness as you will abort your own destiny. At times, you won't realize the goodness of God until you have come out of the so-called overwhelming or uncomfortable season. It will seem as though you were having a series of failures and disappointments, but they weren't necessarily. God is building your spiritual muscles in mind, body, and spirit. He's building you up to be a leader and a vessel for kingdom's sake. Once you have exemplified your readiness, through Christ, He will place you back in the world to represent yourself like Christ. This is where you will continue to learn and grow in the goodness of God. He says you will come out as *pure gold*!

You Are God's Concern

I can never say enough about this topic because money is the least of your worries when starting something that you know God has equipped you to do. God never gives you an assignment that He won't fund. Let me say that one more time. God will never give you a purpose in life that requires money and resources that you do not currently have to complete it. That's one thing I can say and have experienced with God. He will indeed invest time and money into you, meaning He will provide money when you don't have it and resources when you don't know anyone personally. If you ever have a big dream growing inside you and you look at your lacking outside circumstances, it can cost you your future!

I remember many years ago, when I first decided to go into real estate investing, I didn't have the money to get started in the business. I had been laid off, and we were trying to make it off my new real estate agent career. I had not planned properly for my transition to this commissioned lifestyle. So I figured that if I got into real estate investing, I could have income coming in each and every month from tenants. I tried finding the money and even earning it, but it was not easy. I decided that maybe I needed to get some training to learn how it's done. The class was only $99 at the time. I heard this small still voice say, "Never let not having the money stop you from doing anything," so I wrote it on a piece of paper to remind myself when I felt like quitting. Basically I was to pursue my goal.

God started introducing me to people by sending me to certain events. I was learning from others and earning money to buy books and other event tickets. I remember one event that I had gone to where I was mad because my life was not improving to the achievement of my financial goal. I deliberately sat on the last row of the event in case I decided to leave early. I didn't want to be bothered by anyone nor befriend anyone at the time. This one young lady sat right next to me with no seat left empty between us. I thought to myself, "Out of all these empty seats in this place, why did you choose to sit here? Can't you move up front somewhere?"

Little did I know that this was a God-ordained relationship. He had scheduled to get her and me where we wanted to go. This young lady went on to be a mighty woman of God. I learned how He delivered her from financial lack into a debt-free state. I also learned to know of God's great love for his people through watching her life with Him. It was like God had dropped her out from heaven straight into my life without consulting me. That's why I love Him so much! He knows exactly what you need before you ever even know you need it. This young lady paid for my flight, hotel, and seminars for a season because I had knowledge and training that she had not yet received but needed. She had connections that I did not, so this was a perfect match! We basically traded our resources to benefit one another. God connected me with this young lady whom I had never met before or ever seen. We later became great business partners on very lucrative business deals and great friends! If the dream is indeed God-ordained, He will provide the resources to bring it to pass.

You Are a Leader

"Not so shall it be among you; but whoever wishes to be great among you must be your servant" –Mat 20:26

Jesus clearly states that being a leader is not just about ruling over someone but also about serving them. It takes a lot for a person with power to humble themselves and serve their workers as though they did not own the place. This kind of God-given humility deserves much respect. When most people hear the word "leader," they think about a political figure, CEO, a manager or supervisor at their job, or even the president of the United States. But this is not always the case in today's world. A leader can be any person that decides to take control of a situation or circumstance that they feel no one else is willing or capable of doing. This includes stepping up and taking control of your own life. A leader is a person that runs their own affairs with confidence and encourages others to grow beyond their known abilities.

Is this you? Do you feel that what you have can change the marketplace, a person, a people, or a nation? Well, okay, it may not be a nation, but it's possible! Whether you realize it or not, your decision to become a business owner has now placed you in the top ranks of those who are the shakers and movers in your industry.

There is a quote that says, "If you cannot lead yourself, you cannot lead others." Building a business exposes your personal strengths and weaknesses, so you must continue to examine your temperament at every point in your business. Continuing to add to your mental library will cause you more personal and business growth than you could ever imagine. If you want to gain more knowledge about how to be the best leader you can be, then go grab as many leadership videos, books, and CDs by the top secular and nonsecular leaders.

You Are Your Business

Your business is a reflection of *who you are*. If you have a weak mentality, then your business will have a weak infrastructure. Can this be improved? Yes, by getting training or hiring someone who is stronger in the areas you are not. If you are a control freak, then you will run your business with control that others may resent, therefore causing you unnecessary losses. If you are filled with compassion, integrity, character, and decisiveness, then your business will run like a well-oiled machine. This in turn will attract quality people and leaders that accentuate your leadership. Whatever you believe and whatever qualities you possess inwardly will determine how much you prosper, outwardly, in your business. Always remember, God's word says you can do all things through Christ who gives you the strength, knowledge, and power.

Let's examine some internal qualities that can either make or break you if you are not careful and do not take control of them.

For God did not give us a spirit of timidity (of cowardice, of craven and cringing and fawning fear), but [He has given us a spirit] of power and of love and of calm and well-balanced mind and discipline and self-control. ~2 Tim 1:7 [Amplified Bible]

From this scripture, you can see how the world and our past experiences have caused us to take on qualities we were never meant to have. Take fear, for instance, which has come to be better known as **F**alse **E**vidence **A**ppearing **R**eal. Now, let me back up for a moment and let you know that there is *good* fear and there is *bad* fear. An example of *good* fear is when you are presented with an option to step in front of a car while crossing the street or just waiting for the car to come to a complete stop. You know that if you walk in front of a car that is moving, you could be killed or left in a debilitating state. This thought will cause a feeling of fear within you that ultimately will shield you from danger.

An example of *bad* fear would be if you believe you can be president one day, you decide to go and share it with others. They start telling you how this could never be because you don't possess what it takes to be president. (*They are judging you off their limited beliefs of your past skills, present qualities, and old bad habits, or they are jealous.*) They even tell you that the world won't accept you as president because of your past history and possible humiliation from acts of other family members. If you aren't careful, you will take on their fears about your greatness, and you will become fearful that you, indeed, are not enough, therefore shrinking back into society as an average being.

So, if there are any areas of your life that need improvement, becoming an entrepreneur will certainly bring them out. Here is a remarkable quote I heard from Mark Nepo, a spiritual writer and poet, *"Every single being has an amazing, unfathomable gift that only meeting life head on will reveal."*

The definition of a gift according to Webster's dictionary is a notable capacity, talent, or endowment. Whether you know it or not, each and every situation you encounter is an opportunity to grow, even if it feels like a tragedy you'll never recover from. Life is either strengthening you or tearing you down. If you accept the situations and circumstances that come your way as a way to sharpen your life skills, then you will mature. But if you fight every time a situation does not go your way, you will struggle the majority of your life. Just think … if you have ever been really sick and recovered because you chose to fight it, then you are a master of that illness. If you have ever bounced back from a bankruptcy only to become a wealthy man or woman, you are a master of your money. If you have ever faced a divorce that was so devastating that you thought you couldn't live another day only to find and marry the most wonderful person in the world, then you are a master of divorce. What you have overcome is now a cure, a medicine, an antidote to someone else in that same situation.

If you look back over all these situations that you would call crises, these are all wonderful opportunities for you to share your victories with others who feel they will never make it. I saw a Super Soul Sunday episode where Mark Nepo mentioned we have an "unfathomable gift" that only life can help you to discover. So I say embrace the wonderful new change that is trying to enter your life.

Life is what helps us to *see* and *discover* just what we are truly made of. All while growing up, you were able to do things that others were not. What I mean is that something you did or do now comes naturally to you while it is a struggle for others. This is a sign and clue that this is a gift that God placed inside your DNA. It's what makes you different!

I have always been a student of life with introverted tendencies for as long as I can remember. I was always the person that my friends came to for discussions of their cares or concerns. I would listen and offer some suggestions that made them feel great about themselves and even solved some problems. Therefore, they made better decisions to bring about the success they desired. The more they asked, the better I became at learning about people, behaviors, and understanding the outcome of certain actions. I never wanted anyone to leave me feeling worse than when they arrived. (**Encourager**)

Secondly, to this day, I am still a great listener and let others do most of the talking. I guess this would fall under the Law of Polarity, huh? I also grew up liking to teach and to be the counselor of a make-believe camp and school. My cousin still laughs about it today! I loved my little chalkboard, tray tables, and chairs. I also designed the facility out of sheets so that my campers would have somewhere to sleep. (**Teacher/ Counselor**)

Thirdly, as a teen, I grew up enjoying the solitudes of life and reading books and discovering new information. If there was anything I wanted to accomplish, I read books about it until I learned as much as I could. Afterwards, I would go out and do it! What's that saying? "A reader is a leader." (**Learned skills**)

Lastly, while in college, I recognized that I felt really comfortable whenever I had to do presentations. I would be nervous, but I would study, do my research, and bring the information to the class or group. I would feel exceedingly glad when I took questions, and they made me think through my research. I am now teaching financial empowerment to men and women for a non-profit organization. It seems that whenever I had the opportunity to speak in public, such as in church or during a program, I always felt I was supposed to be standing before these people. People would often compliment me. It felt natural to me. (**Speaker/ Teacher**)

I didn't say any of these things to boast about my life but to show you the things that came natural to me. God has already given you everything you need to succeed. You contain who you long to be. You might not know how to bring your gifts out of you or recognize the signs of your greatness, but it's there!

Should I have acted on each and every one of my gifts or skills? Maybe … maybe not, but it would be a choice I could always make. Your gift is something that others ask you how are you able to do it. All you can say is, "I don't know. It just comes naturally to me." You are being identified! You may not even know you have the gift until you keep hearing the same words coming from different people.

If you are still struggling to find out just exactly what you should be doing with your life, then look at the things that come naturally to you. I spoke of how standing in front of people made me feel like that was the place I was supposed to be. Although, I didn't know *how* this gift would take me anywhere meaningful in life, I was still aware it resided within me. At the end of this chapter, you will be given the chance to assess your gifts, skills, and talent for a better indication.

I stumbled across a book I found about Oprah Winfrey by a teen. It was basically an autobiography of her life taken from several reliable sources. In the book *Up Close: Oprah Winfrey Media Queen* by Ilene Cooper, she mentions how Oprah arrived at her start to walking in her purpose. Here is an excerpt of what Oprah said that captured my attention.

"I came off of that stage August 14, 1978, and I knew that I was at home. In all my years of being discontent, feeling like something's not quite right, feeling like I was in the wrong place, in the wrong job, I knew this is it. It felt like home because it felt so natural. It felt like I could be myself."

This is one of the biggest hints that you have found purpose! This is the beginning of a journey that will lead you to the greatest fulfillment of your life. You will incur some ups and downs until you get your purpose perfected. Oprah Winfrey states, according to the book, that she would constantly call on God to help her through *any* situation she could not understand. She says she operated off *instincts*, which are the natural abilities that God put in her from birth. She was constantly told while growing up how good she was at speaking and being in the limelight, which were confirmations of her destiny.

Instincts, GPS (God's Positional System for your life), starts out as subtle hints as to who you were created to be from birth. Some parents have recognized these innate abilities and guided their children to grow these gifts or talents. Instincts are hidden treasures that God puts inside us, and the only way to develop and master them is to find the key to unlock their meaning, which comes from a heightened awareness. So many times, we lay down our own treasure map to pick up someone else's, only to be lead through a series of dead ends. It's sad that not until we experience those moments of long-term disappointments, fears, and frustrations of being off course do we return to find or pick up our own treasure map again. No other time in history has it been more prevalent to discover who we are than it is today! No longer are we comfortable with following the status quo because it is showing itself to be a faulty system in many ways.

Here is another example of the natural ability in a fish. A fish doesn't have to be told that it thrives in water and not on land. It contains the abilities that God put in it to carry out its very existence. If you take a fish out of the water, you will see that its natural ability has stopped functioning, and it will die, after a prolonged period of time. It is being forced to thrive in an environment in which it was never intended to thrive in.

If there is a place that you belong, naturally, and you are not thriving in it, you will live an unfulfilled life. This is the same as feeling as though you are dying in your current situation. You may even feel as though you are a failure in life, although this can be attributed to you not operating in the place that God created you to be a part of. This could also be a sign that you need to seek Him for further instructions on how to break free! Just open your mouth and ask Him to show you the way.

Your natural abilities or gifts are working in your life without anyone having to alert you to them. Natural abilities are often seen in your process of growing up—from childhood. Your gifts are working in your life now or can show up later. A natural ability is something you are able to do without a struggle and even without training.

I know my examples may be a bit extreme, but your gift is something that you were never taught; it's a part of your DNA. If you are trying to monetize an ability that you quantified as your gift to the world and it isn't working, then you may need to reinvent yourself.

Rabbi Lapin told a story in his book *Thou Shalt Prosper* about his daughter growing up wanting to be a teacher. Her capabilities were evident; when other girls were dressing their dolls, she was teaching hers. So, of course, she grew up and became a great teacher. She loved teaching but later realized that she could not reach fulfilment in her current industry because teachers were not making much money or given much opportunity to be more than what was required. So she reinvented herself and started consulting by creating curriculums for other schools that she used in her own teaching environment. She took her natural ability to another level before quitting and thinking she had to give up something she truly felt happy doing. She created her own place that accentuated her gifts even more.

If you quit something you love because of the money, you will go on an endless journey to an empty way of living. Don't make the mistake of not being who you truly want to be because someone told you the income is too minimal in that field. Too many kids get told to go be a doctor, lawyer, or engineer so that they can earn some real money. This is not to bash these great occupations because we all need their services at one time or another. But at least look at whether your heart and soul agree that this is the path that you should take because of your passion or your love to not disappoint a loved one. Can you see how you can make the biggest mistake of your life by giving in to status quo?

If you know exactly what you were created to do, then I congratulate you! Talent can be considered a combination of your gift, your passion, and your skills. Think of a famous or wealthy person who has a natural ability, who love what they do, and who, through doing it for years, have now perfected their skills. Put this all together and this is their marvelous talent you are enjoying today! I can think of many people, such as Michael Jordan, Oprah Winfrey, Warren Buffet, Bill Gates, and Tyler Perry, who have helped and brought much pleasure to our lives.

Now, don't get what you are currently great at confused with that which is your gift. If you have gone to school and you have found you are earning good money doing it, this could easily be misconceived. Maybe your gift became hidden when someone told you to change direction for a more promising career. The best way to know if your current career or path is what you love is by measuring how you feel about the work and the environment. Does your chosen career feel rewarding? Would you volunteer to do this on any day of the week with no pay? Do you continually think of ways to improve your current tasks through creative methods? If not, it may be time to reassess your career choice. Your career choice should make you feel excited to get up and go there every day!

Everything that you do, once you have decided to become an entrepreneur, should line up with the skills needed to run your business. If you are not getting the skills you need, currently, then you should look for ways to acquire them.

Your skills can come through a variety of places, such as job training, educational seminars, workshops, family, friends, mentorship, and just plain ol' practicing it as often as you can. The good thing about acquiring skills is the learning process through which it will allow you to determine your likes and dislikes to empower you to do more of what you love.

Perhaps a better way of summing this all up is to do what you've identified as your gift, love what you are doing, and as long you wake up daily wanting to do it, then your skills will be perfected, therefore creating your talent that can be offered for service to others. Now that's having a passion for a thing!

Let's explore to see if you are utilizing the gifts and skills that will make up your talent to be used in business. *Sit quietly for five minutes without any interruptions before answering any of the questions.* Then, write what comes to mind. It's important to bring back up those memories and feelings to make sure they are true answers.

In the "My Gifts" assessment, it's best that you answer the questions, first, yourself. Then give another sheet to at least three other people who are co-workers, current or past business partners, family members, friends, to help you. Now, take the sheet you completed and the sheets of the others and look for similar responses. See **Figure 3.2**.

Figure 3.2 – Gifts, Love & Skills Assessment

My Gifts

1. What tasks or actions come 'naturally' to you
2. What areas have you won contests, received awards or received public praise?
3. When you were a child, under the age of 10, what sort of things came easily to you? List the ones you really enjoyed doing.
4. What do people tell you they wish they could do like you?
5. What do you love doing but are not currently getting paid to do it?

My Loves

1. What part of your current career do you enjoy doing the most? Everyone has something that they like or don't like about their job.
2. If money were no object then what would be your career or business?
3. What kind of work activities do you enjoy doing and can stay late at work completing without anyone asking you?
4. List all your hobbies that you love. See what work activities can be carried over into running your business such as attention to detail, leadership, customer service or caring, etc.

Compile all the answers together that you have mentioned multiple times for you final hints to your talent.

My Skills

1. If you went to college, what was your major/minor?
2. If you went to a trade school, what was your trade?
3. What other careers were you exposed to such as your mom or dad? (Ex. Mom in banking/finance, Dad an entrepreneur)
4. Who are your mentors? People you look up to and possibly emulate.
5. What positions have you held in the past? List all the jobs & skills. (Resume)
6. What do you read or study in your spare time?

Note: Compile all the answers together that you have mentioned multiple times for you final hints to your talent.

Chapter 3 – God-made Millionaire Exercise

1. Look at your "My Gifts, My Love, and My Skills" exercise and search for similarities in your observations and feedback from others. This could be an indication of one or more gifts. *For example,* I have teaching as my gift, solving problems and helping others as my love, and coaching, training, and computers as my skills. My recommendation is that you focus on the top three. If you have one, then this would give you greater focus.

2. Research those who are currently doing what you love to get the current pay, what it entails, and how it is impacting the lives of others or their customers. Start studying as much as you can about your industry and pick up the knowledge you need to grow. Make a list of at least three of your business heroes.

Chapter

4

The Unfolding of Divine Vision

In the beginning God (prepared, formed, fashioned, and) created the heavens and the earth. The earth was without form and an empty waste, and darkness was upon the face of the very great deep. The Spirit of God was moving (hovering, brooding) over the face of the waters. ~Gen 1:1-2 [Amplified]

When God created the heavens and the Earth, He had a vision of what He wanted it all to look like. I am sure that God did not have to write down everything He needed to remember to accomplish, but we sure do. God is an exception to the rule because He created everything we would ever need in less than seven days. If that were us, we would have to get out the pen, paper, camera, and books, and we would have to find mentors and teams to get anything of this magnitude done in less than seven days. But the basic point is that everyone's time and ability to complete a task is different.

As you can see here, God prepared, formed, and fashioned His Earth. This means, visually, He had to step back, examine this task from all angles, and think this thing through, strategically. He took His time to make sure He had a *plan* before putting anything into place. You also notice that "the earth was without form and an empty waste." This means God started with a clean slate or canvas just as an artist would before painting his or her greatest masterpiece. The scripture says "darkness was upon the face." This means that what God was about to create did not exist already and had not been seen by the naked eye. He also had a lot of space to work with, thus the words "the very great deep." This is my take on God's process for what was about to be His masterpiece.

I mentioned in the last chapter about how The Holy Spirit, God's power and love, was with Him in the beginning of creation. So here is God's Spirit being displayed with His act of creating: "The Spirit of God was moving (hovering, brooding) over the face of the waters." God's process of creation was that He spoke from His vision what he wanted, and then His Holy Spirit went to work, creating and making God's very words and thoughts come to life. This same power is waiting on you to tell Him what you want Him to do for you!

I did some research on "the process of creation" for an artist to see how this might compare to God's process of creating the earth. One company, Art Promotive, did an online article in April 2013 on the creative processes of ten featured artists. After reading the article, I found that each artist has a particular style, manner, or technique by which they create. Some examples are abstract, contemporary, or a style called "ever-changing." Next is having a *medium*, a particular form or system of communication, such as the materials or methods used by an artist, like canvas, digital, or mixed medium. Lastly, each one has a certain *process* by which they are inspired to complete their work. For the "**process of creation**," I chose one special artist whom I thought exemplified a process similar to what God may have used to create the Earth.

"When I start working on a new scene, it's like entering into a fantasy dream. Like starting your own new virtual world. 'Everything is possible' and in the majority of my works I am trying to combine visual realities, with subconscious emotions and philosophical thoughts." –**Tammy Mike Laufer, Israel**

Her words couldn't have confirmed any other thoughts of what I perceived to take place in the mind of God while He was creating. I actually put myself in a place where God created the Earth, virtually, by calling it all forth into existence. I understood her words to emphasize what she would soon see through the workings of her hands, which mostly came from her mind, which was her vision of what she imagined to do. I perceived her emotions to be love and dedication and thoughts of blessings to those who would enjoy her finished work. Of course, God is one of the greatest artists ever.

Here are a couple more of the artists' processes that I think will be beneficial when it comes to showing you how processing your vision can come about in various ways.

"I think about my art all the time, about possible pictures and colour combinations, what tools and techniques I would use, etc. Once I have an idea I start painting. I very rarely do sketches; I paint mainly from memory and straight onto the canvas." –**Teodora Totorean, UK**

"I sometimes think about it and plan it in my head, sketch it out and then paint it. Other times it just begins or comes to me out of the blue. It depends on what is going on in my life or what I'm being influenced by at the time. Sometimes, it's very spontaneous."**Genevieve Esson, St. Louis, Missouri, USA**

How do you get your images throughout your day, week, or month? Are you getting them mostly while sitting in silence, or maybe you get them on the way to work in traffic? In order to be financially free, through business, you have to have some kind of vision about your personal and business life. These artists capture their thoughts, dreams, and visions using different mediums, such as a blank canvas. So don't you think you should have some kind of *medium* to record yours? This could be a journal, a recorder, or a vision board to capture these future moments. As they say, thoughts come and go, sometimes never to be seen again. Now, let's talk about your dream!

Your Dream, Your Imagination, Your Vision

For the vision is yet for an appointed time and it hastens to the end [fulfillment]; it will not deceive or disappoint. Though it tarry, wait [earnestly] for it, because it will surely come; it will not be behindhand on its appointed day. -Hb 2:3

What kind of dreams do you have for yourself, your family, or to help others? Let's look at what Webster's dictionary has to say about the word *dream. A dream is a strongly desired goal or purpose, basically something that you have wanted very much to do, be, or have for a long time.*

Everyone has said this at one time or another: "I sure do wish I could do _____" or "I sure do wish I could have _____!" This is a sign that you are looking for or ready for a *change* in your life. Tell me, when do you dream? Is it while listening to music? Is it while on break or at lunch during work? Is it while you read books and magazines about how you would love your life to be? And when you dream, do you dream about owning your own business, driving your dream car, living in your dream home, or giving large sums of money to your favorite charity? All of these are valid questions and signs when God is knocking at your door to let Him into your life!

The quickest path to getting what you want to show up in your life is for you to take your dream or vision and hold that image or thought in your imagination. It is often hard to accomplish anything by just thinking about it. It is often said that the imagination is one of the greatest tools that a human being can possess. This is the very place in the mind that I believe God held His vision for the Earth and everything in it. The definition of imagination is "the act or power of forming a mental image of something not present to the senses or never before wholly perceived in reality or creative ability."

"Imagination is more important than knowledge." -Albert Einstein

There has not been any conclusive research that has shown just exactly how the mind processes thoughts that reach and start the creative processes in the imagination. I recently read somewhere that the imagination is labeled the "mental workspace." As for myself, I envision the imagination as a comparative model to a blank canvas where God has given us His creative mind to design the world we were meant to live in. This marks it as a place where your most passionate thoughts become visions that are sent to the imagination for processing. The imagination allows us to be purposeful, productive, and powerful through our passion.

For example, you have four thoughts of what you want to happen in your life. You allow three of the thoughts to die because of life and your negative beliefs. But this one thought to build your own successful business just won't go away. This vision could have come to you while you were asleep or awake, such as in a daydream, a snapshot or a photo of you being successful in a chosen field. Now, as time goes on, the vision gets stronger and stronger. Through your internal and external factors in life, neurological urges start to take place in your body. Since this desire is pushing you to make something happen, it has now moved into the imagination, your mental workspace, for processing. Once this dream or vision gets here, there is nothing that can stop you *but* you. As long as you continue to affirm it, through thought, it's yours whether the desires are good or evil.

This is why you have to be careful not to let anyone talk you out of your dreams because they are basically keeping this vision from being processed in your imagination. In the initial stage of your vision, most people may not understand, so they protect you by telling you not to do it. But your next logical step would be to examine your life and where your heart is taking you. If your vision's end result helps not only you but others, then start building models, vision boards, or talking to critical people to help make it all happen. Remember, God gave that vision to you and not them.

Remember when Martin Luther King Jr. said that he had a dream? He was basically having visions of little boys and little girls of different races getting along and holding hands in peace and harmony, which represented the people of the coming world. Because he had a thought, which became a vision that was processed by his imagination, he was able to impact others and bring the vision about. At this point, there was no stopping him. He had even brought thousands—even millions—of people into agreement with him, so the vision was magnified that many times more until it came to fruition. Getting others onboard is an even higher power of manifestation. And though he was killed, the dream still lived on in the imaginations of all those other believers of the vision. When there are two or more carriers of a dream, I truly believe that only God can stop them (or the law if it is illegal). Take a look at this scripture that follows to see what God has to say about the imagination of people.

And the Lord said, Behold, they are one people (acting as one) and they have all one language (in agreement); and this is only the beginning of what they will do, and now nothing they have imagined they can do will be impossible for them. ~Gen 11:6

For a moment, let's talk about *you* who had a vision and let it die for one reason or another. Was it because you let someone tell you all the reasons it wouldn't work, or was it because you thought it was taking too long or it was too late for you? In the Book of Habakkuk, it says, *"For the vision is yet for an appointed time."* This is conditional because it depends on you *believing* and *not giving up* on the fact that this can happen for you, no matter how long it takes! Anything worth having is worth fighting for, right?

As you continue in your walk in faith with God, there will be moments in your life when God gives you glimpses of things He wants to give you, things that are *"yet for an appointed time."* This means that when you have reached a particular place and moment in your life, God will reveal certain things to you through visions or dreams. He will show you things to come and things you have asked Him for.

As stated in the Book of Genesis, Abraham, who was ninety-nine years old, was told that he and his wife Sarah would have a child at a non-childbearing stage of their lives. Abraham laughed at the possibilities, in awe I would say, at something he didn't think could happen *but* knowing only God could make it happen. But what Abraham and Sarah didn't know was *how* and *when* that blessed day would come. So this is where, with your dream, you have to *believe* God and hold the vision in your heart, in your imagination until its appointed time. Remember Jesse Jackson speaking of "keeping hope alive"? Well, this is where *hope* is the fuel that will give you the painted picture you desire. Understand that God is not a man. He will not lie about anything He promises you, so it's guaranteed! As the scripture pointed out for Abraham and Sarah's vision, *"though it tarry, wait [earnestly] for it, because it will surely come."* So it is for you!

Beliefs and Beyond

We all have thoughts of past failures, past limitations, and past judgments that can make us feel as though we can't do a thing. We may even feel we don't deserve the success we want. But aren't you glad that now that God is with you, it doesn't matter what you think when it comes to His promises? He loves you enough to bring you through!

This is where I see so many people have a hard time deciding just what they want their business to look like. I can't emphasize enough how important it is to start out with the information you have because it is going to change or evolve over time anyway. However, you must have a vision and some type of plan to carry it out.

As Donald Trump says, "Entrepreneurship starts with a vision. Follow your own path because it will bring you to the places you were meant to be."

I have known entrepreneurs that have started their businesses only to discover that another door has opened to an even greater opportunity.

Just because they took the first step and did not let fear enter into in the equation, they embarked on a journey that would lead them to that "right" place in business. Always remember, entrepreneurship is a journey, not a destination, because if you are running your business properly, there is always a place for you to make an impact with your product, service, or finances.

The power of the imagination can be seen most prominently in the hip-hop culture of the world. They are constantly singing about getting out of their bad conditions and environment. They spend their time daily talking about how they are about to be the next big star and get rich. With the use of their constant declarations through their songs about success and their visualizing their success before big audiences, they eventually get what they want. Now, if they can gain success without knowing the principles they are using, how much more can you get utilizing these same skills for your success in life, with God's help?

It's time to put your vision into action on paper. Take time to visualize three years from now and exactly what you want your business to look like.

"Begin with the end in mind." ~Stephen R. Covey

For example, compare this exercise to going to a movie and seeing what looks like the beginning but is yet the ending. Movies can start out with scenes that are jaw dropping and have you on the edge of your seat. But in essence, they show you the end and back you up in time to show you how you got there. This is the very same thing that you have to do with your vision for your business or life to bring it to fruition.

It is not necessary at this stage to know every detail of your business; just think about where you want to end up as a result of your success. Sit quietly and just imagine yourself operating in your business one, three, or five years from now. Through this experience, see yourself in your greatest achievements and wealth. I want you to *truly* think of how you are living your biggest dream life ever! Once you've captured that vision, complete the questions below to get your mental motor running. Have some fun!

Determining Your Vision

1. What product(s) or service(s) do you have in your business?
2. What types of clients are you serving? Who is the best candidate for what you offer? If you have specific clients in mind, list them.
3. Where is your business located? Do you work at home or in an office? Describe everything.
4. You've just met yourself on the job. What do you do in the business? Are your duties that of a true visionary who pushes the business forward or a hands-on, employee type of owner that prefers to hire someone else to run the company? Describe each.
5. How much do you and the business earn? (The amounts won't be the same because you have a certain lifestyle that you desire to live and fund. Your business may have employees, overhead, and systems that need funding and for future growth.)
6. Do you have employees? If so, how many? What do they do? What value do they add to the business? What skills and training do they have? Be as specific as possible.
7. Do you want to sell the company at some point? What does this business look like when you sell it? Would you prefer to just leave it for your kids or relatives?
8. What does this business do better than any other? What are you known for?
9. How do you feel about this business? What inspires you about this business?
10. How many days a week will you be working and what hours during the day?

Now, I don't want you to be hard on yourself if you cannot answer all of these questions. This is not something that I expect you to complete right now here on the spot. You may need a little more time because you are just getting started with your vision, or maybe you are perfecting it. But you should expect to be a lot further along by the end of this book.

If you are able to answer all of these questions now, then great! The best is yet to come for your business' progress. I do suggest that you get a notebook and keep all the exercises in one place so that you can refer back to them. In this next section, we are going to get your feet planted on solid ground so that you will be unstoppable!

WHY keeps your Vision Alive

Determining the reason "why" you want to run your own company is very crucial to the survival of your business. There will be moments in your business when you will question yourself as to why you are putting yourself through these various changes, especially in the beginning. It can get kind of rough on some days. I call these "unforeseeable obstacles" that can stop you, steer you, or just slow you down.

You can't give up just because you lost a customer or client or even if you haven't found the right one yet. Even if you had a failed product or service and your bank account dwindled to nothing, you must keep pressing forward. Entrepreneurs are expected to bounce back from these risks as quickly as possible. Anyone who has achieved any type of success will agree that this is all part of being an emerging entrepreneur. But guess what, *you are never to give up*!

Maybe your *WHY* falls into one of the categories below:

> ➢ Personal Fulfillment – You know there is more to life than what you are currently doing. There is a questioning within you, wondering if you are in the wrong place or if you are not being fully utilized in your potential.

> ➢ Make the World a Better Place – You are interested in how the world can be better through creating windmills as a better energy source, creating more green space, preventing child slavery, or creating organic goods (for example).

> ➢ Money – You want to be more financially stable than you are. You are tired of having your salary capped and want to earn unlimited income to be able to be, do, and have the things you want. It's okay to want money because God gives people this desire to make their own lives, other people's lives, or even a nation better.

> ➢ Power – We know that the one who has control over the most money normally has the most power and influence. There is nothing like having your decisions carried out by a large population of people—but make sure it is used to direct the wrongs of the world to become rights that serve many.

> ➢ Lifestyle Change – You've decided that you no longer want to work, live, and play in corporate America 365 days a year. You want to take half the year off and retreat to India or Africa to do some volunteer work or travel for pleasure.

President Obama said at the 2012 presidential nomination: "*We honor the Strivers, the Dreamers, the Risk Takers, the Entrepreneurs who have always been the driving force behind our free enterprise system. The greatest engine of growth and prosperity that the world's ever known.*"

It sounds like you have a civic duty to become a successful entrepreneur so that you can help someone, a people, or a nation to be better than they are currently. With your success and wealth, you will have the opportunity to be a person of power and change that can leave a mark that can never be erased—a legacy.

In *Inc.* Magazine's November 2013 issue, they spoke about the Inc. Hire Power Awards. This award is given every year to the companies with the highest number of jobs created in the marketplace. Creating jobs, I would say, is one of the top two reasons to start a business.

There are more private companies springing up on the scene than ever before. This year's honorees created a combined total of 51,327 new jobs. Now it's time for you to be a part of the growth in the marketplace, even globally!

I know you may not have gotten to the place of hiring employees, but you need to enlarge your vision. You should open up your mind and dream far bigger than you ever thought possible. If your *why* is so you can own a big house, buy the latest designer clothes, drive a luxury car, or become famous, then you are thinking way too small! You have got to get outside yourself and think of how you can help as many people as possible. It's more profitable to concentrate on the *benefits* that people will gain from you and your business. Have you heard the saying, "If you help enough people get what they want, you can have whatever you want"? It's true! Ask any wealthy, successful businessperson.

You may be thinking, "I really want to run my own company because I am tired of making someone else rich. I want to build my own company and earn as much money as I choose." And I would agree with you and would list this as one of your *whys*. I actually started my first company for that very reason. I wanted to run my own show and determine my own salary. In my early ventures I had only temporary success because my business was centered on me making money. But thank God, I no longer am plagued with those selfish motives. I have found my *why* and am now desiring to serve other people and not just myself.

Let's take a look at the *whys* of three very successful entrepreneurs in case you need a little help defining yours.

Howard Schultz. During an Oprah Winfrey interview, Howard spoke about how his father got laid off after he slipped on some ice and hurt himself and was not able to return to work. His father was not given any benefits while working at that current job. Little Howard watched with devastation as his family's income dropped drastically. They wouldn't hire his father back. Howard expressed that he felt his father had not been respected and honored for the man he was by that company. So he got to thinking *there has got to be something better.* Along the way he felt the need to build a company that his father never got the chance to work for. He wanted to build a company where no matter who you were you were treated with respect and given benefits, whether you were full- or part-time. It was exemplified in the Starbucks culture. Howard Schultz is known for providing quality products and services.

Walt Disney saw his sister standing outside a park that she didn't have the money to go into as he and his friend Rudolph watched her desire. He and Rudolf decided they would go into this park and see what it was all about. Walt liked what he saw and decided he would have an amusement park one day, but it would be much cleaner. He started thinking *there has got to be a better way* to allow children and their parents to enjoy the amusement of being at the park together while enjoying a cleaner environment. His vision for what he imagined went to work. One could say this is primarily due to his love for his sister or his desire to see her happier. Hence, Disney World was born.

Mary Kay Ash started her company because at the time the business world was dominated by men. She got to thinking *there has got to be a better way for women to succeed.* She wanted a company in which women had the opportunity to fully utilize their skills and talents so that they could enjoy the rewards appropriate for any goal they were smart enough to reach, even as a woman. Mary Kay Cosmetics was the solution.

As you can see, all of these entrepreneurs had one thing in common: Each one had a thought that became a vision that entered their imagination on how to solve a particular problem they thought needed solving. As a result, it was a solution welcomed by those who are still benefiting from it today!

What have you noticed in the marketplace, where there has got to be a better way of carrying it out? I don't want you to think about making all this money or knowing the right people. I prefer you to "act as if" you already have the resources you need in your possession.

Here are a couple very important questions I want you to really consider before defining your *why*. Now, if you are thinking in the wrong direction, this is a good place to reverse it.

➢ Are you starting a business to prove to someone that you are not a failure?
➢ Or are you starting a business because you want to make a lot of money and live a life of luxury like the famous people you admire?

If you answered **yes** to either of these questions … *wrong answer.*

➢ Are you doing this to improve a part of your life or to help support a parent or other loved ones? (e.g., retire parents, pay college tuitions, improve your income status, give to charity, etc.)
➢ Do you want to make an impact on a person, group, or particular part of the world? If so, will it create an impact or change? (e.g., create jobs, build shelters, do something better, etc.)

If you answered **yes** to either of these questions … *right answer!*

To sum this section up, once you define your *why* for building this business, always refer back to it when times get hard in any particular situation. I don't know how many times I have had to remind myself *why* I wanted to be a business owner. And each and every time, I heard that still small voice reminding me of what good my actions will bring to others. This, indeed, is an incentive to never give up!

Core Values Help Define Vision

But the fruit of the [Holy] Spirit [the work which His presence within accomplishes] is love, joy (gladness), peace, patience (an even temper, forbearance), kindness, goodness (benevolence), faithfulness, gentleness (meekness, humility), self-control (self-restraint, continence). Against such things there is no law [that can bring a charge]. ~Galatians 5:22-23

According to God, these are qualities that define your core values that you have as a result of possessing His Holy Spirit. As you come to experience more of God through meditation in His Word, it will become easier for you to exemplify these values in your everyday living. God calls these "fruits of the spirit." These values help you to build a character that will overcome things that you normally would not have been able to defeat. The Bible says that *as a man thinketh so is he in his heart,* so if any of these are missing, it could cost you your success. Defining your core values will help you find growth in your personal and business life. As that famous saying goes …

Your belief becomes your thoughts.
Your thoughts become your words.
Your words become your actions.
Your actions become your habits.
Your habits become your values.
Your values become your destiny.
~Mahatma Gandhi

I understand that the audience for this book is the emerging entrepreneur and the entrepreneur looking to do things God's way for maximum results. Core values start with you personally and spill over into your business. Core values are not written in stone, and as a matter of fact, they may change over the course of your business' growth as you evolve. Your core values can be considered your qualities that can never be bought.

The dictionary says that core values are the fundamental beliefs of a person or organization. Core values are the guiding principles that dictate behavior and action. They can help your company determine if it's on the right path and fulfilling its business goals, and they can create an unwavering guide to employees.

All through life, your core values or personal values were being shaped. You started to formulate your own through life experiences, and some were given through the influencers in your life. The easiest way to discover which ones were good and which ones were not so good would be to look at your life. Core values anchor you to your truth! If you have not identified your core values, you can be swayed by the wind, possibly in the wrong direction.

What values have you kept in mind concerning your life? Did you believe growing up that the only way to earn a good living was to get a good education and go to work for someone else? These core values of "good education and work hard" are definitely great ethics to have, but the core of each of these must be applied to *your* life. And it must be in an area that resonates with you and not the person who advised you. Your core value may be "work smarter not harder," but you heard a loved one say, "The only way to make it in life is through hard work! Nobody ever gave me a dime or helped me. I had to use blood, sweat, and tears to get where I am today!" This reinforces the fact that you need to struggle your way to success. So whenever you make money doing what you love, you may start to sabotage your success. This can turn into a vicious cycle that will bring detriment to you and your company in the long run. Core values are meant to bring about harmony and unison.

Core values, personally or in business, are about developing a culture or belief that bring about thoughts, words, actions, habits, and values that create an environment and destiny that work for all who are involved, which includes customers, employees, vendors, stockholders, etc.

You must be prepared to stand your ground at all costs whenever any person or group decides to stray away from the core values established for your company. If someone approaches you with some kind of get-rich-quick scheme, your core values will see you through. Core values can be challenged as you start to add more and more people into your organization. If you have established solid core values, your company's profits will reflect it. If your company ever starts to falter or slip in its corporate structure or profits, then quickly refer back to what your founding value principles are for checks and balances. Just remember, your core values, if instilled properly, will continue to drive your company long after you are gone.

Here are four examples of companies with core values that have made them the corporate culture they are today in the marketplace.

Mary Kay Cosmetics – The company's core values are "God first, family second, career third" and "Do unto others as you would have them do unto you."

Apple – The company's core values are summarized as "honesty, respect, confidentiality, and compliance."

Chick-fil-A – "To glorify God by being a faithful steward of all that is entrusted to us. To have a positive influence on all who come in contact with Chick-fil-A."

Walmart – "Save people money, help them live better lives."

Jesus (The Christ) – "A thief is only there to steal and kill and destroy. I came so they can have real and eternal life, more and better life than they ever dreamed of."

Here are some familiar core values you may have adopted into your personal or business life. See *Figure 4.1* to find out what your core values are made of because they are indeed directing your life choices, which ultimately can be defined below:

- A belief in God for the basis of your existence and ability to succeed
- A belief in operating in integrity with customers and employees
- A belief that family is of fundamental importance

- A belief that honesty is always the best policy and trust has to be earned
- A belief in maintaining a healthy work/life balance

Figure 4.1 – Core Values

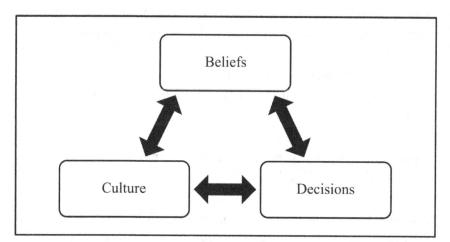

Creating Your Core Values Exercise

1. Take a blank sheet of paper and think of all the words and phrases that you think best describe you and that will spill over into your core values for your business. Come up with about ten to start. You may come up with words like *dependable, committed, reliable, honest, creative, respectful, innovative, motivating, inspiring, or consistent.* Of course, this may take you some time to complete, so don't be in a hurry.

2. Once you are done, go back through all your words and phrases and start to combine those that sound alike in meaning. For example, you might have *honest* and *trust* as two different values as shown in the previous examples. Now narrow them down to about five of your top chosen ones.

3. In order to make sure you have captured the true values that you exhibit from day to day, find five people, such as business

partners, friends, co-workers or family members, to give you their top three values they noticed about you.

4. Take your list and their lists and compare them to see if you are on point with your assumptions. Then examine what you see and what they see. I am sure you will discover new values you didn't know you were exhibiting.

5. Finally, you should have a list that, after careful examination, you agree has defined the good values you want to take into your business.

Your Vision Becomes Your Mission

To succeed in your mission, you must have a single-minded devotion to your goal. ~Abdul Kalam, Scientist

Your mission statement can contain your vision, your *why*, and your core values. This is why defining your core values can help you show your customers and clients what your company stands for.

The mission statement communicates both the purpose and values of the organization. For employees, it gives direction about how they are expected to behave and inspires them to give their best. Shared with customers, it shapes customers' understanding of why they should work with your organization.

Below, I am providing you with some long and short mission statements. Once you create yours, it should be checked and updated whenever needed.

Longer Mission Statements are normally used to define a large corporate culture.

Examples include:

- **AARP** – "To enhance quality of life for all as we age. We lead positive social change and deliver value to members through information, advocacy and service." **(25 words)**
- **Feeding America** – "To feed America's hungry through a nationwide network of member food banks and engage our country in the fight to end hunger." **(22 words)**
- **Jesus (The Christ)** – "I came that they may have and enjoy life, and have it in abundance (to the full, till it overflows)." **(14 words)**

Short Mission Statements can be summed up in one short sentence as shown below.

Examples include:

- Just Do It! (**3 words**)
- To help people be healthy (**5 words**)
- To have our product in every home in the U.S. (**10 words**)
- To treat our customers with integrity and excellence (**8 words**)

Think for a moment about the product or service you are selling in the marketplace.

➤ What do you want people to know that your product or service can provide or do for them?
➤ What is the main reason *why* you created the product or service?

These are the types of questions your mission statement should be answering and then displaying to each and every one of your customers. Now, let's go ahead and get your mission statement ready for your business. Once done, you will definitely want to add this to your website if you are promoting any business services or products.

Chapter 4 – God-made Millionaire Exercise – Mission Statement

_____

_____

_____

_____

Why Most Businesses Fail

The plans of the diligent lead surely to advantage, But everyone who is hasty comes surely to poverty. ~Prov 21:5

When building your business, you must have precautionary measures in place that better ensure your success. God's word says that you should be diligent in understanding what is required in order to build. You must not be in a hurry. Your breakthrough is not based on your ability alone. It is His divine sovereignty and your human responsibility that make the winning combination. *"Faith without works is dead"* is what God says about anything you desire to accomplish. You must put your mind and hands into action, and God will see you through.

In this chapter, you will come to understand the pitfalls of poor business practices that have caused entrepreneurs and small businesses to fail many times over. Even if you have already started your business, you should avoid these at all costs. This chapter is not designed to shake a finger at you. It is basically to show you what to avoid while building your business. You can confidently know that God can teach you how to overcome each and every one of these if you allow His Holy Spirit to guide you.

Let's look at some personal qualities and business practices that, if missing, can lead to your business' demise because *you are your business!*

Spiritual Blockers

No one really spends their time trying to find out exactly what makes them tick. We are mostly trying to see what other people are doing and how they are achieving the things we want in life. We continue to observe and follow them because we want to *copy* who they have become because we believe we can get the same results. We were not created to be replicas of anyone! What we don't understand is that the true change must start, as Michael Jackson says, "with the man in the mirror." We ourselves cause our delays and denials of blessings because we can't identify the things that are keeping us from achieving success. If we would just stop for a moment and let God reveal to us the spiritual and blessing blockers, most of our troubles would diminish. Here are a few spiritual blockers to eliminate from your life.

> ➤ **Un-forgiveness** – A harboring of a disagreement or dispute against someone that may have caused you to feel bitterness in your heart toward them that caused you hurt. Ask God to help you release them as it can be difficult to do on your own.
> ➤ **Sin** – More of an act of wrong thinking that brings about the wrong actions toward others and God. It's the mindset that you don't need God and are going to do things your way. Therefore, things you do become adverse behaviors that defy God's will for your life. Sin occurs more often as a result of not knowing who you are. Jesus became sin and defeated it on your behalf, on the cross.
> ➤ **Self-Doubt** – Not believing that you can be, do, and have what you desire in your heart. Do you believe that someone like you can be a millionaire? Do you believe you have what it takes to run a successful company? Do you believe you are powerful beyond measure? Just know that God says you have all the makings—through Him, not yourself—to do the impossible.
> ➤ **Fear** – The worst fear of all is to believe that if you trust everything you are and have to an invisible God that nothing will happen. Fear is worrying about things God never intended you to be concerned with. Keep your eyes on God and fear will disappear.

➢ **Unbelief** – Not believing that God is who He says He is, which is the opposite of having faith. Not believing that God has a plan for your life to give you a wonderful future. Not believing that God loves you enough to bring you out of your current situations. Any unbelief that you have is directly connected to the voice(s) you are listening to.

➢ **Not Giving** – Feeling as though you don't have enough for yourself, so why should you give to another. Giving does not have to always be tangible money. You can give of your time. Giving, when you have little, of your time or money can be compared to a wealthy person giving out of their overflow. Giving is an act of love toward another, and not giving leads to a drying up of what you already have been given.

➢ **Disobedience** – Not doing what God has asked you to do according to scripture. The Bible is known as a Book of Blessings. If you love someone, you will treasure the advice they give and be careful to do all they say. But if you despise a person, you will not do as they say and therefore will not reap what they are offering as a gift of love.

➢ **Gossip/Judgment of Others** – Although we are all guilty of gossiping, one should not spend precious time talking about others concerning things that are not advancing their future. One has to look beyond the surface of someone to see those behaviors and acts that *are* good. Unknowingly, there is a reason behind the acts of others who behave unacceptably. If you are not willing to help deliver them from whatever it is they may be going through, then there should not be any harsh words spoken about them.

➢ **Lack of Discipline of the Tongue** – In Proverbs 18:21 it says, "Death and life are in the power of the tongue, and they who indulge in it shall eat the fruit of it [for death or life]." If you don't want a particular thing to take place in your life, then only speak those words which prosper you or others. Using the tongue for gossip, as stated above, is the same as speaking death toward another. So don't curse *your* future by declaring what you think you aren't capable of doing. Just letting your mouth speak the first things that come to mind, negatively, about you or someone else is never good. Always speak life.

➤ **Anger Toward God** – Never close off your heart to God because of something you feel He could have prevented or done for you. I have seen and heard so many people get upset with God and turn their backs to Him and lash out at anyone who is remotely close to Him. God will speak to you, in spirit, and give you comfort. He will give meaning to what seems unexplainable situations. But if you close your heart, you will never hear or feel the love of God in your time of need.

Humanistic (Personal) Blockers

There are personal blockers in your life that can stem from not having enough experience or education in areas that are critical for life and your business. Everyone needs to grow in order to stay relevant and current in your industry, especially in business. If you are going to run a business that services others, then it is imperative that you think like a leader. Certain personal strengths are the anchors that ground you to your business. Not possessing one or more of them could create unnecessary failure. What is great about these attributes is that you can *learn* them over time.

➤ **Gratitude** – This is being thankful for the small beginnings. Don't take anything for granted when running your business. These small signs of success end up being the catalyst for building your business empire for generations to come. So get up each morning and be grateful for the smallest of things that God has afforded you in order to see the big things arrive in your life in perfect timing.

➤ **Leadership** – This is the ability to be trusted with a vision or purpose from God and for it to be completed with a chosen people to reach an expected end. Leadership means staying one step ahead of those who dare to follow you. You must seek God for strategies that can defeat your worst enemies. Leadership means that you will continue to educate and associate yourself with those who have accomplished great successes. This may mean going left when everyone else says go right because you are confident in your decision. The true sign of a great leader is their ability to trust God when things seem impossible to become possible. Leaders also instill in those around them the belief that they are well able to do anything as a team *and* find growth for themselves.

➢ **Creativity** – Most entrepreneurs are creative. They can take nothing and make it into something with the help of others. By nature, entrepreneurs are dreamers and carry visions of possibilities. True creativity comes from the heart, and you must dare to be different. Being creative takes a special kind of confidence that you are willing to fail in front of others and try again.

➢ **Perspective** – What is your outlook on life and the situations around you? Are you the type of person that looks on the bright side of things or points out the worst first? Successful business people keep a positive outlook on life and their business ventures. They surround themselves with positive people. In order to be the best you can be, you must open your mind to the possibilities and be willing to see through the eyes of others so as not to limit your growth and possibilities. Wealthy people look at life through wide-angle lenses.

➢ **Learning** – You should always look for ways to improve yourself, whether with a mentor, books, seminars, or by taking classes offline/online. From the beginning, you must be prepared to take a percentage of your business and dedicate it back to you! Life is a continual learning process with infinite wisdom to be gained. Always remember, the minute you stop learning is the minute you become obsolete.

➢ **Self-Regulation** – Are you the type that does not need to be reminded that things need to be done? Are you self-disciplined? If you cannot trust yourself to work without supervision, then you may have a problem with becoming a successful entrepreneur. Oftentimes, you are the sole runner of your vision in the beginning, so learning to control your daily activities for productivity is very necessary to your success.

➢ **Perseverance** – Are you in this for the long haul? Or are you ready to bail out at the first sign of trouble? Maybe your sales are down and you are low on money, so what are you going to do … close down your business and leave your customers hanging? No, you have got to do what is necessary to keep a steady and consistent movement for continued progress. This is what makes an entrepreneur successful. If you don't have this quality, then keep your day job!

Bad Business Practices

It is the unknown that often trips up any emerging entrepreneur when starting a business. It is the thrill of being your own boss and regulating your own time that takes precedence over procedures set forth in a start-up company. Most entrepreneurs take off running with no real research as to why businesses don't ever make it. If we would just study the failures of others, we would better understand the importance of not repeating the same mistakes. In **Figure 5.1**, you can see the staggering percentages of reasons why *people* fail, which in turn, cause the business to fail due to bad business practices.

Figure 5.1 – Reasons Why Businesses Fail

Major Cause	Percentage of Failures
Incompetence	46%
Unbalanced Experience or Lack of Managerial Experience	30%
Lack of Experience in line of goods or services	11%
Neglect, Fraud, Disaster	1%

Source: *Data provided by Statistic Brain- 07/27/2013*

Let's dig a little deeper into each one of the major causes to see what you should be aware of as you build your business.

1. **Incompetence** – unfamiliar with the process of running a business as an entrepreneur. You should always do your research and seek to be the *best* in your industry.

- Emotional Pricing
  - Just because you think it should cost this price does not mean the customer will think so as well. Check industry prices and the quality of your product or service as compared to others on the market.
- No knowledge of the industry
  - Do your research to see who the top people or companies are in your niche. You should be following at least three people or companies to learn from their successes and failures.
- Nonpayment of taxes
  - You have to definitely schedule to pay your taxes quarterly or annually yourself or with your tax preparer. Major banks partner with agencies that will file your business taxes for a small fee. You don't want to get closed down by the IRS before you get started.
- No experience in record keeping
  - If you don't know how to set up your company's daily transactions, contacts, customer information, or product database, then you will not know when there are profits or losses that need to be dealt with. Hire a professional accountant to set up and balance your books on a quarterly, semiannual, or annual basis. If you need to take a basic finance course, then by all means do what is necessary to be an excellent money manager on your own.

2. Unbalanced Experience or Lack of Managerial Experience – only worked in a particular area for a short period of time or not at all

- Poor credit-granting practices
  - If you have decided to become a wholesaler or to carry account receivables, then please put practices in place to *qualify* your buyers. You may want to hire an accounts-receivable company to handle or buy any bad buyer debts to keep cash flowing in your business.
- Expand too rapidly
  - If you are doing very well in your business and decide to open a second office, please make sure you have *systems* in place to warrant your expansion.
- Inadequate borrowing practices
  - It is best to have a business plan in place in case you ever suffer from not enough cash flow coming into the company. You may even need extra cash to buy more inventory or hire new employees. If you don't have the right documents available, then no investor will look at your company. Please don't wait until you need the money to put together your credit worthiness. You should be keeping good records that you can pull from at any time.

3. Lack of Experience in Line of Goods or Services – developed or purchased product or service that one has not sold before

- Carry inadequate inventory
  - You do not have enough items in stock to fulfill your customer or vendor orders. They will walk away and buy from your competitor. You may even be selling an inferior product because you do not know the quality of your product source.
- No knowledge of suppliers
  - You contract with suppliers who may not be the sole supplier of your product. They may be getting it from

an overseas manufacturer, and it may take weeks to get your supply. In the meantime, you did not get a wider list of other suppliers who could provide your product in a quicker and more efficient manner.

- Wasted advertising budget
  - You decided to place an ad in newspapers, magazines, and on the radio, and you even invested in a billboard. But not knowing what mediums are best for your business or service is an ingredient for wasted dollars. You should always choose one medium for six-month increments and then scrap it or move on to the next medium if it doesn't work. With social media today, you will use less money if you connect with your customer in an authentic way.

4. **Neglect, Fraud, Disaster** – This category fits the person or company that clearly has no intention of being in business for long. There is normally deceit, manipulation, and no honor wrapped up in this category. You have seen those millionaires and billionaires that have ended up in jail and shamed by their actions. Even those who run small or large businesses that don't keep their hands and eyes open to what their customers are asking for find themselves filing bankruptcy or going out of business because they neglected a sector of their business. Obviously, this is not the path to take in order to reach a God-made millionaire status!

"There is a flawed assumption that people who are an expert at a certain technical skill will therefore be successful running a business of that kind."
~Michael E. Gerber, E-myth Revisited, Author

Michael Gerber believes that an entrepreneur maybe unsuccessful if they are not fully aware of their role in running a successful business. He feels that there are three roles that one has to play in business, and most of the time it is not the role the entrepreneur thought it would be.

Here are the three distinct roles that Gerber says are functioning within any business, including yours. **Figure 5.2** shows the three distinct roles that Michael Gerber describes in E-Myth Revisited.

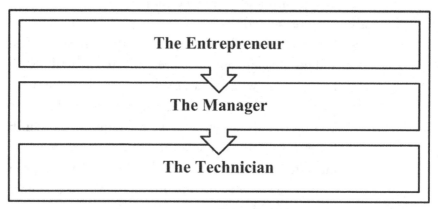

Figure 5.2 – Three Distinct Roles

➤ The Entrepreneur – operates in the future and is oftentimes the visionary. He/she is thinking about or planning with imagination or wisdom.

➤ The Manager – operates in the past and is more concerned with the operational procedures of the company that have been put in place. He/she is more concerned with helping the visionary carry out his vision for the company.

➤ The Technician – operates in the present and is a doer. He/she is more concerned with the daily tasks that are required for any particular day. They are not concerned with the vision or what the operation manual says about company procedures that are outside their job duties. This is oftentimes the person that bakes the cakes in a bakery, mows the lawns for a landscaping company, or stitches the clothes for an upcoming designer line.

Michael believes that many people start their businesses because someone told them they were good at something. For example, maybe you were told you are the best cook in town. Maybe you can repair any car you put your mind to fix. All of a sudden, you have an "Aha" moment because people are telling you that you should open your own business. They tell you how you can be rich by bringing in customers on a larger scale.

You start to listen to what they are saying. You have a thought, that thought becomes a vision of grandeur, and it gets sent to your imagination. You start looking for places to lease to start your newfound business. You get your business license and hopefully open up a separate checking account for your business.

You start letting everyone know you are now in business for yourself and to send you some customers. You get customers, and you are working day and night and loving it because it's your passion!

All of a sudden you realize that you are only one person. You can't keep up with the demand. You need to hire someone else because you are missing out on special occasions with the family. But you find out that there are labors laws and employee payroll concerns that need to be set up. You start getting letters from the state tax office about reporting your earnings for the quarter.

This is where the budding entrepreneur realizes that they have been the "technician" the whole time and not the *true* entrepreneur. He or she did not realize they would eventually have to give up the work they enjoyed doing and hire others to carry it out for them. Their new job would require them to take off the worker's hat, remove the wrench from their hand, and put on the CEO cap of Visionary.

Gerber describes this as a "wannabe" entrepreneur having an "entrepreneurial seizure"—a person who gets so excited about having their own business before considering the cost. So, please consider what it takes to start, build, and run a successful business!

Knowing When to Quit

When it comes to quitting your job, it depends on where you are in life. If you're young, your responsibilities are usually lower. But if you are already in your career and have built a life around others, then you have some life-altering things to consider. If you're like me, it's not easy to just stop what you're doing midstream to change directions. This can cause critical chain reactions that could be devastating. It can include loss of relationships, income, and even your hair. Deciding to pursue your dream can be frightening. This is the part that makes quitting your job so difficult, whether you have responsibilities financially or morally to others or not. Sometimes you have to *consider the cost* of *not* doing a thing as well. God created you to do great things and this includes doing the things that bring you the greatest joy! Honestly, taking the challenge to step out on faith, with a God you have never seen, is the greatest glory to God mankind can ever give. It may not be so easy, but it can definitely be worth it in the end.

I remember one day, while working at one of the largest insurance companies in the nation, I had to go to a sales meeting. I had been working with a customer in the sales department and had just finished up with them. I saw men walking around the office with suits on, and supervisors who normally didn't dress up had on suits as well. They were all congregating in different parts of the office in little huddles. I didn't know who they were, but I knew they had to be some of the top corporate leaders.

I had been sitting at my desk for less than five minutes after finishing with a customer when a manager came over to our group and asked us to follow them to another area of the floor. When our team arrived at the meeting place, we were greeted by an entourage of other staff and management. The VP was actually in the building, and this was why all the commotion was taking place. The VP proceeded to thank us all for our excellent work and how sales had soared in the last quarter, surpassing an all-time high. Collectively we had sold over 1.15 million policies in four months' time for a total of 259 million policies! As he continued to explain that our goal was 329 million by year's end, the managers started to chant and rave to raise the energy on the floor.

I thought what an accomplishment for a company. This was spectacular to me because I thought what if this was my company! All of a sudden the entrepreneurial spirit started to rise up in me again, and I started to think, "Why am I sitting here living in someone else's dream? They had an instinct to act upon their idea of starting this company in order to help people have better and affordable insurance. The owner was solving a problem. Why am I not acting upon my own dream and researching how I can solve the problem of the sector of people I have a heart for?" That small voice deep down inside said to me, "How much longer are you going to continue to run back to corporate America and make someone else wealthy and disregard your own dreams?" Then my self-defeating voice started shouting, "Why can't you just be like everyone else and be happy with having a good job with benefits where you know *when* you're able to go on vacation, go out to dinner with friends *and* buy those things you've always wanted?" As an emerging entrepreneur, this struggle has always gone on inside my head. (Maybe it has yours too?) So what did I do? I put back on my entrepreneurial hat and got to work making things happen once again. If you truly want to be an entrepreneur, then these type of decisions have got to be dealt with, sooner or later. And, if this *is* your pressing dilemma, what are you going to do about it?

This is a dilemma that so many entrepreneurs seem to face when they feel discontent in their current positions and can't seem to take that leap of faith. They are waiting for someone to say, "Yes, I think you should quit your job to pursue your dream of entrepreneurship, so what are you waiting for?" Those words would be music to your ears, right, because someone has finally validated that very thought floating around in your head. But the downfall comes when you heed what is said without the proper preparation for your exit. You have no strategy. Now, I know many people latch onto phrases like the one from Nike™ such as "Just Do It!" That may work for some, but it may not work for others. Some of the greatest entrepreneurs never decided to quit their job in three years, two months, and five hours from a particular day. Normally, when the opportunity presents itself, you have to decide if you are *in* or if you are *out*.

Consider the Risk

Of course, if you are still working full-time, you should be doing your research and gaining experience. There are a few things you should take into consideration before quitting because you don't want to jump ship before you have looked at enough options. I am not being a pessimist here, but I want you to consider some things that you *may* be giving up as a result of leaving your job *before* your profits exceed your yearly salary. Consider the cost by thinking on these four things, which are just a few of many.

Your Credit Ability. Credit should be used only if you are disciplined and as temporary leverage. Having that day or night job helps you get more credit cards, borrow money, or look good on paper to lenders if you feel you absolutely have to borrow money. God-made millionaires understand this concept. As an emerging entrepreneur, you should save cash for your start-up inventory and business expenses and borrow only if you need to purchase more for order fulfillment. It is much easier to substantiate your borrowing if you can see how you can pay it back quickly. If you have a spouse, Plan B could be them keeping their full-time job so that you can still have access to credit cards and loans, if absolutely necessary.

Your Financial Stability. Financial stability as an employee is different from financial stability as the employer. As an employee, continuing to have an hourly salary can enable you to set your sights on things like luxury vacations, an upgraded house, a new car, or even eating out many times a month. You can order online products today and have it arrive tomorrow. As an entrepreneur, you must understand that there may be days when you are not able to buy gifts like you used to. You may need to take those profits and roll them right back into the company. There will be many sacrifices that will have to take place for the sake of your future success. If you have kids, then this will mean having to tell them *no* on many occasions. This decision may even cost you your retirement. Are you ready to take on the financial risks that are associated with becoming an entrepreneur? Maybe or maybe not! Of course, better financial planning equals a lower financial risk. To bring about financial security for your family, make sure you invest in a life insurance policy that would provide for them in case of any unthinkable moments in life that could cause them financial hardship while building your business.

Your Tax-Deduction Capability. I am not going to spend a lot of time here because I do not profess to be a tax advisor. When it comes to tax time, your dual income will allow you to deduct some of those business expenses therefore giving you a bigger tax break. In order to take full advantage of your employee to entrepreneur and possible employer status, you should know what governmental breaks await you. Please check with your accountant or CPA to confirm your deductions. Download IRS Publication 587 – Business Use of Your Home, and Publication 583 – Starting A Business & Keeping Records, if needed.

Your Benefits Comfortability. I cannot say enough about this. You must realize that your wonderful benefits and flex-spending account will go away. Make plans to have a self-employment medical plan all lined up before you prepare to leave. As one suggestion, google "insurance plans for the self-employed" if this will be a benefit that will not be cost-effective. Of course, if you have a spouse that can carry the health benefits, that would be great!

Will quitting affect your retirement plan? Will you be penalized? You want to plan for the worst-case scenario. Check to see if there will be any major penalties for withdrawing your money early. I was penalized about 10 percent for early withdrawal approximately ten years ago, plus whatever tax bracket I fell into due to my age. You may even want to check with your CPA about starting an SEP account, which is a

Simplified Employee Pension Plan that helps self-employed individuals and small business owners get access to tax-deferred benefits when saving for retirement. Use up your health benefits by seeing all your doctors before you leave the job. Don't burn bridges with those you may need again, such as asking for your job back if things don't go as planned. (Of course, going back is never the plan!)

If you are still not sure if you are ready, then check online for various entrepreneur tests. You can go online and Google "entrepreneur personality test" or "entrepreneurial personality test." I have taken a couple, and they are pretty good. I found some areas in me that were indeed my strengths and how I was using them in my everyday life. Just know that as an emerging entrepreneur, you will never know *all* the answers before venturing out on your own, but you must keep in mind that it is a learning process for your development. If you keep an open mind and open heart for the mistakes that must take place in order for you to succeed, you will get to the place that you have only dreamed of, no matter what!

Failure Is a Must

On many occasions I have heard the saying, "Failure is not an option," but I beg to differ. *Failure is not only an option, it is a must!* No one can say that they have not failed at something. The biggest point is did you get back up and try it again? If you didn't, that of course was your option. You have to make up in your mind the reason why it is imperative that you conquer a thing. Just think back, for a moment, on a time in your life where you refused to give up. Then think about the reason *why* you decided not to give up. There was always something driving you to be better at whatever it was you overcame for the victory.

I remember when I first started my entrepreneurial journey. Like my dad, I wanted to run my own company and build a better life. I witnessed him working a full-time job while also running his business after he got off work. He would give up his sleep on occasions and even some of the time he spent with our family, but it had to be done. I later understood this is the point in life where transition takes place and the losses occur. For some, the losses can be time with family, a decrease in pay, sleep deprivation, or even the loss of relationships. But you must understand that these losses are like the casualties of war. To win any battle there has got to be some losses. So with my first business, I followed in the footsteps of my father to try to make that same transition. But things didn't always work out so well for me. The difference between my father and me was that he knew what he wanted to accomplish and in what industry. I didn't. I spent many years knowing I would run my own business but failing my way through to find it.

I had what one would consider five failed ventures. But I never saw it that way because I just kept moving forward. People around me would look at me as though I were crazy for wasting my time on things that never panned out. In some of my more depressed states, I tended to believe them. But I kept going despite their outlook on my endeavors. Someone even told me, "Well, sometimes we think we hear God, and we actually move without His approval." I interpreted that statement as having missed God five times over, therefore making me deaf to the voice of God on every occasion. I believe in some cases you can miss God. But whenever you earnestly pray *before* doing anything, then God will faithfully direct your steps. I often asked God to open doors that I couldn't open on my own in order to show that He was with me. In most of my ventures, I worked with the little that I had and moved forward with the greater faith that had been given to me. I had learned to *trust* God to move on my behalf based on past victories with Him and through His scriptural word. I never depended on *anyone* to tell me when to start or when to quit *any* of my business ventures. I listened for the opportunity to move, instinctively, from one place to another, therefore knowing when it was time to quit. Was I always right? I wanted to think so.

Honestly, no one can really tell you when to quit your job. Only you can make that decision based on your perception of your current situation.

Does your dissatisfaction with your job or life warrant you leaving the security of a full-time job to pursue the unknown? Venturing into the unknown is a risk that every emerging entrepreneur will have to take, at one point or another. The question is, "Are you willing to take that leap to pursue your dream and forego all the *worldly* safety nets that have protected you for so long?" Some would say wait until you have a year's worth of savings in the bank to cover your everyday expenses while others would say stay at your current job until you are making more money in your business than being employed. Before quitting, always make sure that you ask yourself the right questions.

Are you educated well enough in your desired industry to make the leap? Here are some questions you might want to consider if selling a product.

- Have you calculated how much it would cost to make the product, if it is your invention?
- How will you get it to market?
- Have you researched who will want to distribute your product and put it on their shelves?
- How much of a profit margin will you have, and will it be enough if you need to hire other people to help you?
- Is your manufacturer really maximizing the product quantity they are making for you, or are there several other products they are producing for other companies?
- Will you have to order a certain amount of stock each month?
- Do you have a place to store the products, and will climate control be a factor?
- Have you calculated whether or not this product will have a long shelf life, and if so, what is the maximum amount of time it will last before having to toss it, if perishable?

These are just some questions that touch the tip of the iceberg because these questions are only about the product and not your business costs or expenses for each month. I only mentioned this because starting out on your own must take some kind of thought because you are leaving the corporate security behind and taking on all the risks on your own by quitting too soon. Just choose wisely!

I have quit my job on several occasions to pursue my entrepreneurial dreams and was successful in some ventures and not so successful in others. I went through a phase where I seemed to be quitting my jobs every six months like clockwork. I believe this is why I took on only contractual positions and not full-time jobs because I wanted to keep my options open for the right moment.

I left the doors open to my past so that I could come back from the unknown if necessary. But let me tell you when the going got tough, I got going back to that place of comfort! I kept going back to my previous jobs for a two reasons. First, those jobs became my investors when I ran out of money *and* my crutch when I felt defeated. Secondly, employment meant I would no longer have to struggle and press forward toward God's higher calling on my life. It felt too hard at times! I eventually learned that I was ultimately taking flight instead of facing my fears inside. With me, it was because I was not in alignment with a transition that was trying to take place in my life. I believe that when your thoughts start to line up with God's, they start to guide you away from the normal and into the abnormal. This can be scary. This is the opposite of what the world dictates that you should be doing in order to fit in. With me, I should have been doing more of the things that moved me closer to purpose than just going to work to get a paycheck to pay my bills. Whenever that entrepreneurial spirit rose up in me, as I mentioned before, it was time to go on another adventure. But each time, I was getting better and better!

Eckhart Tolle talks about "The Three Modalities of Awakening" in his book *A New Earth*. He says that if you do not have *acceptance, enjoyment,* and *enthusiasm* working in your life, then you are in disharmony with the universe (God). So this means that if you do not have any of these three modalities present in your life when carrying out your job, then you should stop because it is dysfunctional. You are not aligned with your present moment, yourself, or life. He states that this is a psychic dysfunction and is like a disease. Your success depends on what positive energy flows into what you are doing. Now you must examine *why* these modalities are not showing up in your job.

You could feel disconnected from your present job because of unconscious thoughts stemming from external disruptions or because a change or a transition is happening in your life. You are shifting because of an awakening in the mind that is leading you down a greater and more fulfilling path. I compare this to those times when you know you should be doing something else in life besides what you are presently doing. If you are not, in any present moment in acceptance, enjoying and exerting enthusiasm in what you are doing, then there is a problem. Now, if you know these three modalities of awakening are missing from your life, then you are probably working your present job because you need the money. But you must understand that you should also be working on ways to follow the essence of your discontentment to its core for proper direction.

Chapter 5 – God-made Millionaire Exercise

1. Take out a sheet of paper, write down your *WHY*, and frame it on your office wall. This will help you stay on course in those times of despair. This will become your fuel to keep you moving forward.

2. Start to study the successes and failures of other people and other companies, in any industry, to learn from their mistakes. This will make you a much better entrepreneur and teacher to others.

3. Whether this is your first business or not, take mental notes of your failures so that you can learn from them. Put them in a journal because this will help you see how God brought you through it. You will begin to see patterns of how God deals with you and your successes.

Chapter 6

Taking Your Rightful Place

"The road to happiness lies in two simple principles; Find what it is that interests you and that you can do well, and when you find it, put your whole soul into it—every bit of energy and ambition and natural ability you have." ~ John D. Rockefeller

Passion leads to purpose. Find all the things you love and write them down because not all you love is profitable. If you have been seeking God, then you know what category of business seems best for you. So research on Google to find out if people are willing to pay for a product or service of your type. If they are purchasing, then you need to decide if you can buy or produce it at a low enough cost to earn a profit to sustain you.

According to what you wrote in your Chapter 4 vision exercise, here's where you decide which business is best for the benefits you wish to reap from business ownership. You identified your work hours, where you would like to work, and how many employees you have, amongst other things. I want to show you areas of business that you can try on for size to see if they fit you.

Let me share a short story with you about my journey to discovering what business would be right for me. I am not saying that your life will unfold like mine because no two people travel the same road in life. As I spoke of earlier, I knew in my twenties that I felt the desire to become a successful business owner, but I didn't know in what. I had even started having dreams about it. I didn't consult with anyone on what business to go into because I wasn't quite sure. I stepped out one day on a great urge to open a ladies after-five boutique. I rented a space but kept my night job. I worked about four to six hours in the morning and eight hours at night almost five or six days a week. I didn't dare try to work seven days during the night and day and still live! I was also a young mother, although my husband and I took shifts. He even worked there on some days to help me out. The boutique was doing very well and gaining momentum. I would fly to New York every season and stock up on the latest fashions while building relationships in the Garment District of Manhattan. I was having a ball, and it could have been because I got the latest fashions at wholesale costs. My husband had even started delivering some of the fashions to the customers at their homes or their jobs. It was a great angle and made us stand out, but we both became exhausted and decided to hire someone.

We paid minimum wage and brought someone in part-time. It worked for a little while, but the employee was not very responsible. They were not dependable, but we didn't know how to hire a competent person due to our pay structure. We needed them only when we didn't want to come in, which placed them on call, or we couldn't pay them if our profits were low that month. We started to find some of the items missing when we returned to the store on occasion. No one seemed to have witnessed anything. I eventually had to fire my part-time employee and closed the boutique shop down.

I walked away, though, with valuable lessons: I learned (1) that you can't leave your business in the hands of an employee, therefore being an absentee owner; (2) you have to carve out time to grow your business, especially when working a full-time job; and (3) before hiring an employee full-time or part-time, you must have a pay structure that will entice them to stay and to sell more items, such as having a commission-based position.

Although I ended up closing the doors because I wasn't quite ready, about five years later I decided to try it again. My job was threatening to lay me off, and I knew it was coming. I had decided to take the leap of faith because it just felt right! I prepared myself by doing the research to make sure I had enough knowledge to get a momentum flowing. For some reason, I felt better prepared. I didn't go back to the retail business but instead went head-on into real estate. This proved to be a most lucrative business and time in my life. I grew my bank account, gained relationships, and learned much about real estate investing. But in 2005, we lost it all! The real estate economy crashed and so did we. I made the money and spent the money as soon as it came rolling into my bank account. We bought anything our hearts desired. I eventually lost the business, and my personal life went with it. I lacked financial-planning and management skills. This loss is what drove me to finding God, once again.

About two years later, I started another business in which I consulted God for direction. This business was a larger-sized retail store than I had before. I used the same name that I had used for my very first retail store. I started out in a small space and several months later moved to a space two times that size. The store did pretty well, but I didn't study my competition in the area to know that I could not compete with their inventory. I fell in love with my idea and ran with it—not always a good idea, without research. I was working off a shoestring budget, so my inventory and marketing was very limited. What I came to realize is that I did not have enough inventory to make the money I wanted to make. I had not completed a projected income sheet to determine what I would like to make on an annual basis. I didn't care about my salary at that time because I was willing to forego it. If I had done a projected analysis of how much inventory I would need and the profit necessary from each sale, I would have realized that I needed a lot more inventory to accomplish my goal. If I had done that, I would not have had to worry about any competition, but about carrying the right quantity of products.

Once this dawned on me and I could not find the money to invest more into the business, I found myself struggling to survive. I asked God for help. As a result, he led me to take some of my products onto eBay, and they sold like a wildfire in a dry forest! I remember having these ladies get into bidding wars for the products I listed. I started putting in extra products, for a boy or girl, and packed handwritten thank you cards in the mailings. This created even more referrals. I made my rent for the next several months thereafter. It was enough to get me through the last months of my lease. I eventually closed that business down because I couldn't compete and wasn't making enough to fulfill my financial needs. This was another opportunity to learn from my mistakes while trying to find my rightful place.

During the next three to five years, I opened up several more businesses. Each time, I went to God before proceeding, and the doors always seemed to open in my favor. Although these businesses were not sustainable, I still felt my entrepreneurial days were not over. Others looked at me as though these were failures, and for a while so did I. God knew all along what He was doing because He knew where my rightful place would eventually be located. I had a will in me that would never let me give up, no matter what! There was always a drive in me to keep going to find out where I belonged in the marketplace. I knew I was an entrepreneur, but what was I supposed to do with that nagging desire? I started business after business after business. God was still watching over me. Eventually, people started calling me to help them with their businesses and problems they would encounter. I would offer my solutions based off my past knowledge and experience, and it would work for them. Go figure!

What I didn't know was God was building a business database within me, for the emerging entrepreneur, that would be the catalyst for my future purpose. I later realized that I loved helping and training people more than I loved working *in* the business. I learned and came to understand the pain of emerging entrepreneurs and existing store owners who were experiencing failures because they missed necessary steps in building their business *before* opening their doors.

I said all of that to let you know that building your business will not be discovered immediately. Wealthy people understand the process of trial and error. God understands the process of pain that is necessary to lead you to glory! So remember, if you want to be a wealthy entrepreneur, you have to be willing to fail in order to find your rightful place. It may take you a series of failures to get to the true business that is yours, but don't become all caught up in missing the mark. Be vigilant and diligent because each time you are getting closer! Take your time and consult God at every turn, and you can find that right business quicker than you could have on your own. As God's word says below, you should not be in a hurry.

I returned and saw under neither the sun that the race is neither to the swift nor the battle to the strong neither is bread to the wise nor riches to men of intelligence and understanding nor favor to men of skill; but time and chance happen to them all. ~ Ecc 9:11

Just showing up and getting started is the beginning of taking the right step toward becoming an emerging entrepreneur. It's the action behind the thought that takes you to places that you have never been before. And it's not about finding success the first time around but about experimenting with enough businesses long enough to discover your rightful place in business.

Business-in-a-Box

I would like to now expose you to what I call "Business-in-a-Box" to help you gain exposure, knowledge, or maybe even some business experience. These models can help you fail forward faster with real-world circumstances that prepare you for your opportunity with minimal losses. You may not have ever considered going this route, but it may be worth exploring for a season. Please don't think I am saying that you have to become a part of any of these business models, but they were instrumental in giving me great techniques, valuable insights, and relationships that were great resources to me. I will only go into a basic description and some advantages and disadvantages you could possibly have as a result of being a part of them. Remember, before doing anything in business, you must *research, research,* and *research* for yourself!

A big advantage to being involved in a "Business-in-a-Box" is the way you can explore this business with someone else's product or service with much of the marketing already done for you. Your part is to find customers and use a calculated amount of money and a specified amount of your time in order to succeed. Now, a few decades ago, making money in these business models was considered a foolish dream. Anyone who offered the chance to make money through the Internet or home-based products was considered either a scammer or a victim. Today, we know better! With an excellent product and an excellent service, you can do wonders for others, online and offline.

Let's talk about a big disadvantage to this business model. There is said to be a very high percentage of failure in these business models. This is not because they are faulty in their structure but because there is a low **barrier of entry.** This term can refer to *hindrances a firm or company faces in trying to enter a market or industry.* It can also refer to *hindrances an individual faces in trying to gain entrance to a profession.* The prerequisite to entering into the Business-in-a-Box model is minimal, so there is much competition. You do not have to have any specialized skills to do this line of business. It can sometimes be harder to succeed due to many people selling the same products with varying pricing. The truth of the matter is, the harder it is to duplicate what you are doing, the harder it is for anyone else to capitalize off your product or service. Once you become a part of one of these business models, you have to be prepared to "think outside the box" in order to be very successful. You have to differentiate yourself from others, or you will be a clone of the basic level of training that was given to you when you when you first began.

Some of the business models are considered get-rich-quick schemes, and they can involve manipulation if you are not careful, which brings about temporary results. The manipulation comes forth when you don't care about the product or service but just about getting the money. Remember, your personal and business reputation is on the line in any business you start, so always act with honesty and integrity, which should have been one of your core beliefs. Some of the people you will be working with want to see and help you succeed, so represent your product well.

If you are willing to work hard, perform your due diligence, such as researching the company and products for their excellence and adding your uniqueness, then you will have a winning combination for success! Now let's discuss what I consider the top five Business-in-a-Box models. Any of these are great for secondary sources of income and have the potential to develop into primary sources of income.

Affiliate marketing

In affiliate marketing, you get to sell one or more products online through your own website or blog. In simple words, it is a way to make money on an existing website, especially if it already has a good following and visitor base.

The basic concept behind affiliate marketing involves a product manufacturer giving you a commission every time someone clicks on the advertisement to their product on your website. The commission could also be given for each conversion or sale. For maximum success, you need to choose a product that is within the same niche as your blog or website. When you find a product that offers an affiliate marketer program, you can sign up.

Many affiliate programs require a certain fee for signing up, but you can consider that an investment rather than an expense. Besides, you also get a pack of marketing tools with most affiliate programs. It all seems rather simple, but you need to be careful about how you choose your affiliate products; otherwise, it will have a negative effect on your own reputation as well. You should buy the product and test it for yourself first, before offering it to your client list. A great example of an affiliate site is Amazon Affiliates at https://affiliate-program.amazon.com/. You can also find your favorite online products and sign up for their affiliate programs, if they have any, and sell that product on your site. I would suggest making sure it is a product that can add value to those you refer it to. Remember, your reputation is on the line as a business owner.

Direct Sales

Direct sales are another great way to earn a solid secondary income. The direct sales industry is currently valued at around $30 million, so it may seem like a very lucrative way to make money online or offline. However, the high value of the direct sales industry is possibly because of its broad definition.

Direct sales can refer to *any way of selling products* directly to end customers without bringing them to a retail location. Direct selling on the Internet has good potential as a supplement to your income, but it takes a lot of hard work to turn it into a primary income source. On the positive side, there is a very low entry barrier for direct sales. Moreover, you enjoy greater freedom in your work, and the costs for starting up are also relatively low. If you choose the right products to sell, it could even be fun and interesting. Make sure you check http://www.dsa.org for reputable companies to partner with before joining any one of them.

When it comes to direct sales, you work as an independent representative or distributor, or as a sales consultant or representative. You basically have to market your product in many ways. It could be through your website, forums, or even direct conversations or home parties.

Now, when you work part-time for a legitimate direct sales company, you could earn a few thousand dollars every year at the very least. This may not seem like much to most people, so it comes as no surprise that almost 90 percent of direct sellers do their job part-time. Many of them work less than ten hours a week.

Moreover, many direct sellers enter the market because they get their favorite products at discount rates and have some fun while earning a little on the side. Some of these reps do not even bother selling or recruiting; they just enjoy the discounts. As a result, the average earnings of direct sellers come down. The truth is that you can earn serious money through direct sales if you put in enough effort.

There are two great companies that I would like to mention. The first is Mary Kay, www.marykay.com. I had the privilege of joining many wonderful Mary Kay ladies as a representative at Mary Kay Cosmetics for a short while. Her products are excellent, and this explains why the company is still successful today! Her business practices help build your confidence through motivation and education and allow you to earn as much money as you would like in your spare time or full-time.

The second is Traci Lynn. I have come to know Traci Lynn through her ministry and business practices on her television broadcast and the quality of her product and designs at Traci Lynn Jewelry, http://www. tracilynninc.com/.

These two women have created multimillion-dollar companies helping other people, mostly women, to take charge of their lives and careers. These companies are founded on Christian principles of doing things God's way in order to help others to succeed. It's a win-win!

Network Marketing or MLM

Network marketing or multi-level marketing (MLM), is simply a method where representatives of a company reach out to potential customers who would otherwise not be reached through traditional marketing methods. To do this, network-marketing and MLM companies recruit their sales force like regular companies, and this sales force, in turn, recruits more salespeople for their team. There are many network-marketing groups all across the country. You probably know someone, right now, that is a part of this type of business model. Maybe you have even been invited to one of these groups and considered joining due to the residuals you are shown you can earn. This is another model where you must differentiate yourself to fill your sales funnel.

I must say that there are some excellent training programs and business experiences that can be gained from working in any of these business models. The greatest advantage to direct sales and network marketing is the experience you can take to any business, such as learning about systems, sales techniques, and especially overcoming objections.

For more information, visit the Association of Network Marketing Professionals (ANMP) at www.anmp.com and Multi-Level Marketing International Association (MLMIA) www.mlmia.com.

Internet Marketing

Internet marketing is another potential source of income, and if you market well, you can earn good money. This can include selling other companies' products as well as your own online. You do need to have some skills in designing advertisements that can drive traffic to a particular site where the product resides. You must stay educated in the latest technology, platforms, and programs because the Internet changes so often. When you are selecting a product to market on the Internet, you need be very careful. This applies to all the other money-making methods above as well, and it has been touched on in each of the topics. There are a few things to check out when choosing your marketing company.

First, you need to research the age and stability of the company. A stable company means good products and better sales figures. Another thing to look at is how good their services or products are and how many of them are being sold on a daily, monthly, or quarterly basis. You should see some statistics on the sales figures when deciding to select a particular product. Remember, a product in high demand is a better product than those that are likely to reduce in demand.

The next thing to look at is the company's pay plan. See if the commission or payment you are getting for marketing their products is worth the efforts you are making. This is an important point to consider since it represents how much you will or will not be paid. You also need to see if their payments are timely. There is no point in associating yourself with high-earning marketing programs if the payments are not even making it on time.

Finally, you need to see how well the company trains sales representatives and how good their support and business system is. Even if you choose a great company with amazing products, you need to have a system that actually works to convert all those positives into earnings. Check for mentorship and strong training programs because those matter.

EBay

EBay may not be on everyone's mind when they want to earn money online, but there is no denying its usefulness as a money source. Even if you want to clean out your house and earn a few dollars, eBay is a great place to get your feet wet. With the right guidance and enough effort, you can also turn your hobby of collecting or making unique items into a profitable venture and turn eBay into a primary or secondary income source. Some of the biggest eBay sellers began by selling off a few things they did not use. They soon discovered the potential for profit from the website and began running their business online by establishing relationships with online wholesale vendors. If you prefer not to store any products in your home, then carefully research for manufacturers, such as drop shippers, that can send out their products on your behalf. The customer will think it was sent directly from you.

Etsy

Etsy is a marketplace for creative wares and allows only handmade items, craft supplies, or antiques older than twenty years to be sold.

This is what differentiates it from eBay. It can be very competitive in either of these two models due to the many people vying for consumer attention. Finding a way to create something that is uniquely yours is a great way to niche market your way to profits. I would still suggest eventually venturing off to creating your own online or offline store to gain a larger presence in the community or across the globe.

For more information, visit www.ebay.com and www.etsy.com to see how you can start selling your own unique items with targeted traffic. This is indeed a great way to gain visibility that can eventually lead to your own business to differentiate you from the rest.

Your Own Product or Service

Here is where your passion, uniqueness, and creativity can really shine! The greatest way to earn the most profit and dominate in your market is to create your own product, service, or business model structure. If you are constantly looking for ways to improve your life, then you are bound to see something that can be improved or created to make someone else's life better. God is able to give you creative ideas that can bring about witty inventions. This is a great place for the "barriers to entry" to really work for you! The harder it is for someone to play on the same level as you, the greater your chance of success. As a result, you can end up with patents, trademarks, and copyrights that make it hard for others to duplicate your efforts. This makes it very hard for anyone to take your market share without possibly having to buy you out or join forces with you. You can become known as the expert in your industry, such as Coca-Cola, Apple, or Nike.

In order to find the most success out of anything, you must stay in a positive environment. There are many people that may tell you "why" something can't or won't work. Sometimes those around you could be jealous or envious because you have discovered how to rise above your current circumstances. Figure out what gives you the most energy and motivates you. I find that positive songs, movies, CDs, online and offline books, and most of all positive people help me stay motivated and focused. In business, it is most important that you use your time wisely by including motivational tapes and books by those who have gone before you and succeeded in the area(s) you wish to dominate. Never forget to stay connected to God in order to achieve your highest potential.

The true secret to winning at any business model is to learn all you can about the business. You are to become an advocate for the product or service. You are to service your customers with excellence, or you should think about hiring someone to care for your customers. Your customers are your bloodline! You must *believe* in and have a *passion* for the product or service, or it won't work for you. The ones that I have seen make the most money in these business models are those who go on to become leaders and show others how to become leaders, too. The leaders then sell CDs, DVDs, audio downloads, and books, and become coaches or speakers to earn a larger income that can lead to millions. Just selling the product or service alone and never thinking outside the box is a surefire ingredient to being average and earning minimal income.

Chapter 6 – God-made Millionaire Exercise

Prepare to dip your foot in the water by locating within yourself that very something you have always wanted to try as an emerging entrepreneur.

1. Write down a business that you would like to start working in, if possible, either part-time or as a volunteer to find confirmation for your vision.

2. Do research to see if you want to venture out with your own product or service or if you will feel more comfortable having a safety net, such as with direct sales, affiliate marketing, or network marketing, to get started.

3. Once you determine the route you will take, write down three action steps you will take over the next ninety days.

Note: Give yourself time to get involved to make sure you are committed, and document your progress whether by journaling or recording your experience. Before you know it, you will have found your rightful place in the market.

Chapter 7

Your Million-Dollar Idea Starts Now!

Roll your works upon the Lord [commit and trust them wholly to Him; He will cause your thoughts to become agreeable to His will, and] so shall your plans be established and succeed. ~Prov 16:3

You've got an idea that you know the world will love! When everybody sees what you have to offer, your sales are going to go through the roof. "I'm about to be rich!" you might shout to those around you. But did you know there is such a thing as a *good idea* and a *God idea*? Good ideas manifest in the Earth each and every day, but many of them don't work out for their creators. The only way to know if your idea is a God idea and not just a good idea is to take your idea to God. The scripture above says that if you commit your plans (your ideas) to God, they will succeed. God will take your idea or give you an idea that is even better. He will walk you through the journey to make it happen because you entrusted it to Him. God believes in doing something once and reaping a harvest many times over. As a result of your patience and belief in Him, you will be rewarded handsomely.

Being an emerging entrepreneur is a journey. It is not a straight path, but one that is filled with many ups and downs. Don't fall in love with your idea to the degree that you aren't willing to let it go, if necessary. Remember, you have to learn the lessons of life to appreciate the successes that await you. So if you have tasted failure in some form or another, then you are well on your way. Continue to read books on your industry; research people and companies to grow your idea. *The biggest mistake I see is people who are so in love with their ideas that they start executing them before solidifying the validity of the business.* This included me! There can be so much heartache if you decide to spend a large amount of money on something that you have not tested or proved to be a worthy idea.

As you begin to take action, God will lead you through a process to strengthen your weaker areas. No two people follow the same path of life with God, so yours will be tailor-made. You will become a stronger, wiser person as you are taught things about *you*. You should connect with other entrepreneurs through network meetings or groups to stay current in your industry. You will start to notice people who can help you and find resources that can move you further faster. You may even discover that you don't want to be in one business but will be better at another. But how could you ever know that unless you stayed connected to God? Continuous positivity in your surroundings makes for a great breeding ground for successful ideas.

As a believer, you are to continuously stay in your higher consciousness of God in order to see the manifestations of what you will need. The way to accomplish this higher consciousness is by reading His word, spending time with Him, or being directly or indirectly mentored by someone who has experienced results with God. You have to treat finding your purpose as though you were on a secret mission. You have to guard your million-dollar idea by discarding negative voices from those around you. The inner workings of God will start to take place on your behalf as long as you continue to stay in belief. You must trust that He loves you and only wants to see you succeed at whatever you put your hands to do. The scripture says that God goes before you to make your crooked paths straight. God is a light to your path when you can't see *how* a thing can be done. Do you have an idea?

The Holy Spirit of God will start to give you thoughts of even greater ideas of how you can be excellent at what you are about to bring to the marketplace. Expect from God as though it was a sure thing. He will *never* fail you! There has not been one time that I have entrusted something to God and He failed to provide an answer for me. And if I didn't get it, it only meant I was too busy to sit still and hear Him.

I believe that many ideas come to a person's mind but aren't captured on paper or recorded as they should be. I often tell the story of how Michael Jackson mentioned that God had given him an idea about a song he was to write. He said God told him that if he didn't write it, He would give it to Prince. So, I am sure he wrote the song!

Have you ever thought of a great idea and never acted on it, but later heard that a person or company had introduced it into the marketplace? You instantly thought about how your financial life would have been totally different if you had only done it first. I would suggest keeping a pen and paper near your bedside to capture these ideas—these God ideas. You remember the saying, *"If you snooze you lose"*? I get my ideas at various times and places. How about you?

You can get some of your best ideas from the following places and while you are:

➤ sitting in church and listening to a sermon
➤ taking a nice warm shower or bath
➤ waiting in traffic
➤ visiting other cities, states, or countries
➤ noticing what would make a product or service more efficient
➤ watching TV
➤ running or walking
➤ falling asleep or waking up

Now, the first thing you must do is find out if your idea is a unique one. You should research the marketplace to see if there is a similar product or service in existence. The Bible says that there is nothing new under the sun. Basically, we take an already existing idea and modify it to make it better. Let's look at some successful entrepreneurs that we've already been discussing.

- Howard Schultz of Starbucks got his inspirational idea when he took a business trip to Italy and decided to bring the coffee culture back to the United States.
- Sara Blakely of Spanx got her product idea when she realized there were not products on the market that were flattering to wear under her white slacks. She also secured a patent for her idea!
- Cathy Truett – Cathy, owner of Chick-fil-A and his brother Ben came back from World War II and opened their first restaurant called The Dwarf Grill in Atlanta, Georgia but now called The Dwarf House. Through trial and error they wanted to create the best tasting food they could for their customers in Hapeville, Georgia. So they set out to make a better chicken patty and sandwich, which birthed the chain of Chick-fil-A restaurants.

You created a vision of what you wanted your business to look like back in Chapter 4. Now it's time to break that vision down into little chunks that can make it all happen.

This exercise will cause you to examine your vision for better clarity. It's one that I use in my coaching business and workshop to test the validity of your vision. I don't expect you to know all the answers right now, but come back to complete it as soon as you can. You should have the answers already to most of these questions if you've completed the previous exercises. See **Figure 6.1** to better examine your idea.

TAKE IT, TWEEK IT, TOSS IT©

You are only to answer Yes or No to these questions.

1. Does it solve a problem for a particular person or group?
2. Are there a number of people that suffer from this problem?
3. Am I passionate about this idea?
4. Have I shared this with at least 3 people and gotten their opinion?
5. Am I willing to commit at least the next 3-5 years to this idea?
6. Are others successfully doing something similar to this?
7. If so, can I do something substantially different or better than them?
8. Are there too many competitors already selling in my market?
9. Can I build this business on my capital reserves?
10. Can I have a product & customers in 90 days or less?
11. Do I have a background & skillset compatible with this business?
12. Does the business/risk reward match my person risk/reward?
13. If I don't start this business, will someone else?
14. Do I have a competitive advantage on how to get customers?
15. Does it help me fulfill my purpose or passion?

Under this section, you are to *count the number of 'yes'* and rate your idea according to the metric below.

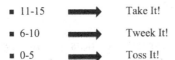

- 11-15 ➡ Take It!
- 6-10 ➡ Tweek It!
- 0-5 ➡ Toss It!

Figure 7.1 – Clarifying Your Vision

The metric is designed to make you think your idea through to see if you have done enough research and development work before proceeding with your time or money. Of course, if you have a score in the range of Tweak It or Toss It, you can surely raise it up to Take It by completing more research. It's a questionnaire that makes you think a little harder about your idea.

On my website www.godmademillionairethebook.com/toolkit, you can find the template "Time To Create" to record your ideas. You can take all the ideas that come to mind and write them here. Whenever you act on any of them, write them in the section titled "Ideas Acted Upon" with your start date and then get to work. You can keep this sheet in your nightstand, on a clipboard, or on a recorder to capture your ideas.

Focus, Focus, Focus

This Book of the Law shall not depart out of your mouth, but you shall meditate on it day and night, that you may observe and do according to all that is written in it. For then you shall make your way prosperous, and then you shall deal wisely and have good success. ~Jo 1:1-8

No one knows like God the importance of focusing on a particular idea until you see success. He has given us a book filled with all the answers we could ever need out of life. The Bible is laced with success principles that are common to some and treasures to others. The above scripture tells us that if you meditate (focus) on His words, you will make wise decisions, become prosperous, and find the success you want. Now, couple that with the wisdom you will find from reading, researching, and studying successful, wealthy people. This will prove to be an ingredient for guaranteed success.

According to Webster's dictionary, meditation is *the act or process of spending time in quiet thought, the act or process of meditating, an expression of a person's thoughts on something.* Focus has a lot to do with meditating on a thing. We talked in an early chapter about holding images in your imagination until they manifested in your life. You accomplish the act of "holding" that image through meditating. Seeing that vision or idea until it seems so real that you know it can do nothing but take place is the basis of manifestation. If you do not have some "me" time, which is synonymous for *meditation,* you will truly live an average life because wealthy people do this on a daily basis. Meditation can include taking scriptures that apply to your current situations and saying until you believe them. You can take personal affirmations that you created that move you toward your goals and say them repeatedly until they become a part of your life. Personal affirmations work for me sometimes, but listening to sermons and success stories raise me up faster. The less attention you give to outside forces that aren't moving you forward, the sooner you will see success.

Mastering your walk with God

Walking with God is something that you learn over time. The more time you spend meditating on His word, the more you will come to know His nature. As a born-again believer, it is up to you to allow the Holy Spirit to be your guide. I often pray that God's voice will be the loudest voice of all that I hear throughout my day. I know you're probably thinking, "Hear the voice of God?" As a born-again believer, you will learn the promptings and the guidance of that small, still voice (Holy Spirit) that tells you to do or say something at a particular time.

Prayer is speaking to God, meditating is allowing God's Spirit to speak to you. -Deepak Chopra

I remember when I first started to wonder how I could learn to hear from God to bring about the ideas He placed in my heart. I didn't understand how I could hear the voice of someone that was not visible to me. As I continued to listen to the word of God through my pastors, those words started to become questions in my mind. So I started seeking the answers through those who were getting results from knowing God. I would read the Bible and other books that pertained to God's divine resources. It wasn't until I started having troubles in my life that I truly got to know God. I had no one else that could understand nor help me out of my situations. My turning to God (which can sometimes be orchestrated by The Holy Spirit) was a chance to know God's power as a permanent help for my life. Think about this: Have you ever wanted to get to know someone better? You would do whatever you could within your power to get in their presence. You would be where they would be, get to know the people they knew, and ask around until you finally met them face-to-face. This is the same thing you should do in order to have a better walk with God. Do whatever you have to do to find time to be in his presence.

Because of the seasons of trouble I went through in my life, I got to know God for my own self—not through the words or hearsay of someone else, but through my own experience with Him. How else can

God show Himself as your present help in your time of need, if you do not give Him the chance to show you what He can do for you? These are the most frightening, yet loving moments you could ever have with God. I learned to close out the voices of others and those who did not know how to help me. I became dependent on God because He sent the answers I needed through sermons, people I met, and even through dreams. I learned to set myself apart and sit at the feet of Jesus.

The best way to know how God is operating in your life is by journaling on a daily or weekly basis. You can also sit back and reflect over your day or week to see how you made it through certain situations in your life. And if you didn't have any major occurrences happening in your life, then that's God too, taking care of it for you. These moments will all be indications that God is guiding you through His Holy Spirit. Oftentimes, I look back and wonder how I made it through tough times, but I know it was because of prayer and thanking God for watching over me.

After gaining more experience in hearing the voice of God, your ideas will become magnified, and your creativity will start to soar. God knows the hidden things in the world. He will show you people and give you the resources you need to flourish. He will show you strategies that can grow your idea exponentially. He will cause you to attract the right people that want to know and help you.

Top Distractions

Now, in the marketplace, there are so many things vying for your attention that you literally have to turn the world off just so that you can hear your own thoughts. Millionaires understand that when it comes to building a business, it is very important to have a single main focus to build upon. Your attention should not be divided and directed toward unproductive tasks. Here are some examples of what I consider top distractions that can deflate your ideas as an emerging entrepreneur.

- Naysayers – listening to others who tell you all the reasons why your idea won't work. They may even tell you about themselves or others who have tried and failed. You must remember the vision is for you, not for them.

- Time Management – The biggest factor when it comes to not managing your time well is lack of discipline. You have to control how you spend the twenty-four hours that we have all been given. Check your weekly activities by creating a daily task list that can help you stay focused on the priorities at hand.

- Email – Your inbox contains others' thoughts and wants. You can lose all sense of time and purpose by diverting your day's mission to tasks that can wait or actually be ignored.

- Cell Phone – This can be a complete time waster if you are not having conversations that are moving you forward in business. You can spend countless hours with friends, family, or co-workers without ever taking one major step toward your progress or success. During business hours, limit your time to scheduled callbacks, especially if working from home. You're in business now!

- Others' Success – You can get caught up in how others are succeeding around you and begin to feel that something is wrong with you because you are not where they are. You must continue to believe that your success is on its way and not allow your distorted perception to stop your momentum.

There are so many emerging entrepreneurs that I encounter and coach that talk about the many businesses they are involved in, simultaneously. This is a recipe for disaster because a *master of many is a master of nothing*. I understand that you don't want to put all your eggs in one basket, but having multiple businesses is a poverty mindset. Your strength and momentum lie in your ability to stay focused!

I have learned over the years to put all my efforts into one project. When that is completed, I then move on to other projects. Wealthy businesspeople understand the importance of taking one idea—according to your individual objectives, skills, risk tolerance, and passion—and focusing on "the" greatest entrepreneurial idea first. You are to take that idea through the process of discovery until it shows you potential and profit. Whenever you're adding new parts to your business, make sure they align with your current business objectives and that you're not adding new limbs that branch off into a whole new direction.

Carving Out Your Niche

At this point, based on your mission statement and vision exercise, you should have better clarity on the market segment you want to dominate. So now it's time to study your industry to define your specialty for more profitability. I always tell my clients and students that if you don't know who your competitor is, then you should not go into business. There are many successful companies that spend millions of dollars per year on research in their industry, so why should you not research as well? As an emerging entrepreneur, you may be operating on a shoestring budget, so why not ride the wave of their research? For those who may be selling the same product or service that you do, match your product or service with theirs and document the differences because there should be some. You should always know the top three people or companies that sell products or services similar to yours, at all times. I hear some of my fellow colleagues say that there is no such thing as competition, and you should never think of it in that way. I think differently because you are not getting new customers. You are pulling customers away from some other company because you have a similar product or service that has a better benefit or price than the one they are currently using.

If you still want to say it isn't competition, then at least consider it a "healthy" comparison. "Healthy" competition is how so many runners, bikers, and swimmers in the Olympics and some businesspeople become who they are. A great example is Sam Walton, who built Wal-Mart on this very principle. He was always pushing to research and out-perform his competitors. He would go into their stores, see what they were selling and what their prices were, then buy it in bulk to gain a greater market share. Take a look at the chart in **Figure 6.2** and assess your competitors. I would suggest going online or into the stores to take a look at their customer types, products, and services currently being offered. You might even ask a salesperson or two what they like about the company or why customers shop there.

Figure 7.2 – Competition Comparison Chart

Factors	Your Business	Competitor 1	Competitor 2	Competitor 3
Product/Services offered?				
Things they do that can take business away from you?				
Industry Focus				
What have you learned from competition?				
Their marketing message?				
Things you do better than the competition?				
Things you do they can't copy or improve				
Things they don't do well				
Strengths Observed				
Reasons clients like them				
How do they position themselves?				
How do they package their service? (with special offers, bonuses, guarantees, payment plans, longer service hours?)				
Perceived advantage(s)				
What are they doing well?				
Perceived weakness(es)				
How do they price their services?				

How to Stand Out from the Crowd

In any business, it is known that the more defined your mission is to your customer, the greater the chance of your profitability in your chosen area. *Niching* has been coined as the term that represents *an opportunity for a business to offer a product or service that is not offered by other businesses* in your own specialized way. But you can actually take this a step farther. There is something called micro-niching, which can be used to better define your service or product. Micro-niching is basically taking your chosen niche and narrowing it down even farther to arrive at what I consider your "secret sauce." This is a very useful method to differentiate yourself from others in your industry. Take a look at these examples.

Example 1

(Start) Niche Marketing: Service → Marketing → Entrepreneurs → Start-ups → Home-Based Businesses

(Finalize) Micro-Niche Marketing: Service → Marketing → Entrepreneurs → Start-ups → Home-Based Businesses → Landscapers →North Texas

Do you see how much more specific your market niche will be if you drill down to a specific group? The best part is you can start with one region to gain business growth and then move on to the next region of customers. This way you can build momentum and build a reputation which will get you more referrals. This can save you a great deal of marketing dollars and time.

Example 2

(*Start*) Niche Industry: Retail → Boutique → Accessories → Women's

(*Finalize*) Micro-Niche Industry: Retail → Boutique Shop → Accessories → Women's → Italian → Leather Only → Shoes, Wallets, Handbags, Belts

OR

(*Finalize*) **Micro-Niche Industry**: Retail → Online Only → Boutique → Accessories → Women's → Italian → Leather Only → Shoes, Wallets, Handbags, Belts

Now, it's your turn! Take one of the four industries of service, wholesale, retail, or manufacturing and narrow your industry down as far as you can go. It may take some time, but engage others to help you. During your research, if you find the market is saturated with businesses like yours, keep narrowing it down until you find what you can do to dominate a particular market. I found this a fun exercise, but it works for my clients to bring them more into focus to see profits sooner. Of course, you have to continue to do your research to ensure you will have enough customers to gain the profits you desire. Don't try to take on the world all at once. Take it one small niche at a time.

Test the Waters

In this section, I would suggest taking your product or service and testing it in the marketplace. By this, I mean pitching your product or service to those you know and those you believe can benefit from what you have to offer. You must move forward with confidence that your product or service is the best! If not, people may say no because they notice your own lack of confidence in it. If you have a quality product or service, then this should not be a problem. Ask them the price they would pay for it and if they feel this is something they would buy. This would include any product models or prototypes you have developed before actual production. If they tell you no, then ask them if they know of someone that could benefit from it and thank them for their time. Don't give up if you receive many "no's" because the "yes" is right around the corner.

Make sure you are not basing your accumulated data completely off the "no's" because this could mean only that improvements may need to be made to your product or service. My suggestion would be to give the first set of services or products to potential customers in return for their feedback. Testing the waters to see if your product or service is well received will keep you from earning a bad company image, and from wasting time and money before you start selling. Remember, you are making sure that you are *not* the only one that needs or loves what you have to offer.

Here are some other great ways that you can test the market:

- Send postcards to a chosen area with a link to an online survey about your business product or service.
- Run a beta test for your services. Offer a discount in exchange for feedback.
- Set up a website with the product or service described and have a survey at the end asking for feedback.
- Crowdfunding platforms (solicitation for money through social media) are proving to be an entrepreneur's dream because it can be used to test your product and make modifications before it hits the market. We talk more about this in the chapters to come.
- Use social media to gain and test ideas on how to perfect your marketing or line of business.
- Cater an event for a local organization to test market your new product or service idea.

I remember when I was in my late teens, there used to be people standing in the mall with clipboards in their hands. I would see them each and every time I visited the mall. I would avoid them because I knew the clipboard, pen, and their ability to connect with me eye-to-eye would mean they would approach me to take the survey. I started off saying no but surrendered because they were offering me a monetary or free gift for my time. They would then take me to a back office with them, and they would ask me if I had ever used a particular product before. I would then answer a series of questions about the product if I was familiar with it. They would give me the gift I chose and then thank me, and I was on my way.

I later realized this was a form of market research. These people had been paid to stand in the mall and solicit the responses of potential customers to help these companies see what they were doing right and how they could improve or introduce a new product into the market. I am not sure what these companies were spending on the market research, but I am sure it helped them in some way to become better and prevent massive losses. I don't see this type of market research any longer. You, too, should find out if your product or service will be welcomed or need improvements before moving it into full production. Testing in any manner is never a mistake.

So what is a good indication that you are on to something? If you find that you cannot keep an item in stock or find a company that is willing to place multiple purchase orders with you, then you've got something special. You have made a particular sector of people feel as though you had only them in mind when you discovered the idea.

Understanding Your Customer – Target Market

And when Jesus heard it, He said to them, Those who are strong and will have no need of a physician, but those who are weak and sick; I came not to call the righteous ones to repentance, but sinners (the erring ones and all those not free from sin) ~Mk 2:17

Jesus' target market was sinners, those who did not understand how to live their lives according to the knowledge, peace, and love provided for the world's well-being, throughout the Bible. The entire time he walked on this Earth, he was teaching to those who needed his help. The righteous ones, such as the Pharisees or the religious people in the world, did not receive Jesus' help because they felt they were already perfect.

What you have to offer is not for everyone either. Your product or service is made especially for the one who needs it. First, avoid telling yourself that anyone and everyone will buy your product or service. Yes, anyone can do business with you, but not everyone is going to become a customer of yours. Determining your target market is not meant to exclude other people from the purchase of your product or service. Rather, it allows you to be more specific with your marketing dollars to determine a niche market that is more likely to buy from you. The majority of your money will be spent in this area. As a result, you can increase sales and decrease the number of competitors in your market. When trying to penetrate the market with your brand and product, you must think of that "perfect person" that would use what you are selling. For marketing purposes, pretend that the ideal person is sitting right in front of you as you are describing your product or service benefits.

Your product or service should have one of the following benefits to offer your ideal customer. Which one of these categories would your product or service fall into?

- To Save
    - Money
    - Time
    - Effort
- To Increase
    - Income
    - Investments
    - Personal relationships
- To Reduce
    - Liabilities
    - Expenses
    - Taxes
- To Improve
    - Appearance
    - Confidence
    - Productivity

To be honest with you, your customers are not buying the product or service; they are buying the *benefits* of what it can do for them. They buy these things to make their lives easier. The sooner you advertise the benefits of your product, the quicker your customer will understand *why* they should buy from you.

When trying to penetrate the market with your product or service, you must understand something about your customer, such as what problems they need to solve, what habits they have, and where they hang out. If your target market is not finalized before you decide on a product or service, then expect to waste plenty of your valuable time, money, and energy on the wrong audience. Remember, you are attempting to find out *why* your chosen customer will want your product or service— instead of the competition's—so marketing dollars are at stake. At this point, you have determined that your customer is either dissatisfied with what's in the marketplace today, or they're in need of what you have to make an annoying situation better.

Here are a few things you should consider when seeking your target market:

Analyzing Your Product or Service

Think of the ideal person that can benefit from your product or service. How will they use it in their daily lives? How will it make their life better? What are they using now that you can improve upon with your product? When you thought of the product or service, whom did you have in mind?

Demographics

This would be the age, gender, family size or composition, educational level, and marital status of your ideal customer. For example: Your ideal client might be single, female, middle-class, age 18 to 24, no children, college educated, and earning more than $50,000 per year.

Geographics

This pertains to your target market's location, size of the area, density, and climate zone. It can include a city, state, or country. For example, you can limit your landscaping service to the 75034, 75067, and 75033 zip codes.

<u>Industry Needs</u>

Is your product or service a missing ingredient in the marketplace today? Have you noticed a task that you are doing that a product can take the hassle out of it? Is there a service that can be created to save people time or money? What problem are you solving in the marketplace today?

<u>Psychographics</u>

This equals your ideal client's activities, their loyal characteristics, their repetition of need, and their lifestyle and behavior. They value their time and consider it their single-most limited resource. They like planning for their future. They are very involved with safety and security measures. They love researching on the web for product information rather than magazines or newspapers. They really stand behind a product they select and will defend it to anyone that says otherwise. Understanding your customer in this area will make them your advocate for your product or service. This is considered an indirect referral, which helps to build your target market.

Channels to Find Your Target Market

There are many places that you can look to discover ways to identify your target market. Here is a list of some great places to start to get up-to-date information regarding them. You may be using one or more of these already, so it shouldn't be hard to identify those who fall into the category of your ideal client.

- Personal Observation
- Government Studies
- Chambers of Commerce
- Trade Associations

- Trade Periodicals
- Libraries
- Local/International Media
- Social Media

Chapter 7 – God-made Millionaire Discussion Exercise - "Knowing Your Target Market"

Here are six questions to consider along with examples to help you delve deeper into finding your target market. Let's use high-end handbags as our product.

1. Who is going to buy your product or service? You will generally know this when you decide on the product or service to sell. Are they male or female? What age range or class? Make sure that you don't say that your handbags appeal to anyone because you don't want to have to mail your catalog to "everyone" just to make one sale. That is not money well spent.

2. Will you market to businesses, to consumers, or to both? You must decide on this because there will be two different approaches and marketing methods to appeal to either one of these groups. When marketing to other businesses, there may be a need to set appointments instead of sending a standard brochure.

3. What traits do you think your "typical" customer or client will have? Do they buy often? Staying on the handbags, your ideal customer would be a woman in the prime of her career who is conscious of her look and who wants to stay ahead of the style trends. She is not afraid to pay a high price for a handbag; she welcomes it to show off to her friends. See? You must know this about your ideal client. This is why you would test the market to gain a better understanding and then tweak your marketing efforts.

4. Is the need for your product or service not currently being met, or is it already saturated? This is the most advantageous way of

creating a new product or service. We'll stick with the handbags as our example. Ask yourself if there are handbags with Beyoncé on them on every corner. If you see the same product you are selling in the stores, online, or in magazines, then this market is saturated. You can attempt to cash in on it by coming in at a little lower price since you may have no overhead. This product may not be a long-term business for you. This may be a seasonal item, so you may have to get in, make your money, and get out.

If you see that there is a need for a certain problem to be solved by a product, then by all means do the research and create it. One place you can visit is www.thomasnet.com, or you can Google to find manufacturers that may be willing to work with you on the creation of your product. For example, Sara Blakely of SPANX did it! She realized there was nothing on the market that properly addressed the reduction of panty lines showing in certain garments. She found a manufacturer, and she paid him $5,000. He split the rest with her and took a chance. His daughters actually saw the need and vision Sara had and convinced their dad to take on her project, which she later patented for a barrier of entry to others considering copying her.

5. Is there something about what you have to offer that will allow you to beat your competitors? Do you offer a money-back guarantee and they don't? Do you offer to clean their car after every oil change with no additional cost? Will there be free gift wrapping or shipping? Do you send birthday, wedding, or one-year anniversary 50 percent–off coupons? What will you offer your customers as an added value? (*For example, Zappos® has a 365-days-a-year return policy.*)

6. What unique value will you offer to your customers? It is also known as your USP—Unique Selling Proposition. This is your *uniqueness* that sets you apart from the competition. John down the street might sell roller blades to his customers, but you realized that John does not offer any kind of support once that customer buys from him. Here's your opportunity to build a relationship with the customer by offering follow-up tips,

tricks, upcoming events, and advice on how to keep their skates maintained to last an additional two years. So you just saved them money, and now they will be back to buy again. You are now showing the customer the value of continuing to do business with your company. A great barrier of entry would be to design your own wheels that are patented and possibly licensed to other skating facilities.

Chapter 8

Creating Your Million-Dollar Plan

For which of you, wishing to build a farm building, does not first sit down and calculate the cost [to see] whether he has sufficient means to finish it?–Lk 14:28

You can see that this scripture can pertain to calculating the cost of money, time, or having the skills to run your own business. You cannot expect to be a success if you do not have anything written down, such as a road map, to get you to the success you desire. I cannot say this enough: you will need to calculate pricing, products, your time, money, and strategies to achieve your end results. Companies that pick a strategy, stick to it, and then modify it over time seem to excel most in their business.

A business plan is a written plan of your vision in action. It is a living document with a purpose to create or distribute a better product or service. A business plan gives you your strategy to dominate! A strategy is the pattern of decisions and actions that, when repeated over and over again, determines what the business will be. It encapsulates the most viable parts of your business into its simplest form. You've heard the saying "Fail to plan, plan to fail," yes? Your prosperity is a planned result of your thoughts and actions. No millionaire has ever stumbled into success without putting something down on paper.

Do I really need a business plan right now? If you answer *yes* to any of these questions, then you need a business plan.

1. Do you want to protect your personal assets (your home, car, savings, your peace of mind)?
2. Are you entering into a business with family members or friends?
3. Would you like the option to raise capital through the sale of stock?
4. Do you, or will you, have investors or partners?
5. Does or will your business:
    ➢ Sell goods or services to the public and/or other businesses?
    ➢ Bring customers into your home, office, or store?
    ➢ Have employees?
    ➢ Take on debt?

Most people never consider the majority of these questions when becoming an emerging entrepreneur. Half the time, we are thinking about how to get this business up and running and where the money will come from. If you are already financially set in your endeavor, you are not in the majority. This is where the rubber meets the road, and so many potential businesspeople fail because they give up too soon. If you just take the time to put something on paper or in the computer about your vision for business, others can follow and provide the necessary resources.

Advantages of Writing a Business Plan

There are some great reasons to get started with your business plan, and one of them is to display your vision to others in a tangible manner—like a blueprint. Whether you realize it or not, you are building your future; therefore, you need to know when you are on or off course. Most people think that a business plan is not really something you should worry about until you have a business that is making a profit. This is far from the truth!

Putting together your business plan early in your venture can give you a road map to see if your idea is viable. You may go through the motions of writing your plan only to find out how much work may actually be needed to get the business up and running. The business plan will cause you to take a deeper and closer look at whether the market will receive it and if profits are possible. No one ever achieves success by accident. Once you see that what you are doing is definitely going to positively affect the marketplace, a plan of action is needed to assemble a team of competent people to assist in your future growth. You cannot grow to a level of maturity where your business earns millions without a process.

In an earlier chapter, you wrote out your vision of what you would like your business to look like. You thought out your personal and business desires in detail. Your business plan will now make everything clearer to include other people, start-up costs, profitability, and the pricing of your products and services. This will allow you to bring about actionable steps that lead to an active company. Also, if you ever need additional funds because your business is growing by leaps and bounds, then you can use your plan to bring in investors or partners.

There is nothing like having your business plan up-to-date whenever you come in contact with a potential investor. You never want to tell an investor you will have to get back with them later. You should have a copy of your business plan stored in such places as your email, cloud storage, Google Drive, or Dropbox for file sharing. Investors will be impressed by your ability to do business when the opportunity presents itself.

Two Types of Business Plans

For those of you who are not thrilled about writing a business plan, you will be pleased to know it is much simpler than you think. When writing your business plan, decide if you want to focus on your ideas, to bring ideas in from others, to ensure your team is on the same page, or to communicate your plans to an organization. Most likely, as an emerging entrepreneur, you will want to focus on your ideas. You can write a full business plan or a one-page business plan, although I feel both will be utilized eventually.

Comprehensive Business Plan

This business plan will give you and any prospect an in-depth look at your company overall. It can be easily incorporated into your company's growth for anyone to follow your vision. It also allows you to have more clarity about where you are headed, and it details your goals for measurement. If ever you need to bring in key people that can help make your company more profitable, you can detail their duties here as well. In previous exercises, you completed some of the initial portions of your business plan that can be used here. Once it's completed, this will give you a comprehensive business plan that allows you to see the validity and profitability of your vision. All you need to do is plug the information into your spreadsheet or program. You will want to include such items as:

- ✓ Executive Summary – outline of business, the team, the proposal, why you will succeed, what the rewards are, any risks and how they can be minimized. *This section should grab the reader's attention, which can be your make-or-break moment with the reader. You must sell yourself because if you're looking for an investor, this will cause them to continue reading or toss it to the side of the pile. It should be no more than one page—and it must sell!*
- ✓ Objectives – detail what you need and want to accomplish. *This section can include your vision and ideas for your business that you completed in Chapter 4. It should include things like wanting to be a one-person business vs. a big corporation. How many employees, suppliers, vendors, or manufacturers, etc. will be needed?*
- ✓ Market Analysis – market structure, competitors, trends, competitive advantages, distribution method to your customers, trends, technology, and any barriers to entry. *This section forms the background for your proposition for the information you are formatting for the prospect's review.*

✓ Product/Services – description of your product or service, benefits to your customers, tests and approvals, copyrights, patents, and trademarks. *This section will show if your product is viable and feasible at this time, or a projected solution to a specific target market in the future. You must explain any manufacturing, packaging, or distribution that will be needed and the time frame to bring it to market.*

✓ Marketing and Sales Strategies – detail your marketing objectives, establish your marketing strategies, and describe your selling tactics and unique selling proposition (USP). *This section can discuss your promotional and advertising techniques to get your product seen or heard. Having a great marketing plan can help you spend your marketing dollars wisely and track the strategies that actually bring in profits. Poor marketing can cause you to close your doors for unnecessary reasons.*

✓ Management Section – organizational structure, strengths, and skills of key people on staff. *This section is very important to a prospective investor. This shows the strength and backbone of the business. If not properly staffed, the investor may walk away. You can include yourself or use the resume section below.*

✓ Financial Projections – cash forecasting, balance sheet, profit-and-loss statement. *This section is where you may want to involve your financial person or CPA to complete the numbers to ensure they are feasible, unless you are good with numbers.*

✓ Your Resume – Objectives, experience, education, special achievements, associations, awards. *Don't forget to include your credentials when presenting or sharing your business plan. You are a vital piece of the business, and you need to show you have a background that can carry the business. If you do not, then it is very important that you have highly qualified people listed under the Management Section to show where the business strength comes from. Unlike a traditional resume, you would list statements of accomplishments to validate each section.*

There are many software programs available that enable you to input your information and save it for future use. I am the type of person that believes in systems, and if something has already been invented for maximization of time, then by all means use it. I suggest using the latest version of **Business Plan Pro®** by Palo Alto Software, Inc., or you can hire a reputable person. As an emerging entrepreneur, of course, the difference between the two is your *time* to research your market or having the *money* to pay someone to do it for you. I have used Business Plan Pro® on many occasions, and their templates are excellent. And, no, they are not paying me, but I give credit where credit is due without needing any kickbacks. Most of the time I have been able to find a comparable company in the software, and I was able to alter the data to fit my company. Once done, I would suggest you have an accountant or lawyer look over your information for accuracy. You can also visit www.score.org or www.sba.gov for more business-plan templates.

Single-Page Business Plan

As an emerging entrepreneur, let's go ahead and get something on paper so that you can have a checklist of things that need to put in place. This will help get you motivated and excited about the unfolding of your vision. You may find it easier, in terms of both time and money, to put together a one-page business plan for right now. Make sure you put as much pertinent information in it as possible. Once again, most of this information has been gathered in previous chapters, so you should have most of it done. Here are some of the main points that should be addressed when completing the questions. Feel free to add to the list, if needed.

1. **Your Vision:**

   ➢ What product or service will you sell?
   ➢ Who will be your buyers?
   ➢ How will your product or service help people?
   ➢ What market need or common problem will your product solve for your customers?

2. **Goals:**

> ➢ What goals do you want to achieve in terms of market share and sales revenue, and in what time frame? (*e.g., 5 to 8 percent of the toy industry and $125,000 in sales per year*). What products or services do you want to introduce to your customers in the next six to twelve months?

3. **The 5 P's of Profitability:**

The 5 P's are the main areas that can compose a business, such as product, people, price, placement, and promotion. Write a brief summary of the strategies you want to implement in each field.

> ➢ *Product:* What products or services will you initially offer? Will there be any future products that complement your current ones? What are your product-development strategies, if any? Will there be a premium version? Will you offer any complimentary or freeproducts?
>
> ➢ *People:* What person or people will you need to help carry out your vision? Do you want to spend all your time running your business? Will bringing someone with a specialized skill into the business help you cater more to your customers?
>
> ➢ *Price:* How will you price your product or service? If your product is already in the marketplace, how will you price your product initially to draw customers to you? Will you be using discounts or premium pricing?
>
> ➢ *Placement* (distribution): How will you deliver your products to your customers (*e.g.,* selling it online, selling it in a shop, offering the service face-to-face or across the Internet, partnering with other businesses)?
>
> ➢ *Promotion:* How will you promote your product or service? What will you use as your channels of distribution (*e.g.,* advertising via the Internet, some personal selling, direct marketing, seminars, creating an affiliate or referral program)?

4. **Budget:**

What will your budget be to support and execute your business idea? How will you finance your business idea?

Prepare an estimate of the following four items:

> ➤ necessary start-up capital covering start-up costs
> ➤ income projection for the next twelve months
> ➤ cost calculation for the upcoming twelve months
> ➤ your net profit at the end of the first twelve-month period

5. **Income sources, revenue projection:**

List your main income sources and estimate the revenue that each of them will bring in for the next twelve to thirty-six months (e.g., sales revenue from your product(s), commissions earned, interests, etc.).

6. **Costs and expenses:**

Make a list of your main expenses, including production costs, maintenance costs, and any outsourcing costs. Estimate the cost for each item, or give a combined estimation of your expenses for the next twelve to twenty-four months.

About halfway through writing their plan, most people discover that they want to change either their assumptions or their directions for the business. Understand that it's okay to complete your first business plan using your predetermined ideas. Your next version should be a much clearer depiction of your business as you continue to improve your strategies. Your business plan will evolve as you evolve.

Establishing Your Goals

The Spirit of the Lord is upon me, because he hath anointed me to preach the gospel to the poor; he hath sent me to heal the brokenhearted, to preach deliverance to the captives, and recovering of sight to the blind, to set at liberty them that are bruised, to preach the acceptable year of the Lord. ~Lk 4:18-19

In this scripture, we see that Jesus had goals that he needed to accomplish while He was here on the Earth. He knew exactly what he needed to do, and it is assumed that it was to be done within the three years or so he walked with his disciples. Jesus is still accomplishing this goal today but through us! With every purpose or vision there are goals that need to take place to measure your progress to completion. A goal is something that you are trying to do or achieve. In business, it is necessary to set goals, such as gaining a 3 percent market share within the next twelve months. Also, you can plan to have a $100,000 revenue growth with one of your products or services within six months.

You want to make these goals so that you can push yourself and keep yourself accountable to progress and profitability. I would suggest you take some time and set some goals for yourself and for your company. You can use the following to help you make better decisions. This is a well-known formula that has been used for many years because I learned it while working in corporate America. This is a great way to become an expert at creating and completing all your goals. If you make sure you have the necessary characteristics included in your goal, then you will see the results you desire.

Specific (knowing exactly what you are trying to achieve)

Measurable (knowing goal's completion date)

Action-oriented (making it doable, using verbs)

Realistic (making it actually achievable)

Time-based (giving it a deadline)

<u>My 90-Day Goals – (Start-up Company)</u>

Goal #1 – Obtain my business license completed by _____ (*date*).

Goal #2 – Calculate my start-up costs by _____ (*date*).

Goal #3 – Decide on my business name by _____ (*date*).

Goal #4 – Complete my full or one-page business plan by_____ (*date*).

Goal #5 – Research top 3 competitors in my niche market by _____ (*date*).

You can continue to duplicate this model for your six-month, twelve-month or three-year plan if you like. It may be necessary for you to complete your goals and give them to a friend or relative so that you can be held accountable for your actions. You may even want to reward yourself every time you complete one goal or all the goals for a sense of pleasure and accomplishment.

Business Plan Competitions

Business plan competitions have been around for decades now. These competitions are hosted all around the world. More and more colleges are requiring that they have the best type of business plan competitions to help their students. This has and will continue to be a great way to get others onboard and help you gain more exposure and money to complete your vision. At these competitions, you have the pleasure of connecting with like-minded individuals and the ability to create partnerships. Many times these competitions offer classes that can help you write a better business plan. The difference between the people that win and the ones that don't is simply practice. You remember the old phrase, *practice makes perfect*? Well, in this case, it normally does. Here are some winning strategies to take into account when preparing for your first business plan competition.

Six elements that make up a winning pitch:

1. **Your Story.** If you can put into words your heartfelt reason for creating this company and the problem it will solve, this connects others to your vision.

2. **Powerful and visual.** Allow your recipient to "see" a painted picture of what your business can do to help change lives from the old way to the new way.

3. **Clear and Concise.** Make sure you speak in a language that is not filled with abbreviations and jargon from the industry. Speak in clear and concise words that anyone can understand, anyone who may not be in that industry but who has the money to invest in great ventures.

4. **Defined Goals.** If you are asked how you are going to carry out your plan, make sure you have short actionable steps that are not too detailed for the short period of time you have to explain.

5. **Hook, Line, Sinker.** This is where you want to have a powerful line planned for the end of your pitch. You want to leave them hanging and asking for more because you have less than a minute to capture their attention.

6. **Practice Makes Perfect.** This makes all the difference in the world. Practice your pitch for the short meetings and practice your pitch for presentations in front of audiences or competitions. Once you have the varied versions solidified, you will exude confidence when preparation meets opportunity.

To learn more about where to find business plan competitions you can visit www.bizplancompetitions.com.

Your "Win-Win" Pitch

The term "elevator pitch" has been around for a long time and is widely known in the business world. This is the act of giving a key individual or company a glimpse into the benefits you are able to offer your target market. Although it's been suggested to shout from the mountaintop what you do, I think you should consider the return. When looking to grow your business, there are strategic ways that you should approach a potential partner or investor. I want to give you my three strategies that should be considered *before* attending an event to share your amazing business.

> ➤ Strategic Approach #1 – Networking for partnerships or relationships

When you have determined that you need to surround yourself with others who are experts in the areas where you need help, then prepare to connect with them. When I say *prepare,* I mean plan out a couple sentences or lines that you will say to each person as you float around the room. Anything in business is always a numbers game, and you must have a system in place. The more people you meet in a strategic setting, the greater the percentage that you will meet whom you actually came to meet. Here's an example of what you can say to those you encounter in that room.

Hi, my name is _____. Please tell me how I can help you grow your business. At this point, you have thrown a curve ball to this person because I am sure that they do not meet someone every day that actually is interested in helping them instead of themselves. Also, this allows you to see who would make a great partner by their ability to articulate where they are in their business, which may be a chance to add your services or products to their operation. Plus, if they have gotten past a problem that you are having, then this is the source and relationship you have been looking for to guide you through. This will allow you to know whether or not you should go into detail about your company or move on to the next person in the room. Next!

> Strategic Approach #2 – Networking to gain new customers or clients

We can all use more customers because they are the *bloodline* of our business. Without them, we have a very expensive hobby, right? This is where I think some people miss the boat. When trying to find new customers or clients, it is very easy to look up networking events and visit as many as we can, trying to convince people how great our product or service is. This is *not* a strategic approach. So many people leave networking events, seminars, and conferences without one single new customer. The goal is not to see how many networking events you can attend in one month, but how many events contain the people that would benefit from what you have to offer. Ask yourself this question …

Is my target market going to be at this event I am planning to attend? This is assuming that you already know who your target market is. If you don't, you may want to go back to Chapter 7. If the event you are scheduling is not one in which a speaker has gathered together your target market, then do not go to this event. The problem you seek to solve will not be welcomed by this group. You will leave frustrated because you did not get what you wanted because you did not plan well to receive it. Your plan should be to go where your time will be better utilized and more profitable. You might want to attend an event where a speaker selling a similar product or service is speaking or teaching. You can go and discover new problems your target market is asking of the speaker. What a great benefit if you already have the answer they need with your product or service. It is much easier to sell to those who showed up because of a need you can solve than to convince someone that they should try your product to test the results.

> Strategic Approach #3 – Networking to gain capital resources

This strategic approach is geared more toward finding out what you have to offer that will benefit a people, group, or the world. In this scenario, you want to have a preplanned speech or short "win-win" line that can bring great interest to those who hold the fuel for your desires. I saved this one for last because there is more planning that needs to go into this process of presentation. We just covered several ways to gain financial resources, but this is only to show you a way to *present* your idea or company to the people who can make it happen.

It is said that you have only thirty to sixty seconds to give your spiel about your company to a person that can make all the difference in the world to moveyour company forward. Do you have that short, sweet, and to-the-point win-win pitch ready? As you know, when preparation meets opportunity, there will be nothing that can stand in your way!

Have you ever watched *Shark Tank*? This is a great way to see elevator pitches in action. You can view episodes on YouTube or check out their show on your local cable channel. People who weren't ready failed miserably. You must know your company, your financials, and why your product or service is going to work or is needed in the marketplace. Be ready if you dare to pitch your business on the show.

If you ever miss having an excellent opening pitch ready, it could cost you thousands or even millions of dollars of investments.

Right now, you might be saying, "But I don't need to ask for money because I only want to sell on the Internet." This can be so far from the truth even if you are starting your business from home. If your vision for your company does not include growth that you cannot accomplish on your own, then you are*thinking too small* and need to THINK BIGGER!

I know I am going off on a tangent here, but give me a couple minutes. There are plenty of million-dollar companies that are operating from a home office. Today, you don't have to have a slew of employees to run a multimillion-dollar company. I suggest you get your mind wrapped around the fact that you, too, will need a winning pitch. If your vision of growth is any less than that, I consider that a hobby.

Your win-win pitch should be somewhere around thirty to sixty seconds, but if you are participating in a business plan competition, it could be as long as five minutes. If you've noticed, people with money don't have a lot of unplanned time on their hands when you meet them for the first time.

I want to prepare you with a script that I feel can help you start to formulate a pitch that describes your company and how it can help the industry and target market you have chosen. You can fill in the blanks and type your answers to practice this later.

Here's an example:

I work with _____ (ideal client) who struggle with _____ (problem) and would like to be/have _____ (ultimate result). What makes me different is _____ and because of this, my clients/customers get _____ (benefit/solution).

My example would be: (60 seconds)

"I work with emerging entrepreneurs who struggle with fear, failure, and the frustrations of starting a business and would like to be more confident in their ability to succeed. What makes me different is that I take them by the hand and lead them step-by-step through the business building process. Because of this, my clients get so much more confidence in their abilities that they catapult themselves and their business to greater growth and profits in less time."

My example would be: (30 seconds)

"I work with emerging entrepreneurs who are tired of not getting the results they want and are ready to supercharge their efforts by getting a step-by-step process to achieve their results."

You will be surprised that as you start to articulate WHAT it is you do and WHY you do it, you will become more focused on the necessary actions needed to move your business in the right direction. Try a dress rehearsal if necessary, and record yourself so that you can hear the flow and articulation of your words in order to become better acquainted with your pitch. Don't forget to practice with family and friends until you feel most comfortable.

Chapter 8 – God-made Millionaire Exercise

1. Decide what method you will use to record your business plan strategies for your new venture. If you already have a business plan, then dust it off and update it to reflect any changes in vision you have discovered for your business.

2. If you have not completed the various exercises in this chapter, then go back and really think about the answers you gave. Possibly share them with others who can better clarify your path to purpose.

Your Business Breakthrough

Joshua said to the Israelites: "How long will you wait before you begin to take possession of the land that the LORD, the God of your ancestors, has given you?" -Js 18:3

It's time to announce your presence to the world ... by name! It's time to breakthrough to a new level in life. People everywhere need to know you have arrived in the marketplace and have something unique to offer them. But the first thing you must do is think about your company's structure. God wants you to go out and claim your territory by solidifying it through an entity and other legal structures. Choosing a business entity can be very instrumental in building many protective barriers around you and your company. In your research of the different entity structures, you can discover which is best for you. I am not proclaiming to be a lawyer or an expert at entity structuring, but I did research my options when forming any business I ever started. A thorough examination of the advantages and disadvantages is most advised for the legalities behind their formation. Since you plan to deal with the public, you will want to be exposed to some reasons why you may want to form an entity structure.

- Stakeholders
- Tax planning
- Funding or financing strategy
- Protection of personal assets

- Building an inheritable asset
- Owners the main/sole source of effort
- Looking to build and sell [Exit strategy]

If any of these reasons resonate with you, then I would suggest you start the paperwork as soon as possible on your own or with a licensed professional. Many emerging entrepreneurs don't form an entity until they feel the business is earning a substantial profit. In other words, when the money starts to come in, they feel this business might just work, so why not protect their personal assets before it's too late. I've always been the one to form my entities from the start of my idea because the cost is quite minimal when filing myself. When the business started earning a sustainable income, professional help was needed to make sure the entity I had formed would serve me well.

Selecting the Right Business Structure

Once you start presenting yourself as a business or a proprietor under a business name, you can be held liable for any guarantees you make about your product or service. Even if you don't feel comfortable with forming your own entity in the beginning, you should at least know what your options are for tax and business purposes. This is a partial list of the benefits of selecting any of these entities, but I suggest you *seek an attorney for additional information and advice.*

Sole Proprietorships

This is a business owned and operated by one individual where there is no legal distinction between the owner and the business. You are personally liable for any misfortunes in your company. Once you present yourself as being in business with a product or service with a business name, you have legitimately formed a sole proprietorship. You don't have to file any paperwork, *but* it would be great to solidify your company name in your town or state. If you are starting to receive profits, then I would officially get a license, permit, or any other required documents.

Benefits
- Reduced cost of business
- Easier and cheaper to start and discontinue without fees
- Easier management
- No filing required with state (*check your state*)

Limited Liability Companies (LLCs)

This is the most widely chosen entity by entrepreneurs according to Christiansen Davis Bullock, LLC which I learned during an entrepreneur course at the SMU Dallas campus. It's a business entity that has certain characteristics of both a corporation and a partnership or sole proprietorship (depending on how many owners there are). By law a partner cannot quit but must dissolve the corporation. All pertinent agreements should be documented in the Operating Agreement.

Benefits
- Limited liability
- Flexibility of profit distribution
- Lower admin/documentation burden
- No annual meetings
- Pass-thru taxation

Partnerships

This is an arrangement where entities and/or individuals agree to cooperate to advance their interests. In the most frequent cases, a partnership is formed between one or more businesses in which partners (owners) co-labor to achieve and share profits or losses. This can be oral with no filing with the state, but there should always be a partnership agreement between all parties. The reason I say this is that there could be disagreements between partners and no way to define the resolutions to a problem. Partners should sign a partnership agreement to outline how to divide the ownership interest, profits, losses, voting, and liquidation of rights. I have been acquainted with some emerging entrepreneurs that indirectly formed partnerships with friends, coworkers, or even family members, but who never set up any agreements to settle any possible disputes. It is not a happy ending for either business owner. Also, what happens if one partner is sued or dies? How will their interest in the business be handled? These are questions that should be discussed and documented with your attorney.

Benefits
- Ease of formation
- No filing with the state (*check your state*)
- Multiple partners means a wider pool of skills and knowledge
- Increased ability to raise funds because multiple partners may be able to contribute more funds and their combined borrowing capacity may be increased

C Corporations

A corporation is considered to be a person who is completely separate from its owners. Owners are known as shareholders because they own only a share or part of the organization. Like a person, corporations may own property and assets, take on debt to finance operations, and sell shares to raise money. I have seen where entrepreneurs have filed as a C Corp in order to protect their assets from possible suits, but you must understand that there is something called "piercing the corporate veil." This is where the courts can determine if your personal finances should be considered based on a lawsuit or crime committed. So no entity formation is free from having to pay the price for the intentional or unintentional acts to all parties involved.

Benefits
- Limited liability
- Permanency
- Transferability of ownership
- Access to capital

S Corporations

This structure has more corporate formalities that have to be adhered to than the other corporate structures. You have to issue stock, elect officers, and hold consistent board of directors' and shareholders' meetings. If you are a small company, then I would suggest consulting your attorney to see if this should be your business entity. Owners have limited personal liability for big debts. Business losses can be used to offset against other income, reducing and even eliminating your tax burdens.

Benefits
- Ability to better plan for the taxation of corporate profits at the individual taxpayer level
- Shareholder may be able to offset personal taxable income from other sources against S-Corp losses.
- Must have annual meetings
- Articles and by-laws must be documented

Choosing Your Business Name

Now that you have been exposed to the different types of entities as a precursor, you can start to think about your business name. This will be the one that you file at the courthouse or through your attorney. You can choose your business name at any time during your business setup. I would suggest that if you're creating your own product or service, then solidify the process of protecting it first, before proceeding. You may find that as you test the market, your potential clients can help decide—based on the product's look and feel—what your business name should be. It is an inexpensive way of building your business brand if your product or service will be your leading generator. Your business name should closely relate to what you want your customers to identify you with. The more clarity you provide to the marketplace, the quicker they will think of you when they are ready to buy.

You can create your own brand in the marketplace through your excellence of value in product and service. Your ideal customers will come to know you through their experiences and spread your name, therefore creating brand awareness, such as with Coca-Cola or Apple. We'll talk more about *branding* a little later.

Protecting Your Name

If you name your business before filing your entity structure, you should consider the fact that this name may already be taken in your state. If so, you will have to change everything that you have printed as marketing material. I have seen people go to court because they chose a name someone else already had and were being sued to stop using that name. I would suggest doing a name search in your local and state business directories and yellow pages, which is only a quick and economical way of doing this. It is up to you to seek legal counsel. While you are at it, if you think your product or service will need protecting, then you will need to do a check and register the name under federal and state trademark laws. Try checking your state trademark register and federal register.

So how much time and money should you spend trying to protect your business name? It can depend on the following factors.

> ➤ Size of your business
> ➤ Size of the market you're in
> ➤ Type of product or service
> ➤ Expected growth and expansion

Let's say your business will be local and in only one state. You wouldn't have to bother as much as someone else who wanted to do business in all fifty states. You still should take into consideration the fact that the Internet has businesses coming online by the hour. So if you ever decided to expand outside your state, you could be met with the same name. Of course, you may not know your expansion possibilities at this point, but through the vision exercise, this should have been evident. I would suggest you do a search online for your chosen domain or website name before committing to your business name. A *domain name* is simply a clickable link that you choose that identifies your company and purchased from an authorized dealer to sell website links to represent your company on the web.

Some of the most widely used domain and hosting companies are GoDaddy.com, Hostgator.com, iPage.com, or Bluehost.com. I am a person that believes in finding a good deal. So I recommend doing a Google search for any coupons that are readily available for any one of these companies. I have gotten a *.com* domain for as little as $2.20 for one year of service. It's a great idea to buy the domain name as soon as you can if you are sure of a particular business name or identification. A big mistake of mine was checking back a week or two later only to discover my chosen name was already taken by someone else. What a bummer!

Hint: *A good domain name should be memorable, clever, and easily spelled so that your client and customers can find your site readily.*

Business Registration

I know we spoke about this earlier, but if you've decided to incorporate your business on your own, then visit your state's website or local office. The procedure to register your business will vary by local, state, and even federal laws. Remember, in order to form a sole proprietorship or partnership, in some states it is not necessary to file legal documents; an oral announcement can be acceptable. If you are not paper filing with your state, seek an attorney or legal counsel for any liabilities that may result. Remember, I initially filed my own entity structure by using the disk inside many of the entity structuring books on the market today. It can be done, but be very careful as I am not an attorney and therefore cannot be responsible for your outcome versus mine.

Of course, you will find different requirements for a home-based business versus a commercially zoned business, so check with your local and state office. If you are registering your business for a commercial space, then other licenses and permits will be needed.

Business Insurance – Covering Your Assets

Planning to have any type of insurance for your business is not the first thing that any emerging entrepreneur is thinking about. You are more concerned with making sure you have a quality product or service and whether you have the cash and customers to begin. When we obtain insurance, we are buying something we hope we never need, but we are glad we have it when we need it. While performing sales in the insurance industry, I quickly learned the benefits of having insurance to cover any and all your valuable assets. If your cash flow is abundant when you start out, then I would suggest researching your options with an insurance agent to see which ones would be most vital to you now and in the future. Remember, insurance is one of those things that when it's too late, it really is too late!

<u>Types of Insurance</u>

> **Property & casualty** – Just as you insure your house, you should insure your business. This protects any product or anything property related, such as theft, fire, explosion, vandalism damage, and destruction of equipment and inventory.
> **Liability** – In such a litigious society you should most definitely consider this policy. It covers against anything you might be liable for, such as if someone gets injured because of your negligence or another employee's negligence. If this happens, your business is covered.
> **Worker's compensation** – Not all states are required to carry this insurance, and not all employers are required to carry it, such as businesses with five or fewer employees. It insures against employee injury while on the job. This can be expensive. Check your state insurance commissioner's office for more information.
> **Errors & omissions** – This is mostly needed for service-based professionals, such as CPAs or real estate agents. It protects

---

against any potential professional mistakes that cause a client or customer some damage.

➢ **Health** – It is always good to make sure you, as the business owner, are covered for, at minimum, your basic well-being. There are several insurance agencies that can extend coverage to entrepreneurs. Many of them can be found online or through other business colleagues. If you decide to hire employees instead of contractors, then you will need to purchase health plans for them, too.

➢ **Life & disability** – This is another important insurance that allows peace of mind for any entrepreneur, spouse, or business partner. It ensures your business and family are protected. If you ever decide to apply for a business loan, most lenders will require you are covered.

➢ **Business overhead** – It's designed to cover income when normal business operations are disrupted by fire, flood, or some other type of disasters. It covers expenses in case of owner disability. How great is that!

Setting Up Your EIN Number

It is not necessary for you to have an (EIN) employer identification number for all business entity types. For a sole proprietorship business, since you are personally liable, your Social Security number (SSN) will be adequate. If you want to open a checking account, your SSN will be required to open it. A federal tax ID number (EIN) is acceptable for a business bank account, but some banks may require your SSN as well. Certain states require specific identification numbers for local regulations, so check with them. You can apply online or call the IRS and receive your identification number the same day. According to the Internal Revenue Service, if you answer "yes" to any of these questions, you need an employer identification number. You can find these questions on the IRS website and much more. (*See Resources*)

- Do you have employees?
- Do you operate your business as a corporation or a partnership?

- Do you file any of these tax returns: Employment, Excise or Alcohol, Tobacco and Firearms?
- Do you withhold taxes on income, other than wages, paid to a non-resident alien?
- Do you have a Keogh plan?

Are you involved with any of the following types of organizations?

- Trusts, except certain grantor-owned revocable trusts, IRAs, Exempt Organization Business Income Tax Returns
- Estates
- Real estate mortgage investment conduits
- Non-profit organizations
- Farmers' cooperatives
- Plan administrators

Hint: A resale number is needed for wholesale and retail businesses. If you prefer to pay taxes on your purchases up front, then a resale number is not necessary. Consult your CPA or attorney for more information specific to your business.

Chapter 9 – God-made Millionaire Exercise – "Define Your Business"

1. Decide on a name that will uniquely describe your business. The more it correlates with your service or product, the better.

2. Contact a lawyer or do some research to find out what entity structure works best for you. You can start as a sole proprietor and move upwards, but it can be hard to move from one corporation type to another during growth. Seek legal counsel when necessary.

3. Think very carefully about deciding whether to purchase insurance or not. You must consider whether you need protection for your family from your business when dealing with the public.

Chapter 10

God-made Millionaire Money Mindset

A feast is made for laughter, and wine maketh merry: but money answereth all [things]. —Ecc 10:19

The Bible clearly states that money can answer all things. When I read this in the Bible, I heard the sound of angels singing! I knew my questions and desire to not live paycheck to paycheck another day had been answered. Yes, even God, the maker of everything, understands the value of money in the Earth *and* to you. As you know, if you are terminally sick, money can buy you the greatest doctor in the world. If there is an injustice to any person or people, money can help implement new laws and change old ways. Money can allow you to provide shelter and food for a developing country and, of course, your family. Most importantly, money can change your economic status from not enough to more than enough in order to be blessed and to be a blessing. So, if God knows the value of money to mankind, then why do some Christians not have enough to take care of their life without it being a struggle?

Although this book is about being a millionaire, God's way, it still needs to cover such things as your personal financial management skills. Anything that you need God has already provided. If you don't have it, it is because you have not *believed* He has already provided it for you. The greatest remedy for *any* lack is to find supporting evidence or scriptures that pertain to your need and say it over and over again until you believe it. If it happened for those in the Bible and maybe those you know, then that and more can happen for you. *Your faith is your currency in the Kingdom of God.* Did you hear what I just said? Your faith is your spiritual money in the Kingdom of God! You do not need actual cash to buy any of the promises that God has made to you before you actually obtain them. Anything that you are lacking in material and spiritual needs, you can buy with your faith, first, and receive it according to the word and the will of God. When I say "will of God," I mean those things that are *good* for life, for you and those you will impact. Thank God for not giving us *everything* we ask for because we could kill ourselves in a moment's notice!

Let's talk for a moment about your personal finances and your business finances because they are actually working together to bring you success. Most people get into financial situations and debt because they are not educated on how to handle money. This is not something that was a priority in everyone's family while growing up, so it is easy to have fallen prey to a corruptible system passed down through the generations. It may not have been the fault of any one particular person. Most people learn the hard way. I did!

Personal Finances – Preparation to increase you income

If you are starting your company because you feel your way out of limited earnings is to start your own company, then you are right. This is indeed one way to gain access to a new financial lifestyle. But then there is always a way for those who prefer to invest money into stocks, bonds, and real estate to make a new life. These are all great ways. But this book is about becoming a God-made millionaire through the world of entrepreneurship and doing it using God's system. And to succeed, you must have a feasible plan of action on how to get there, and you must have an appropriate financial risk attitude to be able to manage it. As a Christian, there is something that God expects of you before becoming a business partner with you. He expects to be able to trust you with not only *your* portion of the money but *His* portion as well. You see, God is CEO of the heavens and the Earth, and He *always* knows where His money is going. He gives it freely to those who can be trusted and takes it away from those who cannot through universal laws that are already in place. As a matter of fact, due to the Law of Compensation (*Chapter 2*) that has been put in place, it will not be God directly taking it from you, but you yourself through your actions.

God will gladly get involved with most any business that is benefiting not just you but a multitude of people. He is not a one-sided God. But He expects you to know how to handle your personal finances *before* He will commit to helping you raise the capital you need to start and sustain your business. And one of the great things about your entrepreneurial journey is that He has already provided the educational path to get you trained and ready! All you have to do is trust and believe that He knows what He's doing.

Now, this next section is for you to get an understanding of where you stand financially with your money management savviness. I want you to think for a moment about your financial management skills. Take a look at figure 10.1 and answer the questions. This will help gauge your financial management skills. You must be honest with yourself. As an emerging entrepreneur, you want to make sure that you are ready to handle the incoming wealth God has stored up for you. Some of these questions may seem very fundamental, but this is where the trouble begins, so measure them against your current habits.

Figure 10.1 – God-made Millionaire Money Assessment

1. When was the last time you balanced your checkbook successfully without forcing it to balance?

2. How often do you balance your checkbook? (daily, weekly, only when I am out of balance or received an overdraft)

3. When was the last time you sat down by yourself or with your spouse and took a really good look at where you stand with your finances (meaning more than a glance at your bank statement?

4. If you have a spouse, do you both have a checking account separately or jointly? If separate, are you both in agreement on *how* the household funds are spent? Or is it more like, "You spend your money and I will spend mine but pay me your half of the bill money when they are due"?

5. You've hated you haven't been on a vacation in two years because you are trying to get out of debt. But your best friends just asked you to go to a place that is high on your vacation list. You have a choice between going on thatmost-wanted trip for $3,000 with six affordable monthly payments or paying down your credit card debt with a balance of $4,150, which would you choose?

6. Are you paying yourself first? Are you placing 3-5% of your earnings into a savings account or setting aside at least $25 a month until you can do more?

7. You have filed your taxes and found out you are going to receive a refund of $2,500. What is the first thing you are going to do with the money? Go shopping, take a vacation, and buy that new gadget you have always wanted or pay off some debt?

8. If you had your timing belt or transmission to go out on your car, could you pay cash for it, need to borrow the money or use your credit card to get it repaired?

9. Do you feel that giving 10% of your time or money to God is not necessary?

10. Do you believe that investing in stocks, bonds or mutual funds and real estate is a great way to create multiple streams of income or is this for wealthy people only?

With these questions, there are right answers, and "I'm not there yet" answers, but I am sure you felt what *should* have been your answers. These questions were asked just to get you to see where you need to renew your money mind. But I want you to think about your answer to question #10. If you believed that creating multiple streams of income is *only* for the wealthy then because you do not *see yourself* as that person, you have to work to do. Wealthy people understand that you do not put all your eggs in one basket. You must diversify your wealth into many areas for continuous growth in case one funnel dries up. If you start your business with scrambled thoughts about managing your money, then your business will mirror those same thoughts, which will hurt you and your business in the long run. If needed, take some time to look over your personal finances and see where better money management may be needed. Take some money management classes for free—I did.

There are many mobile apps that can help you manage your monthly spending habits better. I have been using a free app called Mint.com by Intuit to follow the flow of my money in my personal finances each month. It offers me information on my account(s), budget, alerts, advice, and any investments I have. Other great personal finance apps you may want to look into are the *iReconcile app*, *Expenditure app*, or *MoneyBook app*. These apps also have a paid upgrade option that can give you more features. This app, along with better monthly financial planning, has helped me see where I am spending too much money and going over the budgets I've set for myself and our household. There are paid financial advisors that can assist you with keeping track of your finances and getting out of debt faster if you feel the need to have personal counseling.

Know Thy Money Self

Every financial decision that you make is emotionally based on your past. This may sound crazy, but think back for a moment over your life and how you handled your money. Were you a spender or saver? Were you the one that tucked money away while your siblings spent every dollar they had? Or were you the one that couldn't wait to head to the store to shop and maybe splurge on others? Once you define yourself, where did you get this type of mentality about your money? Was it from a parent or the person you spent the most time around? Your attitude toward money determines whether it is used wisely or foolishly.

If you came from a family where you always heard, "No, you can't have that! What do you think—that money grows on trees?" Or maybe you heard, "You never know when something is going to happen, so you better save all you can for that rainy day." Here's a good one, "Money isn't everything!" That one used to make me mad because I didn't have any, so it was everything to me because I didn't have enough of it. These thoughts may have come from your parents or even your friends. Because of this type of confusion, as you grew up, you took on whatever money mindset you were accustomed to hearing. If you felt deprived of having the things you thought were nice and saw that your friends had them, then you probably vowed to never deny yourself anything. Therefore, whenever you get money, you go and do whatever you have to do to have what you want to have—even if it means going into debt to enjoy it.

If your parents got divorced and your mom couldn't support the household, then you may have vowed to never be caught without your own savings. This can cause you to hoard your money and deny yourself the joys of life. Both of these attitudes about money are based off a *fear* of something that happened in your past. If either one of these situations is you, then just know there is hope! All you have to do is realize that your thinking is erroneous and prepare for the switch. Your money mindset needs reconditioning in order to point you in the right direction. If you start to take the time to track your money, this will show you where changes need to be made. Use the forms located at www.dollartimes.com and look for the "Free Printable Budget Worksheet" for downloading. On this site, you can create your own budget worksheet and even find calculations on a few "bad habits" that can be very costly. If you are more mature in age, please don't get depressed by the Millionaire Calculator on the page because there is more than one way to grow your money.

Remember, money is nothing more than a means of exchange for something you feel is valuable (and is therefore hopefully going up in value). Controlling where your money goes is the ultimate money management skill that can be rolled over into your business finances. Keeping your emotions under control when making a purchase is a true sign of mastery.

Defining Your Needs vs. Your Wants

I know this principle is simple, but I wanted to take just a moment to revisit it in your life. It is widely known that buyers make purchases based on emotions. If a salesperson can appeal to one of the five senses, then more than likely a sale will be made. Now, when someone is trying to sell us on something, we tend to have a little more control before we say yes because our subconscious goes on alert to see what this person's goal is, such as earnestly caring or just trying to make a commission. But when we are out on our own, we tend to lean toward our life's values to make that ultimate decision. What I want you to do is to take each and every purchase that you've made and ask yourself if this is a *need* or a *want*.

A *need* is basically something that falls in the category of housing, food, transportation, and "have to have." I would go so far as to add your emergency fund to this list. A *want* is something that you would "like" to have. This is assuming you have met all the necessities in your household, so now you have room to buy an item that brings you possible joy. The reason I say "possible" is that you can make the purchase and never use it again! This is where I interject and say that if it has been six months or more since you last used it, you need to sell it or place it on eBay to put the money toward your *needs* list.

As a good rule of thumb, go back over your past purchases after downloading and completing the budgeting worksheet. Better yet, go back through your most recent receipts to label them "wants vs. needs" to grade yourself. Start putting into practice the act of putting off items that you would "like" to have until you have met your long- or short-term goals that matter. This is not to say that you cannot have fun; you can create an entertainment fund for the household to stay sane.

Plan to pay down before you start up

If you want to find financial peace while building your business then I would suggest taking a look at your *unsecured debt*. So what exactly is "unsecured debt"? Unsecured debt *is debt that does not have a tangible asset attached to it, such as an auto loan or credit cards.* You should stop adding to unsecured debts as well, and stop borrowing against it for the purchase of new things. These are items that can take a toll on your life *and* your business, especially in the start-up capital phase. Take a look at the following monetary examples.

- Credit cards
- Student loans
- Personal loans
- Personal liens
- Tax liens/Income taxes

Now, you might be thinking that if you have to pay all of this off *before* you start your business, you may never get started. The choice to pay off any or all of these items is going to be your decision, if any of these are active in your life. From this list, I would say that your student loan might be the largest of the debts. You may not want to pay off your student loan right now, and that is still your choice. With student loans, you normally can get a forbearance, which allows you a grace period to get your finances back on track. There is also an option to declare an "economic hardship," which allows for a lower payment for an extended period of time. You can certainly check with Sallie Mae or whoever is financing your loan. I struggled to pay this off for quite some time, but both of these options were my way of making it through while I worked on my business. Just keep in mind that if you choose these options, your interest can continue to accrue, therefore building more debt.

As for your credit cards, you may be thinking, "I've heard I should use these to start my business as start-up capital." As I spoke of before, this is your choice because there are many entrepreneurs that started out this way and made it. Credit cards balances can accumulate quite rapidly if you are not tracking the expenses. If you choose to use credit cards, make sure you at least find the lowest rates before applying. If you have any liens pending against you, you certainly want to pay those off immediately. As for income taxes, if you have any that are unpaid, it would be a wise decision to clear these up *before* your profits start to roll in. You definitely don't want Uncle Sam as a partner in your business!

I mentioned these few unsecured debts because they can come back and bite you at any point in your business, if left unattended. And if you ever run into rough waters, it seems that some creditors that were unpaid in your past, come back to haunt you at this most inopportune time. Ask me how I know. As I mentioned before, your personal and business financial habits are connected just like twins! Whatever you feel or go through in your personal life, good or bad, will most likely be felt by your business.

When I started my real estate investing career, I ran into an unwanted financial problem. I got desperate to get a tenant in a vacant rental property. I didn't do my due diligence by running credit checks and background checks on this particular family. Critical and big mistake! I did it because I wanted the financial pain to stop. This family needed a place to live, and I needed someone in my property. I had been paying the mortgage on that vacant property, and it was coming from my personal household finances, putting our family in a bind. I allowed the tenant to pay the first month's rent and a low security deposit. During the time they were in the property, they were always late. Go figure! I allowed this to go on for almost four months until I had to evict them and found myself even deeper in debt! The property had been vacant for two months. I owed two mortgage payments plus late fees. Our family was still recovering from the money we used earlier to pay the vacant property's mortgage before they moved in. Our credit cards, my student loans, and our family vacations were gone until we could recover from this ordeal. The creditors were calling, the mortgage company was calling, and we were living off scraps. We were struggling to keep the lights on! If we had taken the time to make sure we had no personal debt, then the mistakes that were made in the business could have been less of a burden. It was a very disheartening and lesson-learning moment in our lives and finances.

New Debt = New Threat

I must say that deciding to pay off all or some of your personal debt before going into business all boils down to *your financial risk tolerance.* If you believe you can build your business without paying down or paying off your personal debt, then I would categorize your risk tolerance as high. This circumstance was a bummer for me, but I knew this business could be very profitable. I didn't know taking on the debt of buying rental property would be a threat to our already accumulated personal debt. I just knew I wanted to realize the entrepreneurial dream! The greatest lesson to be learned here is that bringing current debt into a new business that may be incurring new debt is a formula for possible financial disaster, if you are not careful.

Setting Money Aside For You (*Me-Money*)

I asked the questions in Figure 10.1 if you were putting aside some money for yourself each week, payday, or month. There is nothing like feeling you are important and should be awarded first since you are the one earning the money. Everyone wants to feel loved and cared for in life. I would greatly suggest you take a designated amount that you can live with or a percentage of your check to put in each one of these funds to get you started personally and in business. These funds will not cover your entire life's financial needs, but they will cover some unexpected needs that may arise in the future. The biggest reason that I have seen that people do not have savings put away somewhere in an account is that they have chosen not to have one. As long as you have some kind of income coming into your household, you have money to invest in your future. Now, it may not be the amount that you consider to be enough to put away, but something is better than nothing. I have to say that if you are not saving, then you are a victim of yourself. Here are a few funds that you can create for yourself. You can even change the name to something that will motivate you to get started today. Don't forget to envision *why* this fund is so important to your future!

> ➢ **My *I'm Covered* Fund** – This fund can be used for such things as the loss of a job, an illness, or a major expense. One of the questions earlier was whether or not you would have the money to repair your car if the transmission or something major went wrong on it. This is just one of the many things that could happen in your life. You would use this fund to put away your first $1,000. Even if you have only $5 or $10 left over at the end of each paycheck, please deposit something in here rather than nothing at all. I would go so far as to advise you to pay your monthly minimums on your debt until you have funded this account. If you don't have the cash ready for an emergency, you will resort to getting a loan or using your credit cards to bail you out. A full emergency fund should be at least 3-6 months of your monthly expenses. In order to lower that amount, you can use the "Snowball Effect." (Our family used it to get out of debt twice, and to buy our second home.) Go to www.daveramsey.com for more information. It's a simple concept and it works!

> ➢ **My *Entrepreneur* Fund** – This can be considered your own personal investment in *you* fund. If you can have a "Christmas Fund" account, why can't you have a fund for your future self? You are the *greatest* investment that you have. Some people, like me, have taken on other jobs in order to earn additional money to put here. This is the best way to save for your start-up costs to fund your new business. So many emerging entrepreneurs have invested $500 in their humble beginnings only to become a thriving corporation, years later. Whatever you put here can be used for seminars, trainings, and any educational courses that will move you forward in business.

> ➢ **My *Financially Free* Fund** – This fund is the same as setting up a savings account but with a more goal-oriented name. If you

don't have enough to add to this fund yet, don't be concerned with it. It would be much better to have your "I'm Covered" fund completed first then move on to saving additional monies here. Maybe you can put your first $25 in here, in order to excite you to fund it faster. I created this fund as a way to give God a place to funnel my monetary blessings. As the wisdom of God directs my path, I knew the money would start coming in through profits. You want to stand back from the fund and let it flow—in a pressed down, shaken together, and running over kind of way! Can you see it for yourself?

➢ **My *401(k) or IRA* Fund** – In today's economy, there are many who feel they cannot afford to contribute to the company's matched retirement plan. This is far from the truth. This represents a way to reduce your taxable income since contributions come out of your pay before taxes are withheld. Having the ability to contribute money to an account where a company will match you dollar for dollar is a blessing. So don't see it as another way to give away more of your money. Today, if you are working for a company that offers a 401(k), there should be several funds, depending on your age, into which you will be placed a higher or lower risk category. The company knows that the older you get, the less risk tolerance you have because of the closeness of your retirement age. If you are not sure how your money is being invested, then ask for more information on the types of investment fund categories that are being offered by your employer. Another thing most people don't know is if you change jobs, you can keep your 401(k) where it is, or you can roll it over into another 401(k) or an IRA account. If you roll it over, it is best to have a custodian over this process so it will be seamless; otherwise if you do it by withdrawing it and re-depositing it, there will be taxable consequences.

If you are not able to contribute to a 401(k), then find a way to fund through an IRA account. There are two types, the Traditional or Roth IRA account. Both Traditional and Roth IRAs let your earnings grow tax-deferred until you make withdrawals just like the 401k plan. Any contributions of money to these accounts are based off your gross income from your federal tax return for that particular year. Visit the IRS website or talk to your tax advisor for more information.

If you check with your bank or credit union, you should be able to start and name any of these accounts accordingly. I was able to go online and rename them once I opened an account with my bank and credit union. There is nothing like having a written plan of action that you can go back and monitor for your future success. You'll be proud of yourself in the long run because those around you may have opted out of creating a financial plan of action. Debt-free living is liberating to one's heart and mind!

Business Finances - Preparation for Profits

I must start off saying that most entrepreneurs do not like dealing with this part of the business. But I feel it is necessary to know what your accountant or CPA is doing with your books and especially your numbers, if you choose not to do it. To deviate just for a moment, this is how the many music artist and entertainers ended up broke because they never checked their financial statements. If they did, they would have been prepared to switch gears before the fall. I don't want financial failure to happen to you so please follow along with me.

As an entrepreneur and business owner, you must get comfortable with managing your cash flow. If you are not keeping track of your costs, expenses, and what assets you have on hand, then you can find yourself out of business very quickly. This is one very reason why I mentioned keeping your personal banking account separate from your business account even if you have not started making any profits yet. (If you are concerned about the monthly banking fees, early on, just know there are ways to avoid then. Shop around.) Becoming skilled at managing your cash flow will allow you to know when any changes need to occur in any process or procedure within your business.

In your first year or so, you will be reinvesting most of your profits. I feel that most entrepreneurs starting out are more concerned with getting customers than making sure their financial structure is in order to receive all the business they desire. So, I want to expose or reacquaint you with the simplest explanation concerning the balance sheet and the profit and loss report. These are probably the two most important reports that will be reviewed to determine the health of your company's future. Let me give you a quick overview of what I am talking about.

The Balance Sheet

It provides you with a snapshot of the assets and debts of the business and the equity or ownership value of the business. Your health check of this report should be monthly, quarterly or annually. The balance sheet contains your company's assets and liabilities. It can show if your business is overleveraged or in a good position to expand. The easiest way I remember from my college days is *assets – liabilities = owner's equity* or *assets = liabilities + equity*. Both sides of these equations must balance thus creating a balance sheet.

Assets are broken down into two categories: current assets and fixed assets.

- *Current assets* - basically cash, accounts receivable (money the business intends to collect from its customers that were extended later payment dates although they received the goods or services they ordered. Basically the company or person bought it on credit) and it includes your inventory. This category is considered anything that can be converted into cash in one year.
- *Fixed assets* – these are items that are more permanent such as equipment, company vehicle, fixtures, machinery, and real property.

Liabilities, in its simplest form, are things that take money out of your pocket. They are better known as expenses. This is broken down into three categories: current liabilities, long-term liabilities and owner's equity.

- *Current liabilities* – are considered short-term debts that a business must pay-out within one year. This includes accounts payable (bills the company owes) and taxes that are due.
- *Long-term liabilities* – are long-termed mortgages or lease agreements as well as any business loans.
- *Owner's equity* – whatever is left over after liabilities are deducted from the assets. This is the net worth of the business which would be paid to the owner(s) if the business were ever sold. This would include any money the owner invested in the business and any stock that was sold to the public.

Here's a sample:

Cash	**$ 500.00**
+ Accounts owed to it	**$ 600.00**
+ Inventory	**$ 80.00**
+ Equipment	**$ 300.00**
= Total Assets	**$ 1,480.00**
Debt Accounts it owes	**$ 200.00**
+Loans it owes	**$ 150.00**
+Taxes it owes	**$ 75.00**
= Total Debts	**$ 425.00**
Total Assets	**$ 1,480.00**
- Total debts	**$ 425.00**
= Owner's equity*	**$ 1,055.00**

*Ownership percentage = 0.71283783 which is ($1055/$1480) = over 71% equity in business.

Looking at this example, you can see that when all debts are paid off and deducted from the assets there would be $1,055.00 left from say a home-based business owner in their first week, month or year. This is a basic model, of course, but any business in the world, small or big, could use this simple method to determine their net worth.

Profit & Loss Statement (also P & L/ Income Statement)

As soon as you make your first sale, this statement will be used. The profit and loss statement is broken into two basic parts: *Income and Sales Income sections.*

Income

- Service Income – what you are paid after performing a service for a customer (consulting, repair a vehicle, etc.) Sales income is received from selling a service of a particular type. Service income can be derived from simply deducting the expenses that are associated with the making the income.
- Sales Income –this involves making sure you deduct the cost of inventory such as storage, insurance or losses and what it cost to make or buy it from the actual income from selling the product. Inventory costs is also known as the cost of goods sold.

Gross sales income	**$ 350.00**
- **Cost of food**	**$ 75.00**
= **Net sales income**	**$ 275.00**
Operating expenses (overhead)	**$ 200.00**
+ **Interest payments**	**$ 50.00**
= **Net sales income**	**$ 275.00**
Net sales income	**$ 200.00**
- **Net expenses**	**$ 100.00**
= **Net profit**	**$ 100.00**

This is a simple and basic explanation of a profit and loss statement because it can be more in depth depending on the size of your business but can be used no matter how big or small the company. If you have a service-based business, with no inventory of any kind sold to customers then the formula would be: Income – expenses = net profit. If you have a product-based business or a sales/service combination then: Income – costs of goods sold – expenses = profit.

If these examples are still not drawing you in to know more about financial statements then the good thing is there's software that can do it for you. I use the online QuickBooks version which is about $9.99 per month or you can buy the full version if you choose. There is also Peachtree Accounting for larger companies and I found Sage 50 Pro accounting software. I have only used QuickBooks throughout my entrepreneurial career because it works for me. I always like to offer three choices so you can make the final decision. Just know the software can calculate incorrect figures if you enter incorrect information. So, it is always best to know firsthand how your financial management system works so you can spot an error whenever it rears its ugly head. Also, check with your tax professional to help you setup the proper categories within QuickBooks for your specific business. I found my software at http://quickbooks.intuit.com/online/.

Note: NEVER should you be caught in the dark about whether your company is thriving or dying.

Business Checking Account

In order to form excellent habits when it comes to money management, you should start with keeping your personal monies separate from your business monies. By this I mean you should open a business checking account as soon as possible. When I first started out, I ran my business from my personal checking account. As a sole proprietorship, this is more acceptable to the IRS, but if you have formed a corporate entity, then this could be considered a no-no! For accounting purposes, it makes it so much easier to see where your business monies are going if they are separated into their own account. Good habits formed up front will keep you from misfortunes and wrong habits in the future.

Finding a bank that fits your business needs will take some investigation. I have found that most *local community banks* are great for smaller companies. They are looking to help the community as well as the small-business person in the surrounding area. As an emerging entrepreneur on your way to small business status, this is a good time to build a relationship with a potential investor. As a strategy, you might consider moving your money from your commercial bank to the smaller local bank to get to know those in the branch. This will give you the opportunity to test their services and get advice from the personal bankers and advisors on staff. Remember, banks don't loan money when you need it. They give you money when you are already making great profits and looking to expand. A lender's main concern is to gain interest on their money and get paid back their money!

Although I am not an advocate for credit cards, I would suggest choosing a bank with "cash back" reward programs and other perks. I would pick at least three banks and compare them for your personal and business needs.

Ways to Fund Your Dream Business

➢ Bank Loans – Keep in mind that banks don't lend money to businesses that need it but to those that are experiencing growth or need to expand. Banks and lenders want to be sure that there is a predetermined way to get their money back—and with interest. If you have what the bank requires as collateral and really need the money to open your business, then by all means attempt it. Always make sure your personal credit has been checked and corrected, if necessary, before approaching the bank.

➢ Family/Friends – Ask family members and friends to donate to your dream business. Most loved ones that are interested in your well-being will want to see you happy. WARNING: Be careful in this area because a few family and friends have been lost as a result of borrowing money. My advice is if the person(s) you are borrowing money from cannot go without their money for an extended period of time, then DO NOT borrow the money. No family member or friend is worth losing over such a small matter.

➢ Second Job – Many people have been so driven by their passion that they have worked a part-time job to pay for their vision. Once you have saved up enough to start your business, then quit the position and devote your time to building your business.

➢ Retirement – Depending on the type of retirement account that you have set up, you can utilize it to start your business. If you directly pull it out without knowing the rules, you can be taxed heavily. You can appoint a trustee to roll your current 401(k) into another qualified plan for business use. This is a great way to keep you from borrowing against your home. Many franchises are started this way, utilizing approved rollover plans that are administered by an authorized organization. The ERISA (Employee Retirement Income Security Act) of 1974 allows emerging entrepreneurs to legally start a business with retirement funds. I always suggest seeking legal counsel to make sure you are abiding by the rules to avoid unnecessary taxes and penalties.

➢ Microloans – According to the Small Business Administration, the microloan program provides loans up to $50,000 to help small businesses and certain not-for-profit childcare centers start up and expand. The average microloan is about $13,000. (*See Appendix A for a list of Microloans for Women*)

➢ Crowd Funding – the funding of a project or venture by raising many small amounts of money from a large number of people, such as friends, family, acquaintances, typically via the Internet. You can tap the online community through word of mouth, social media, or just letting others everywhere know what you are trying to accomplish. They would then go online and pledge a certain amount. Some sites will allow you to keep *any* amount you collect, and some will require you to give the money back if your monetary goal is not reached. So be sure to read the requirements and any restrictions from each site. Here is a list that you can research to see which is best for you.

- Crowdfunding.com
- Kickstarter.com
- Gofundme.com
- Crowdrise.com
- Indiegogo.com

Determining Your Start-up Costs

Do you know how much money you need to get started with your business? In this section, you want to calculate and take into consideration your start-up costs—the amount of money it's going to take to get off the ground. In the beginning, many of your items are going to be nothing more than estimates, so do the best you can. Once you have completed this list, you should have a better understanding of the costs you're up against. This will also help to calm a spouse that may have some hesitations about your newfound business idea. Here are a set of questions and some helpful hints that can keep you on track. If you would like a template to plug in your numbers, then visit www.godmademillionairethebook.com/toolkit.

- ○ **Will you need to hire specialists, like a lawyer or an accountant or marketing expert?** You will definitely need to check around or get referrals from business colleagues. If the thought of everyday business receipts and keeping up with filing quarterly taxes drives you crazy, then I would suggest hiring a bookkeeper. Your accountant can help you find a great person that they've possibly worked with before. Sometimes they may have one on staff. Of course, if you have knowledge in any of these areas, you can save yourself some costs by doing it yourself. If you are looking to incorporate your business without the large costs, then visit www.legalzoom.com before hiring that lawyer. I have used LegalZoom® and so have some of my business colleagues on several occasions, but do your own due diligence to ensure they are a match for your needs as compared to others.

○ **Will you need to buy equipment or office furniture for your clients if they visit your home office?** You do want to have a specific area of your home designated for your business. Of course, there is nothing wrong with working out of your bedroom, but if your client needs to sign papers or set up a last-minute appointment, you want to be prepared. I often booked study rooms at the local library. It worked wonderfully because it was private and even contained a whiteboard, table, chairs, and a computer!

○ **What supplies or stock will you need on hand for day one?** Do you need to purchase beginning inventory? To start your business for the first time, will you need notebooks, paper, pens, and a bookshelf to house your books? Do you need to stock a certain quantity of your product to establish yourself as a customer with a new vendor? Will you have to pay a monthly fee to drop ship your products to your customer? You want to plan carefully to make sure you do not order too much or too little to keep on hand.

○ **How much will your website cost you, and are there any maintenance fees or recurring fees?** You must indeed have a website; it is a necessity. It is your piece of real estate for any business owner. This is the place that your customers go for anything they want to know or see about your business. That is why you have to keep good, up-to-date content on your website. This is where WordPress comes into play because you can update it and let your customer know what is going on in your business, such as new products you're offering.

If after going through this list, you see that you are over budget, then you will want to step back and cut some of your costs. Maybe you can get a friend or family member (qualified) to do your bookkeeping. If you are stocking your product, just make sure you buy in bulk if the purchase price is lower. Always compare at least three companies for pricing before purchasing a product or service from them. Wherever else you see you can cut back, do it for now, but make sure it does not compromise your quality and excellence.

Guaranteeing Your Weekly, Monthly, or Yearly Profits!

Whether you believe it or not, you can predetermine how much money you want to make in any given time. Now, you have to be willing to put in the work. As a matter of fact, you should *always* plan on setting goals to reach a desired amount of income to keep you excited about being in business. In Figure 10.2, I am going to show you a great template I use with my clients and in my business to stay focused on reaching my set yearly financial goals. Once you start to put anything down on paper in its simplest form, you can work miracles to get things done.

Sample

My Yearly Projected Financial Goal is $100,000 for Year 2015				
Your Product or Service	Sales Price	No. Units Sold	Total Monthly Sales (sales price X number sold)	Total Yearly Sales (total monthly X 12 months)
Initial Consultation	$47.00	10	$470.00	$5,640.00
"How To" Pkg 1	$99.00	5	$495.00	$5,940.00
"How To" Pkg 2	$149.00	8	$1,192.00	$14,304.00
eBook - *25 Ways To Dominate!*	$27.00	25	$675.00	$8,100.00
Audio			$0.00	$0.00
Coaching Program - Diamond	$297.00	15	$4,455.00	$53,460.00
Teleseminar	$9.97		$0.00	$0.00
Webinar	$9.97		$0.00	$0.00
Membership/Continuity	$29.99	35	$1,049.65	$12,595.80
			$0.00	$0.00
			$0.00	$0.00
			$0.00	$0.00
			$0.00	$0.00
			$0.00	$0.00
			$0.00	$0.00
			$0.00	$0.00
Total Estimated Annual Income	$668.93	98	$8,336.65	$100,039.80

Figure 10.2 – Yearly Projected Income

As you can see, this spreadsheet allows you to add products and services that will help you reach your yearly financial goals. The entire sheet is based off of your monthly sales goals since it is much easier to gauge than daily or weekly. You will be amazed at how you can project and calculate the number of items you need to sell for success. List your products and/or services in the column *"Your Product or Service."* It doesn't matter if you have only one or two products; just go ahead and start somewhere. (Get my bonus template called "Time To Create" to list any creative product or service ideas that come to you throughout your day at www.godmademillionairethebook.com/toolkit) and come back to this sheet and add them in.

I always find that seeing the numbers help me to push to meet my set goals. Remember, these numbers are just hypothetical and being used to set examples of how to use it. Now, I thought it would be best to add a column to calculate the cost of producing or buying the product handmade or wholesale. Most entrepreneurs forget to calculate this number therefore never knowing how much was actually made on the sale. You need to know how much you've spent and how much of the sale is *actually* profit!

As you build up your creativity and knowledge, you will eventually sell each and every one of the items on your list. Now, in the column marked "Sales Price," list how much you will be charging for the item. Of course, your prices may go up in the future according to your deliverance and customer needs. The *"Number of Units Sold"* column is based on a monthly projected figure in case you need a certain number per month to accomplish for your goal. This column will give you the option to play with the numbers to see how many sales you need to make each month.

The *"Total Monthly Sales"* column will show you how much you will earn in one month. The "Total Yearly Sales" is the "Total Monthly Sales" multiplied by twelve to give you the yearly sales for each product. This makes it so much easier for you to push to reach your projected yearly goals on schedule. Once you have entered all the number the last two columns of "Total Monthly Sales and Total Yearly Sales", it will auto-calculate for you based on your entries. You could call this your very own product and service sales forecasting worksheet.

You can find this template and many others at <u>www.godmade millionairethebook.com/toolkit</u> to start you on your way much faster!

Not charging what you are worth

I had to include a section to discuss overcoming the feeling of "I don't want to charge too much and risk losing the business" syndrome. I want to address those just starting and those of you who may have already started your business but are not enjoying the financial fruits of your labor. As Christians, we seem to feel that we should give our services away for free because it's what God would want—especially if the person says they don't have much money. I went through this "aw, let me help you for free" stage for quite some time. And I must say it does nothing for your morale or checking account. Now, you might do this for a while in order to build your business, but eventually you must start to charge. If you are still working for an employer, then it will be less stressful financially to give away low or free services to gain credibility. But if you have begun your business because you got laid off or you just took that leap, then no monies received can be an issue for services rendered. After you realize that your time spent on work is rising and your bank account is dwindling, then you know it is time to set up a chart of product and service pricing. Do you feel that what you are providing for others is worth your getting paid? If so, it's time to charge what you are worth. If not, you might want to keep your day job or get one.

As a start-up company, you may be wondering what price you should charge for your product or service. The right answer is to offer a *quality product at a fair price.* The best way to find similar products is by checking with your competition or your customers to see what is selling.

Of course, if you are offering a feature or benefit that other companies are not, then you can test charging a higher price based on the value you are giving. When we talked about "Finding Your Target Market" in an earlier chapter, we talked about testing the market. You can ask during this phase what the customer would pay for a particular product or service of a certain type. You may even ask them if they know someone else that is selling something similar to what you are offering. This will allow you to go to that place of business or their website and check out their pricing. Now, don't try to price according to the big brand-name stores. They can buy their products in bulk. In order to not undervalue yourself, don't price your product low to get more sales if you will not make enough to be able to restock for better pricing.

Don't price what you're selling as if it were a commodity. Think of pricing in the sense of your operating expenses, the relationships you build with your customers, or the value of your time, service, perspective, and expertise. As an emerging entrepreneur, hopefully you are not mimicking another person or company. If you look at someone else's pricing comparatively, you could be coming to the wrong conclusion. You don't know *why* their prices are what they are. You don't know if they are making a profit that will enable them to stay in business for coming years. If you are a high-volume seller like Walmart or Big Lots, then you are selling a commodity and therefore should have competitive pricing. Just know that if you are not the cheapest price on the block, be prepared to explain or show your customers why. Actually, if you have to explain it, then you are not delivering. In order to get customers to pay the higher price for your product, you must create a greater demand based on unique and customized experiences.

Just for a moment, think of all the places you've ever spent a large amount of money. It was because of the experience, an expected way of feeling, or the product was top quality. Every vendor, store, and online shop has a label that you have created in your mind as to *why* you continue to buy from them. Just examine your checkbook and think of reasons that keep you going back and opening your wallet to that establishment. Then you will see how you can equate or raise the bar on your own business mission.

Higher Prices = greater customer service + a greater experience + a quality product

The consumer's perception of your product or service is what makes it worth more! You can use your excellence in customer service to make up for the lack in other areas of your business, momentarily. I have found that people will shop with a particular store although their product may be mediocre. Why? Because they are treated as though they are being catered to in an individual way. With this, they will come back time and time again. Consumers value attention!

As for services, you should check with those offering similar services and price according to what makes you uniquely different. Are you doing anything that the local companies are not? In my opinion, when it comes to providing services, you should present yourself as a *boutique* business model. The boutique model is a business that offers one-of-a-kind services that are hard to find in other places. You want your clients and potential clients to see you as a specialist and expert in your industry. You also want your marketing pieces, your website, and anything you put out into the marketplace to represent you in the same way. A boutique persona equals boutique marketing and services. If your prices are low, then you may not be taken seriously, but if you have the goods to deliver, then your pricing should reflect that. With your higher pricing, the greater the guarantee you should offer your customer or client in return. It's a win-win!

Here's something you may find beneficial in your business comparison. You can visit the SBA's (Small Business Administration) site to try the **SizeUp** tool at www.sba.gov/tools/sizeup to compare yourself with the competition in a specific area.

Chapter 10 – God-made Millionaire Exercise – "Define Your Business"

1. If you are not already tracking your personal expenses, then find ways to become a better money manager. Make sure you know where every dollar is being spent while defining your wants vs. needs.

2. Compare at least three banks to make sure you are getting the best interest rates on checking, savings, and credit card accounts.

3. What are some ways that you can fund your business without breaking the bank? (Apply some of the ways offered to you in this chapter and start raising capital.)

Getting Supernatural and Personal Mentorship

"Instruct a wise man and he will be wiser still; teach a righteous man and he will add to his learning." –Prv 9:9 (KJV)

God gave us one of THE greatest books in the history of the world chocked full of wisdom and teachings that can outlive our lifetime. It's a book that teaches you *how* to do and overcome just about *everything* that could come against you. The wisest man in known history was Solomon. His wisdom, from God, can be seen throughout the Book of Proverbs. It's a true book of a mentor leading and guiding God's people to be victorious in their approach to everyday life. As the scripture states, a wise man (person) knows when to be heard and when to be silent. A wise man knows when it is time to put away his intellect of knowing it all and put on his clothes of a student in order to become even wiser. You must find someone that has been where you want to go and sit at their feet, or in today's language, find ways to be in their presence, either paid or non-paid, as an apprentice.

The Bible is full of mentoring examples, such as in the Book of Acts. We see that Philip is sent by the Holy Spirit to mentor the eunuch who is trying to understand the scripture while reading from the Book of Isaiah. Also, Paul, the apostle, mentors a young boy named Timothy while he is in prison to continue God's work under the guidance of the Holy Spirit.

There are many ways that you can get the mentoring that you will need in order to be a success. Anyone who has ever been considered an expert, guru, famous, or number one in their industry has sought out a mentor. I don't care who you are; we all have someone that stretches us to be more than we are today. As a Christian, of course God is the one who is constantly pushing you to be greater than you were the day before. I am going to give you some examples of what kind of mentoring you can receive to move you forward faster in your business.

The Holy Spirit

Whether you have ever considered it or not, God's Holy Spirit does most of your life mentorship. When you have a situation in which you see someone else and it dawns on you that the person you are seeing is actually you, there is a quote that says, *"We meet ourselves time and time again in a thousand disguises on the path of life"* by Carl Jung.

God-made Millionaire Moment

I remember one day I was helping my son who was having a very hard time in math, his least favorite subject. I was trying to explain some of the concepts to him, but he would get very frustrated and upset. I had a whiteboard for my office, and I would have my son work his math problems out at the board. Plus, this would help him get over his fears of going to the board at school. He would sometimes resort to crying, and his attitude would become very negative. He was basically giving up on himself, and therefore failure would soon follow. As I stood there looking at him with love, wanting to help him so badly to conquer this situation, the Holy Spirit spoke to me.

He said, "You are looking at your son and how he is frustrated, crying, and mad about how he is having a difficult time understanding this subject. But this is an example of you and your current situation as well. I want you to get an understanding of where you are with your financial crisis and not let your attitude cause you to be defeated. I am with you and will show you how to overcome this situation therefore getting the victory."

Lesson Learned:

This is the wonderful small voice that comes at the precise teachable moments in life. I didn't want to look at it or learn anything from it. I just wanted the problem to go away. This was my clue to turn my heart and my trust back to God. Sometimes we don't realize we have taken on the resolution to our own problems. But, if you are indeed walking with God, you will have one-on-one mentoring moments that get you back in focus with Him. He is your heavenly guide!

Your Pastor

If you are in a good Bible-based church, then you can understand how pastors are helping you prosper in life through the word of God. In the scripture we find the following words:

"And how are they to believe in Him [adhere to, trust in, and rely upon Him] of whom they have never heard? And how are they to hear without a preacher?" ~Rom 10:14-17

Let me share how God can use a pastor or leader to show you the way. I arrived to attend the New Year's Eve service of another church but could not find the church's address via my GPS. I kept thinking, "Now what are we going to do?" That small, still voice, the Holy Spirit, prompted me to find out where The Potters House was located instead of going back home. The Holy Spirit of God will guide you exactly where you need to be. He was there in the midst of our being physically lost and leading us to our next place of guidance.

Let me tell you, things *always* work out for your good when you trust God! I had come to Texas for a job because things seemed to have dried up in Georgia for my business and any part-time work I was doing at that time. I decided to take a job in Texas so that we could pay off our debt and would quickly return to Georgia. I got to Texas, and Bishop Jakes says he was led to teach on the subject of "purpose."

I thought to myself, "I left Georgia to start working full-time and forget about being an entrepreneur, and now God wants to talk about purpose through you?" That meant that I would have to start thinking about entrepreneurship again, and I was done with that part of my life! Little did I know that moving to Texas was *not* the end of my life but a continuation of what God had already started, in me, while in Georgia. My passion for entrepreneurship was rekindled under the mentoring of Bishop Jakes.

As Bill Winston, the pastor of Living Word Christian Center in Chicago puts it, God should be nicknamed "Jehovah-Sneaky." He said this when he spoke at The Potters House in 2014. This is because God is known as leading you to do one thing that seems troublesome but that ends up producing outcomes that are excellent. He has made a way for everyone to hear His word and live a victorious life! In 2 Chronicles 20:20, God says that you shall prosper as a result of believing His prophets, which includes your pastor, preachers, and spiritual teachers.

If you are sitting under a pastor like the great ones I have had the blessing and privilege of sitting under, then they are mentors as well. I know for sure that most pastors have spiritual mentors, or shall I say spiritual mothers and fathers, that speak into their lives. *Any* person who is in the ministry of God, and who is exceptional, has wise counsel that is feeding into their lives. This goes for those who are considered *great* men and women in the world. So, for the exceptional person that you are, you too should have a mentor to be an intricate part of your life. Remember, all you have to do is ask God to send you the right mentor and He certainly will!

Divine Dreams

In a dream, in a vision of the night, when deep sleep falleth upon men, in slumberings upon the bed; Then he openeth the ears of men, and sealeth their instruction" ~Jb 33:15-16

Although we talked about dreams in an earlier chapter, I want to discuss dreams in the way of spiritual guidance and mentorship through God's Spirit. Through dreams, your mind continues to work out actual solutions to real life and work problems that tap into your innate creativity and problem-solving skills to do so. Now, don't think of me as strange because I believe in dreams from God because I actually do. God gives us dreams as road maps to overcome different things or circumstances in our lives. This is one mentorship approach that is *truly* divine and foreign to others. I know you may be thinking that you have dreams occasionally, but they are weird and very hard to understand sometimes. You might have dreams where you are being chased, flying, or falling off cliffs. You may even have dreams where you are with people that you haven't seen in a long time or have never known. But I am here to tell you that your dreams are sending signals, signs, warnings, and wonders that can help you in your life journey.

In order to receive these divine dreams, you must be sensitive to God's presence in your life to understand the promptings and revelations that come from them. These divine dreams can come only from the Divine God. Your Spirit, while being connected to God's Spirit, is what makes the communication and the interpretation of the dreams possible. Otherwise, the dreams will have no meaning, and you will wake up and ignore them while life continues to happen to you. As Job explains, God speaks to us through dreams, and they show us things to come that we may like or dislike but are divine signs with true meanings. While we are asleep, God opens up our minds and seals our instructions for the days ahead. Sometimes because we are so busy doing things during our day, He has to wait until we are asleep to get a word in to us. You may even recall sometimes knowing you had a dream but you may not remember a single thing about it. I consider this kind of dream one that is for an appointed time that makes the steps of a godly person sure.

When I first started having dreams, they didn't have very much meaning to me unless they were about people I knew or contained something I could relate to. But most of the dreams we have keep us guessing as to what they mean. I have come to learn that the closer you get to God or in a God-consciousness, the closer you will get to understanding the meaning of your dreams. Although His ways are not our ways and His thoughts are higher than our thoughts, He downloads His thoughts to us as prophecies of our life experiences to come. God never reveals things of our past. He is an ever-moving-forward God. Something amazing will start to happen in your dreaming if you write down and start to pay attention to your dreams. Start to look for patterns in them.

If you are a dreamer and *really* want to know what your dreams mean, then ask God to give you the interpretation of them. He wants you to understand what he is conveying. It is known that dreams can give you warnings that you are sick in your body, which mine have given on occasion. Dreams can warn you about things you have procrastinated in carrying out that may need immediate attention. People have visions of things happening to people in and outside their family. These dreams are downloads from God to give you an insight and wisdom for yourself or a special message that is intended for someone else's benefit.

"That dreams, or, as they were then generally called, visions, were a means of supernatural instruction, if we believe the bible at all, is proved by Jacob's dream, the several visions of Ezekiel and other prophets, as also of later date, the Revelations to Saint John; and there appears no reason why this mode of divine communication should be discontinued in the present day." -Edgar Allan Poe, An Opinion on Dreams

If you are indeed a follower of God, your dreams will serve as milestones in your journey of purpose. I have had many dreams that foretold of circumstances that had not yet happened. Most of my dreams are about me and the things that need to change or will be a part of my destiny. I remember, when our family was about to go through a very dark moment in our lives, God was downloading all sorts of dreams about a war and a battle I was about to enter into. He even revealed the unknown person to me. God showed me that He was going to fight the battle for me although I thought I wouldn't make it through.

Now, I didn't know all of this when the dreams first started happening. I thought they were very strange. But I have come to know that you should write down your dreams and be on the lookout for patterns that match them. As you become more aware of the experiences that occur in your life, later on you will start to understand the interpretations of them better. In that dream, God revealed that this person was going to try to harm me, but he would not be successful.

Several months later, we had to move into one of our rental houses due to a financial downturn in our lives. What we didn't know was that the neighborhood where the rental house resided had become a neighborhood with gangs. We were terrorized and vandalized for three months. Our home had been broken into about four or five times, and the police said it was a zone that was known for that kind of behavior. They were literally telling us we should move because they were not going to do anything. On the final break-in to our home, there were traces of blood where they had cut themselves coming in through the window they had broken. They stole our valuables and left the place in disarray. Of course, we decided enough was enough. I knew the people that had lived in this home because they were past tenants of mine.

For some reason, I was led to ask some kids in the neighborhood to describe all the people who had actually lived in the house. They said that there was a couple and some kids plus a son that had just gotten out of jail, and they described him. The description was of the exact same person that was in my dream. They also told me that the tenants we had evicted along with the son had rented a place just behind us on the next street over. This explained the access from the backyard where he came and went without being noticed by anyone. God had warned me about him although we never met face-to-face. They described this young man just like I saw him in my dream! But now that I have been dreaming with God for quite some time, I am more aware of the dreams and ask God to heal me or give me strength to endure. The only thing about these dreams is God never tells you when they are going to happen, so most of the time you won't know until it has happened.

God-made Millionaire Moment:

I had a dream where God showed me I would write this book. In 2005, He flashed a picture of the book while I was yet crying out to Him in desperation in a corner of what was an empty spare bedroom. I had given all the furniture away to a friend who was in dire need. God showed me a descriptive picture of this book's title and book cover. I stopped crying for a moment and smiled at the thought of what God allowed me to see. I remember getting up off the floor and heading to take a shower. While I was in the shower, it dawned on me that God had not told me what the contents of the book would be. From that moment forward, my life started to spiral out of control. I continued to go through financial tragedy after financial tragedy. Day after day I would cry even harder. One day, I pulled up with my son to Costco to buy a few products. My son would not get out of the car. He is normally a good child, but this day he would not cooperate. He cried and cried and would not get out of the car. I remember deciding to just go home and forget about this day.

As I sat in my car crying over my financial troubles, I saw a lady and a woman who looked to be her mother loading their groceries into the trunk of their car. At that time, I was parked next to the return cart bin. We caught each other's eye. I hurried and turned my head so that she wouldn't see my tears. She headed toward me to return her shopping cart. I was murmuring to myself that I hoped she did not see my crying and would not come over to the car. I don't know why I felt she would, especially since I didn't know her. She knocked on my car window and asked me if I understood a message she was to give me. She said, "God told me you are going to write a book." I burst out in tears, once again. I told her that yes, he had shown me in a vision that it would be so. I didn't think much of it because I didn't have anything to offer anyone at that time in my life. My husband and I were struggling to make ends meet. We were actually on the verge of losing everything we owned! I heard what the lady (messenger) was saying to me and remembered what God had shown me. But I couldn't accept the message because of all the chaos that was happening around me. I thought, "How could this be so for me?" At the time, I felt empty and didn't have enough energy or confidence to add anything to anyone's life.

Lesson Learned:

God was basically letting me know that in the midst of my troubles, He had a greater plan for me. If you surrender your life to God to help you with your purpose, then He will show up in many different ways to confirm he is still with you and His promises still stand true. God is masterful at showing us the end from the beginning and backing our lives up to show how strategic and perfect His plan is for each and every one of us.

God will make amazing promises to you in dreams about things you have *only* imagined and that *only* He can bring to fruition in your life. God wants to be your mentor so that He can teach you how to live a more meaningful life. Dreams are remarkable ways to live a more fulfilled life as long as you don't disregard them when He gives them to you.

I would like to list some scriptures that speak of those who had dreams from the Bible and from other biblical experiences. I'm sure God has given you some prophetic dreams, although you may have dismissed them as irrelevant to your life. Take a quick look at those who encountered God's goodness through dreams.

Biblical

"Now Joseph had a dream, and when he told it to his brothers they hated him even more." ~Gen 37:5

"But as he considered these things, behold, an angel of the Lord appeared to him in a dream, saying, "Joseph, son of David, do not fear to take Mary as your wife." ~Mt 1:18-25

"And in the last days it shall be, God declares, that I will pour out my Spirit on all flesh, and your sons and your daughters shall prophesy, and your young men shall see visions, and your old men shall dream dreams."
~Acts 2:17

<u>Divine Dream Solutions</u>

It has been said that Elias Howe, who invented the sewing machine in 1845, struggled to figure out how to get a needle to work on the sewing machine. He later had a dream where he was taken captive by a native tribe of men who danced around him with spears that had a hole at the top point of it. When he woke up, he realized that he needed to place a hole at the top of the needle to get the thread through to complete the sewing process.

Madame C J Walker was an international multimillionaire entrepreneur, philanthropist, and social activist in the 1890s to 1919. She was having problems with an itchy scalp and started losing most of her hair. She started experimenting with different ingredients to make her own cure. She said she had prayed, and one night someone came to her in her dream and gave her the ingredients she needed. She said she woke and looked up the ingredients. Some of the ingredients came from Africa, but she ordered them and mixed them all together. She said her hair started growing so fast that she tried it on others. It worked! So she decided to start selling it and the rest is history!

I challenge you to start placing a journal or notepad next to your bed as you long to solve the problems that seem to overtake your life. Your Divine Mentor is waiting for you to ask for His help. As you seek God for answers, He is always sending them to you, sometimes in the most uncommon ways, such as billboards, kids, commercials, and words in books. The answer you seek just might be in your next dream.

Why Would I Want or Need a Mentor?

You might be thinking, "Why would I need a mentor?" Did you know that some of the greatest minds in the world have gained their notoriety from well-picked *coaches* and *mentors* to make their dreams a reality? God has ways to send mentors into your life as well, and it can come through unconventional methods. Most of my mentors were those who are located in books, CDs, audio downloads, and television personalities. Most people think of mentors as someone who is either paid or free of charge to gain experience in a certain area. Although your mentor does not have to be in direct contact with you, most people prefer them to be. But listen to one girl who used her imagination, internal instincts, and guts to find her mentor.

I watched *The Gabby Douglas Story* on Lifetime. As she became more and more involved in being a gymnast, she began to see herself doing more. She outgrew the average classes she was taking and set her sights on something bigger. She dreamed of working with one of the best-known coaches, Liang Chow, after seeing him with gold medalist Shawn Johnson. While she was reading what looked to be a magazine about her sport, she was still imagining working with Chow. To her surprise, he showed up at one of her practices. She was using her *imagination* to see herself as an Olympian, and therefore I believe because of her intensity, people and resources started to show up. As a result of holding that vision of winning in her heart and mind, she ended up achieving mentorship from him. Gabby knew that she was good but could be greater. She locked her sights on the gold medal, and her heart led the way. Coach Chow told her to forget what she knew about her routines and skills because he was about to take her to a whole new level! She was ready. He taught her things she never knew she could do. This is what a mentor can do for your life and dreams when you place a demand on getting the resources you need to excel. Due to the Douglas family's faith in God, their hopes and sacrifices for Gabby became their reality, and they all reaped the harvest.

"Sometimes you have to believe in someone else's belief in you until your own belief kicks in. -Les Brown

Once Gabby reached the new level in life that she had dreamed about, it was much harder than she realized. This is what happens to us when we reach a new level in God. We are excited about it, but we don't realize the challenges that come along with it. Gabby started to feel the sacrifices that had to be made on this new level and found it hard to continue. She found it so hard that she even decided to quit. This is the point where the mentor steps in to guide you. A good mentor will look beyond your emotions and carry on with the beliefs they had in you when they first took you into their fold. Her mentor, Coach Chow, believed in her when she didn't believe in herself. If you look back over history, people with exceptionalism as a part of their values seek mentorship. Nobody knows everything there is to know about their profession, so to be good at it, one has to push forward for the gold!

You might be at the point in your business where you just can't seem to get any traction to keep a steady pace. Look around you to see where you can find a mentor to help move you forward. Of course, it can depend on your finances and the time you have available. But just know if you are striving to be a God-made millionaire, then you need to seek counsel in the various channels that are available to you.

Direct and Indirect Mentorship

Where no wise guidance is, the people fall, but in the multitude of counselors there is safety. Prv 10:14

> ➤ **Advisory Board** – There is nothing wrong with putting together your own advisory board or mastermind group. You can get some of your business colleagues or the professionals you are paying to be a part of it. I have found that your accountant, lawyer, church members, or chamber of commerce can bring very valuable information and advice to your business.
>
> ➤ **Attend or Create Your Own Meetups** – In this day and age, there are so many Meetup groups being started on a daily basis, there are bound to be some to meet your interests. I have found that choosing a group that is more structured will get you the

best results. Also, you can create a group in which you can give back, and those that you resonate with can become part of your advisory board or even a mentor of yours. A small monthly or semimonthly fee is required, but this can be taken care of through membership or one-time fees. Look through the list at www.meetups.com.

➢ **People You Admire** – I have had many mentors in my lifetime that I have followed online or actually on television. Once I locked in on someone that was doing what I wanted to do, I would find out where and when they would be in the public eye. If they came to town, I was there in the front row. If they were on television, I would watch or record the program. If they wrote a book, I would devour the information and apply it to my life. Sometimes, I had the money and at other times I would find non-monetary ways to follow them.

➢ **Books, Books, Books** – You've heard that saying that "*Leaders are readers.*" This is so true because if you don't read about your chosen field and the people who dominate it, how can you ever apply excellence to your life or business? It is great to read the autobiographies of successful people to see how they achieved their success. There is nothing more motivating than reading about how someone overcame an obstacle that you may be dealing with at that moment. I have found so many words and stories that have reignited my fire when I wanted to quit. Check out your local library or become a member of the largest one in your city.

➢ **Seminars and Conferences** – Look for any seminars and conferences that are happening in your area and even in other cities, if it's possible. I can't tell you how many great friends, business partners, and mentors I have found in this setting. There will be so many knowledgeable people in one room that you are bound to find someone that resonates with you and has wisdom that you can take back to your own life and business. A great place to start is by setting up Google Alerts to come directly to your mailbox with your desired searches.

It is said that those who receive mentoring get great results and go on to mentor others to succeed in life. There are many advantages to hiring a coach or mentor, such as improved professional identity, higher salaries or profits, greater professional competence, decreased job stress or role conflict, and an increase in career satisfaction. Having an exceptional mentor helps you to be an exceptional being.

Chapter 11 – God-made Millionaire Exercise – Follow God's Guidance

1. Schedule time in your day where there are no interruptions so that you can hear from God.

2. Find a quiet place where there is nothing vying for your attention.

3. Sit and reflect over your life to see if you are where you want to be. If not, seek direct or indirect mentorship.

4. Ask God to become your mentor and show you more about your life.

5. Write down your dreams and reflect back over them to see if you have already experienced any of them to better understand how they work in your life.

Chapter

12

Organization- A Key to Wealth

"There is a time for everything, and a season for every activity under heaven."
~Eccl 3:1

This chapter is about getting things in order in your life and business, to clear any clutter from your mind, so there will be oneness of spirit, productivity, and time management to move you forward toward your ultimate vision. It has been said that there is a direct correlation between the way you handle all the thoughts that govern your life and how you handle your everyday life. If you struggle with making decisions and your life seems to be in disarray, then look around to see if your surroundings shout the same thing. A true indication would be how you handle problems that arise; how you keep your home, closets, dresser drawers, and office organized; and even the cleanliness of your car. I would go so far as to even include the people you surround yourself with on a daily basis, such any complainers or gossipers. Are the people you surround yourself with helping you bring structure to your life, or are they adding confusion to your situations? Whatever inferior habits you have accumulated internally will eventually manifest themselves externally in your life.

This chapter is not to beat you up, I assure you. But it is geared toward bringing any organizational hindrances to the forefront so that they may be dealt with now instead of later. I want you to have your business challenges minimized so that your brilliance can shine as you are taking this leap of faith! Until everything flows over into an orderly and productive manner, there will be no realization of your desired success.

FOCUS the New Time Management

"You get to decide where your time goes. You can either spend it moving forward, or you can spend it putting out fires. You decide. And if you don't decide, others will decide for you." ~Tony Morgan

Focus is the greatest form of time management there is for anyone that is trying to achieve a particular result! Everything you pay focused attention to, on any given day, is what you will see spring forth in your life. As you have already figured out, where your attention goes, your time goes. Most emerging entrepreneurs starting or growing their businesses spend a lot of time doing *busywork*. This is work that takes you into unintended areas that causes you to exert energy in an unproductive manner. You spend so much time on these tasks that at the end of the day you have actually accomplished nothing. Ultimately, you ask yourself, "Where did all my time go today?" Without a structured plan to design your day for wise time usage, you can lose your profitability before you even get started. If you are like me, you are starting out with a small budget and not really a devised plan. This is where you must truly focus because you want to make every effort count that is spent building your business.

There are so many things that can steal your attention if you're not careful. You can be lured into the smallest of things that can rob you of big results. This is what we call *"**those bright shiny objects**"* that come in different forms that seem to call our name when working from home. Time management, for the ladies, can mean having to clean a part of the house you deem dirty, or maybe doing a favor for a friend because they know you *"**don't have a real job.**"* You can even be enticed into watching TV shows you didn't have time to watch because you had a job. I've realized on occasion that if I found my business was not going well, I would resort to watching shows that are displaying the lives of others that I want to live. Now don't get me wrong because I feel it's worth it to find inspiration throughout your day, but when you start to live vicariously through the characters of entertainment and forego your own tasks, this becomes a problem.

Another problem I faced while working from home was surfing the web. I would check emails that had links that would lead me to other people's websites that had free offers! Before I knew it, I had signed up, downloaded the freebie, and read through the material—and an hour or so had passed. So now I was off task. In order to combat those so-called bright shiny objects, I would suggest first of all that you say NO and stay on schedule. You can bookmark the desired information or use Evernote to save it for a later time in your day or week. If you are really serious about time management, you can try time-management software to find your weak points. Just Google the top time-management programs and subscribe to their free trials. Test which one works best for you.

I challenge you to sit down and write out a daily schedule that you would like to follow for **ONE WEEK, but the true challenge is thirty days.** Then look back over your week and gauge just how much you accomplished in the given time frame. The only way to measure your productivity, however, is to have written daily, weekly, or monthly goals that you can measure. Continue with what brought you productivity and remove the tasks that did not. I would go so far as to add those tasks if you will be doing them often as a part of your documented duties so that you can possibly outsource them later. If something becomes routine, I add it to my organizational chart as a job description of a future employee's position. *Be willing to continue this process until it has been mastered.* This means that you have to brush off *any* distractions that are *not* on your list. If you need to perform an unexpected task during your daily regimen, then work it into your already composed scheduled to track your time. Don't let your days dominate you; allow yourself to dominate your days. Remember, you're the boss!

Take a look at Figure 12.1 to see how your day might look. I would suggest using an egg timer, your iPhone or Android's timer, iTunes, or a Google Play app to time the tasks you complete throughout any given day. Then, take any calendar, Outlook, Google, Day Planner, or whatever time-management source you use, and map out blocks of time, such as the following below. Also, keep in mind there is an app for everything. Of course, yours may differ daily, but it helps to be routine in order to build a system that you can follow to maximize the twenty-four hours God has given you. If you are working a full-time job and have only nights and weekends, I think it is even more important that you map out your time because family and friends can quickly plan your time for you. Focus is still the key!

Figure 12.1 – Attention Management Schedule

Sample Daily Schedule	
4:30-6:00 am	Morning run, prayer time, shower, etc
6:00-7:30 am	Get kids ready for school, get breakfast and pack lunch(es)
7:00-8:00 am	Review/write your tasks for today and place them in order of priority
8:00-9:00 am	Return phone calls that impact my business immediately - followups
9:00-10:00am	Check emails to ONLY respond to strategic partners and stop
10:00-11:00am	Read information about your industry and stay current
11:00-12:00 pm	Check & respond on Social Media, Facebook, Twitter, Pinterest
12:00-1:00 pm	Lunch with others/Brisk walk/Mid-day praise to God
1:00-2:00 pm	Scheduled tasks/Other Priorities
2:00-3:00 pm	Make connections by phone, check email, schedule future meetings
3:00-5:00 pm	Finish tasks and priorities, return phone calls and check other emails
5:00-8:00 pm	Prepare dinner/dinner with friends, homework w/kids, family time
8:00-9:00 pm	Special time with spouse or special loved one to enhance relationship

As a full-time emerging entrepreneur, you have more time to manage than a part-timer, so avoiding the simple things can maximize your time. Make sure that you turn the volume on your cell phone to silent as the alerts, rings, and beeps can take you in a direction that you never scheduled. Technology today can have you scatterbrained with all the information capabilities that are vying for your attention. It can diminish your focus by leaps and bounds! I can't count how many times a phone, iPad, or Google tablet had emails, missed phone calls, and alerts that took me in a direction that I didn't recover from until hours later. My suggestion is to check emails only during the scheduled times you set on your daily calendar. Whenever you have completed the tasks you set earlier, then go back and fill it in with unexpected tasks.

I implore you to take a lunch as it will cause you to unwind and avoid any upcoming stresses or concerns that can cause burnout during your day. Taking your lunch or scheduled breaks can make all the difference in the world to your progress and thinking abilities. Even if you choose not to eat during this time, use it to ask God if there is anything you have forgotten or need to do on this day to move you forward. You'll be surprised at how much more you get done as a result of seeking His guidance. Since I still believe in writing things down, I would like to share what I call my *Daily Task Sheet* with you. Whenever I have to be away from my home office, I just transfer my tasks to my electronic devices. If you would like to get a copy of the template then visit

www.godmademillionairethebook.com/toolkit.

Here are some wonderful tips that I want to share with you that I think will help you make the best and highest use of your time management. Just following these five suggestions can bring profits into your business at any given time. I believe that these will be eye-openers that free you to be bigger, better, and bolder than you ever imagined!

Live in the Now. If you're thinking about that business call you have to make while your child is sharing a story about what happened at school today, you're missing the joy in the story. Living in the moment doesn't have to be at the exclusion of the future; you can be aware of that business call and still give your child your 100 percent attention. Likewise if you're talking to a client, you don't want to be thinking about what movie you're going to see this weekend. Give each moment your full attention, and then move on to whatever is next on your schedule, plan, or agenda.

Ask for Help. As an entrepreneur you're not required to do everything yourself, and you don't want to expect this of yourself. It's just not possible, nor does it lead to a productive and profitable lifestyle. You're not required to be a lawyer, accountant, salesperson, copywriter, customer service representative, public relations expert, marketer, and so on. Your job is to focus on your strengths and get help in the areas where you need it.

Learn to Say No. Sometimes, whether you're talking to a customer, or a business associate, or a potential partner, you have to say no. Being an entrepreneur isn't about pleasing folks; it's about making your business the best it can be. If there isn't a benefit for you and your business, then it isn't worth your time. Trust me, people will say no to you. It isn't personal; it's practical.

Let Go of Perfection. Perfection doesn't exist. Even in the bluest of skies, there are clouds, airplanes, pollutants, bugs, and birds that can change the scene at any time. Pursuing perfection takes too much time, and it drains your productivity. I have found that as women we tend to want everything perfect before we move forward with most anything. As a man, you are far greater at letting go of the sensitive side of things because of the way God wired you. But perfection is indeed a façade, and doing your best at any time is far greater than doing nothing at all. Do your best and let it go.

Remember to Take Care of Yourself. A balanced life isn't complete without some thought toward your health. This isn't a book on how to eat right and take care of your body; however, it is an important part of living a balanced and happy life. If you're too sick to work, then you're too sick to play. We all get sick from time to time, and it's usually a sign from our bodies that something is out of balance. Take care of it, and it'll stay in balance.

It's Time to Delegate

If you find yourself not wanting to do a task or having to do the same task repeatedly on a daily basis, then it may be time to pass the task to someone else. Procrastination could be the culprit that is running rampant in your mind. Take a look around your business and see what types of tasks you keep putting off until tomorrow or even next month. I want you to know that it is okay to not want to do *everything* in your business unless you are the type that feels no one can do it better. (Of course, this is an ingredient for burnout and can lead to you disliking your business venture.) But ask yourself why you are hesitant to start a particular project. Could it be that you feel inadequate or that you do not have the best resources? Or could it be fear? Whatever your reasons, it is time to face the music. I always carry in my heart the words of Paula White, pastor of Without Walls in Florida, *"You can't conquer what you won't confront."* It is completely necessary to stare that task dead in the face and decide you are going to do it or you are going to hire someone to do it. Remember, you must move on to the next task on your list without any holdups. Most of the time, it just boils down to getting some training or mentoring or being real with yourself, admitting that you truly dislike dealing in the details of it.

There comes a time in your business when you are no longer able to handle everything and every position in your company. As a suggestion, when I first started my company, I created an organizational chart of the positions that I would eventually have. *Figure 12.2* shows you what your organization may look like as you start building your business. You will take on many roles and wear many hats. In your initial stage, you are not even sure what job positions will be needed in your business because you are busy working hard to keep expenses low in order to have momentum. But create a chart of the tasks that you are completing now and would like to possibly pass on to your hired help.

In *Figure 12.2a*, I show you how to realize which tasks you are completing throughout your day can be delegated to someone else. If you can't keep up with your own tasks because your business is growing, this is a great place to consider hiring contractors or employees. I suggest creating an organizational chart of all the duties you are involved in with a plan to add in people at a later date. Another key point, as you add people to your team, is to have them document their daily duties in order to create an employee manual or job description for future use. This can save you time and money!

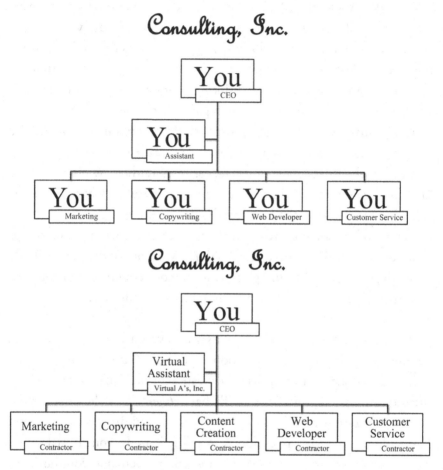

Figure 12.2 & 12.2a – Organizational Chart

Hint: If you pay any independent contractor over $600 in one year, you will need to report those payments on IRS Form 1099-MISC. Make sure you send them a copy and the IRS a copy for tracking purposes and compliancy.

In the chart I show an addition to your team of a virtual assistant. As far as finding a virtual assistant, you can easily go search for "*virtual assistant*" on Google to find one that fits your needs. It is best to check with your colleagues that can refer you to those they have used in the past or are currently using. Virtual assistants are very knowledgeable—more so than people think. They have connections to other business owners that could possibly be a client of yours or even a partner. They have a vast knowledge of various systems and software programs that will benefit you and your business. Actually, I've found that hiring them is a win-win because the top virtual assistants can educate you and introduce you to key people to grow your business. The right virtual assistant can be what God calls a "help meet" because it is not good to do things alone.

Outsourcing – A Millionaire's Profit Machine

As time goes on, you will have more clarity and find more time to add in fun activities, such as travelling, shopping, and even having upgraded lunches and dinners with family and friends.

On your way to becoming a God-made millionaire, you will find that time is THE most valuable asset that you have. Each and every waking moment of your day is an opportunity to earn an additional dollar by serving more people, so why not make it all count? The customers in your niche deserve to have your full attention because, after all, you are in business to serve them, right? As the visionary or CEO of your company, you are concerned with the bottom line, especially during start-up, but you should be concerned with finding more ways to be efficient by surrounding yourself with people who believe in your vision to make your company number one. Outsourcing can save you time and money. Some people would argue the point here because this method cuts out the full-time employment opportunity for those in need. I am not saying that you should carry this method throughout your business' lifetime, but I am saying that this is a quick way to build money and momentum to get to the place where you can hire a full-time staff if that is what you want. Hiring a direct specialist is just another step to achieving the American dream!

Outsourcing is basically contracting for products or services that reside outside your company. In the 1990s this was the wave of the future for most large organizations. It meant a loss for so many good and committed employees, although most contractual jobs paid more for those who specialized in certain fields. Back then it was devastating to be laid off after giving so many years and so much time and energy to a company that seemed not to appreciate it. Today, outsourcing is a wave of the future for the emerging entrepreneur. Outsourcing has many advantages, such as costs, increased efficiency, focus on key areas of weakness, better technology, access to skilled resources, time zone differences, and last but not least, faster and better service to your customers.

As I mentioned earlier, you should have an organizational chart, although it may be small at first, that you can add to as you realize new positions that can ultimately benefit the company and your customers. It may be necessary to Google the tasks to find out what position name and duties you can give the assignment. If you have decided that your company is not going to be a hobby but a business that brings benefits to others, then you'll want to sit down and list the duties that you are constantly doing on a daily basis. The suggestions given below will help take your productivity to a whole new level. Millionaires understand doing mundane tasks can take them away from what they do best, which is guide the company to its designated goal. I consider most of these duties repetitive and ones you can outsource immediately to a virtual assistant. As for the DIY (Do-It-Yourself) entrepreneurs, I have included other options to assist you along the way.

* ❖ Setting appointments – Are you good at scheduling your clients? If your business requires meeting with customers or vendors, then you will need to have some type of contact management system. You can use Outlook, a software program that manages contacts,

or just a plain, old desktop organizer to add notes. You want to make sure that you are appropriating time between customers. There's nothing like missing an appointment with a potential client because you did not schedule wisely by allowing time for travel between clients. Having an assistant schedule your appointments is a great way to maximize your time and make a great first impression with your potential clients. *DIY: timetrade.com, simplyappointments.com, Google Calendar, phone apps*

❖ <u>Ordering stock/supplies</u> – Who is going to be responsible for ordering your supplies? Will you have a system in place to know when your online orders or your on-hand inventory is low? Most online shopping carts have the option to input how much inventory you have on hand and most POS (point-of-sale systems) will provide the same. But if you carry physical stock, someone has to count it. This is a great place to take a manual inventory or hire an assistant to come in once a week to compare and count inventory. *DIY: Try fishbowlinventory.com or inflowinventory.com*

❖ <u>Bookkeeping</u> – Are you going to do the bookkeeping and be in charge of your own accounting? If you know you are not good with numbers, then this is a good place to outsource from the start. Most emerging entrepreneurs place receipts in shoe boxes and wait until the last day of the quarter to file their taxes. Don't let this be you. Late filings cost you profits and Uncle Sam will thank you! A virtual assistant or your local CPA office can assist with helping you find a good bookkeeper to handle your financial system and filing of taxes. *DIY: BookKeeper 2014, QuickBooks, Outright.com*

❖ <u>Marketing Materials </u>– Who will promote your product or service? Will you be promoting by mail or Internet or local shows? Who will create your marketing and write your brochures? Don't skimp here! This is definitely a category to spend as much time as needed because the bulk of your budget dollars will be spent here. It would be a wise investment to hire a virtual assistant to get you the help you need to set up and order any marketing materials you need to advertise your opening or a new product or service. Most virtual assistants have a rolodex of contacts they can refer you to for magnificent marketing pieces. *DIY: elance.com, odesk.com, guru.com, fivver.com*

❖ <u>Office Filing</u> – Can you walk into your office and find *any* document you need in a matter of seconds? It is very important that you or an assistant get all your important papers in a systematic filing place. I have tried the accordion filing container, shoe box, and manila file folders for my documents, but eventually I moved to a designated and categorical place in my office that housed them more efficiently. If you need to purchase a desk, then why not get one with separate drawers made for hanging file folders? It was one of the greatest things I could have done to keep me organized. I label them and place each necessary document in it until I need it again. I also have various file containers on top of my desk for everyday files that I use most often. *DIY: efilecabinet.com, thepapertiger.com, dropbox.com, edocorganizer.com and neat.com.*

❖ <u>Answering the Phone</u> – Who is going to answer the phone if your customer has a question about your product or service or delivery not received? If you are still employed full-time, this can be a problem because you cannot answer your phone at a moment's notice. I would suggest getting a virtual phone system or service to make you look more professional. And please call the customer back as soon as you can to let them know you care. Customer service is the bloodline of your business! *DIY: freedomvoice.com, onebox.com, ringcentral.com, or evoice.com.*

❖ <u>Chores around Your House</u> – Some people may consider this option a little vain, but I don't. Entrepreneurs who are serious about building a multimillion-dollar business recognize the benefits of *not* doing tasks that do not maximize their time for business building. Add up how much it costs for you to have your lawn mowed, house cleaned, and some occasional errands run against picking up a new client, closing a business deal, or adding new solutions to your business. In the end, you will see that having someone come in to help around the house once or twice a week can do wonders for your time spent growing your customer base. *DIY: Check your local listings to weigh the costs.*

❖ <u>Checking and Replying to Email</u> – Checking and replying to email can be an easy task even for the emerging entrepreneur because you can check your email at any time or anywhere on your electronic devices. You want to make sure that you have an email address that is representative of your business and not something like yahoo.com or hotmail.com. I am not bashing these, but they are not really what a potential customer would take as a serious business email address if they decided to work with you. It just doesn't speak professionalism, in my opinion. I can say that Gmail has more business systems in place than any of the other email providers, but using your own domain name, such as <u>billy@wesellcars.com</u> is much better. It is most imperative that you reply to your customers as soon as possible or at least within twenty-four hours. If you cannot, then this is a great place to incorporate a virtual assistant to take care of it for you. If you have a "Contact Us" page on your website, then your email auto responder should notify your customer of the timeframe in which someone will get back to them. *DIY: aweber.com, simplycast.com, verticalresponse.com, constantcontact.com.*

In conclusion, outsourcing is a great way for you to look like a large organization while you actually operate out of a home office with no employees. Your business will look streamlined because you are building a team that makes your company that much more valuable to your customers. Plus you'll get to experience a little more freedom of time, money, relationships, and peace that will help make you become a better person!

Chapter 12– God-made Millionaire Exercise

1. Find ways to better organize your office or home office for better efficiency. Use a systematic approach to label all your files, folders, books, and your product inventory, if any, to take note of what you have on hand when needed.

2. Look for distractions throughout your workday and list them. Then make a conscious effort to avoid them and gauge how much more work you get done.

3. List routine or unskilled duties that can be delegated or outsourced to a specialist. Research at least three virtual assistants to compare pricing and the services offered for a possible hire when ready.

Chapter 13

Building Your Online Global Presence

"If you build a great experience, customers tell each other about that. Word of mouth is very powerful. ~ Jeff Bezos, CEO and president of Amazon.com

In order to venture out into the World Wide Web with your business, you must be prepared to stand out. According to Internetworldstats.com, there were over 3 billion Internet users as of June 2014. The United States held the top spot for quite some time, but over the last year or so, China has doubled its Internet users. And coming in with a close third is India. With this new burst of users each and every month, the emerging entrepreneur now has access to billions of users that can be segmented into a target market that equals great profits! If you're operating only in a local market, you are leaving thousands maybe millions of dollars on the table.

Just imagine getting $5 each from just 1,000 Internet users per month over a twelve-month period. That's $60,000 per year! If you are unemployed, the possibilities are huge because you can use this time to devise a plan to present your service or product to them. If that number is too small for you, then how about getting $497 each from just thirty new clients, recurring per month, for twelve months for your professional services? Would $178,920 make a big difference in your life today? In order to earn this money from your potential customers, you must be prepared to serve them.

What I would like to talk about first is something that I feel is a number one profit maker in *any* company that wants to excel in profitability and visibility. That profit maker is simply the "customer experience." As Jeff Bezos, president of Amazon, has learned over time, how you provide for your customer will determine just how much repeat business you will gain over time and online according to the opening quote. Your online business has to be streamlined for the customer's ease of use and online experience. This online experience starts with your customer knowing where to find you in the global world of business.

With everything in the world evolving around social engagement, it would only be fitting to plan a website with an online strategy that captivates or motivates any new clients to become lifetime customers. So before telling you all the great ways to set up your website and make it esthetically pleasing with great traffic results, I would be doing you a great injustice if I skipped the preparation part. You would not be as effective as quickly as you would like to be.

Today ecommerce is the most common way to do business across the globe. No longer do you have to get out of bed and get dressed and drive across town to make any kind of purchase, big or small. Most large organizations have figured out that people are willing to open their wallets and buy gladly from companies online that deliver exactly what they want to buy.

This is a vast land of milk and honey that God has made available for all those seeking knowledge, skills, personal and business relationships that bring about the monetary success of those wanting to expand into new territories. The Prayer of Jabez fits nicely into this category. "Yes, Lord, expand my territory!" you might be praying! The ecommerce world has closed the gap between, you, the solo entrepreneur, and the big-box businesses that used to dominate the marketplace. It's now fair game for those that have something valuable and beneficial to offer others.

> *"Now Jabez called on the God of Israel, saying, "Oh that You would bless me indeed and enlarge my border, and that Your hand might be with me, and that You would keep me from harm that it may not pain me!" And God granted him what he requested." ~I Chronicles 4:10*

If you consider yourself a non-techie, don't be afraid because I will explain ways to help you along. As for you who are just starting your business and/or are ready to jump right in and get your website going, then this is a great chapter for you. For those that have a prefabricated, or what I call "a website in-a-box" structure, then this is a great way to differentiate yourself.

Before we get started with your website, I want to offer a big direct marketing, multi-level marketing, or network-marketing secret to you. You will become a much bigger success if you build your own website to complement your organization's website. This will display your personality and any expertise, awards, or events you attend to show your involvement in the organization. You want to always give your current and potential customers a very present and magnetizing experience with you. (Social media is great for this as well, but we will talk more about that in the next chapter.) A website says and shows that you are an expert in your chosen field. The organization-given website is basically a way to help you with your marketing and your business purchases to make it easier for you. These companies know that if you have most of the work done for you, you will be more apt to join and become successful faster. But, again, I believe that if you create a website with testimonials, pictures of you, some of your customers using the products or service, you will have a much better chance at success. This will allow you to attract new customers and new representatives for your team.

Another idea for you is when setting up your website, you can always link the company's website from your "Products" tab. Be careful not to list the company's products directly on your website because they may have a rule against you doing so. Your supplemental website is a place to give away *free* tips, tricks, a newsletter, or any events that you may be hosting to gather your ideal customers. If you take a look at the leaders in your niche, they most likely have another website that showcases more about them. This is the only time that I would say that you should have a website centered around showing only you, your new lifestyle, and your many accolades or rewards you have earned to solicit new clients and customers.

Primary Objectives for Your Website

With all of that said, let's take a look at your *primary objective* for creating a website. You might be saying, "It's to show people what I am all about or to convince them to buy what I am selling." I must agree that these are objectives that are most certainly viable for bringing your business online, but as a newbie to the online world, you want to make sure your efforts to bring about the results you want in a faster manner aren't thwarted.

List Building – If you are looking to build a list of target customers who are indeed interested in what you have to say and to sell, then this is the way to get it down. You want to have a *free offer* that will entice your visitors to know more about what you do. You want this free offer to be something of great value. It can be an eBook, a free CD, a newsletter, an audio download, or the first two chapters of a book that is coming out soon that you are writing. Once you build a list of 500 or more, you will have an audience that is ready, willing, and able to buy what you have because you have proven you can deliver what they need. In order to get started with your list and to have a place for them to sign up to receive your free offer, visit www.aweber.com/**Forms.**

Content – Are you looking to show only what information you have available on a global issue, local issue, or a cause that you are passionate about? Maybe your website is going to deliver a certain type of information to your target market. A better example would be if you have specialized knowledge in a particular area and are now selling it as your profession; then you would use a *blog* to display your expertise. This is a way to put you at the top of the industry gurus by keeping your audience "in the know" regarding what's actually happening and what strategies you have to help them overcome. In the next section, we will discuss blogs more.

Establish Credibility (Corporate) – If you have decided that you want to do business with such audiences as executives or corporate companies, then this objective will serve as your resume. It is not appropriate to place an opt-in box here because most corporations never sign up for newsletters and freebies because you first have to be screened by someone before you even get to them. So you want to make sure that all the information you want them to know about you can be found on your website as they will research your credibility in various areas. If you have spoken at past events, have knowledge in a particular area, or have any audios, then make sure samples are displayed prominently on your website.

Establish Credibility (Entrepreneurs) – The objective here is to promote your expertise and services. When using your gift, skills, and talent to help all types of entrepreneurs to better themselves in their profession, you want to exemplify *why* you would be the right person. In most cases, you are offering your services, along with tangible products, to display your credibility to help you close the deal. There may be many experts in your chosen field, but what makes you different? Your ideal client might have this question, so you want to follow it up with any media appearances, testimonials, or social media comments to show you're the one they most definitely need to help them. I would also suggest that an opt-in box would work well to have them get on your list to receive any future products or newsletters to further establish a long-lasting relationship. This kind of website will be about your brand and what you want to be known for in your industry.

Selling Goods/Products – This site is to do nothing but sell a specific type of your products or products in a certain market trend, such as seasonal items. It's basically an ecommerce website to display your merchandise. The website can sell to the general public for retail pricing or as a wholesaler with discount prices for other retailers. You can highlight the product of the month and offer to keep customers in the loop by having them sign up to receive special discounts, new product arrivals, or any reviews of the product of the month. So using an opt-in box here would certainly serve the greater good to move your products faster and to have the customers feel as though they are special by being the first to know about your products. A great example would be Amazon.com, BestBuy.com or Zappos.com.

Building Your Virtual Online Walls

Now that you know your primary objective or reason for building your website, let's find the best way to present your website in the online world. Before you can build your website, you must know what type of presentation of your website will resonate with your ideal customers. Think of it like this: if you had a physical building, what impression would you want to give to your current and new customers? What would you want them to feel, see, and think about your place of business? It's the same when they type in your website address, which is like driving their car to your company. Once they take the time to drive there and get out of their car and walk into your building, what will they see? Will they be impressed? Will the advertisement that got them there match the product or service you offer? Most of the time in business, the decision to buy is not always about the content itself but about how it's packaged. This strategy is most important in the online world.

As a home-based business owner, your website is your piece of real estate as opposed to an entrepreneur that is operating out of a physical location. Just as you would have someone caring for the cleanliness of the store and its being open on time, or even making sure the day-to-day operations are running smoothly, you need to be aware of the role of website maintenance or developer.

Whenever a potential customer comes to your website, they should be greeted by you or by a video validating why they should stay on your site. This is most important because if your potential customer misunderstands how you can help them, they may never visit your site again. So your site should be set up to appeal to your target customer and engage them in what you have to offer.

If you are currently running your business from a commercial location, then the process of expressing what you have to offer is much easier because you know what your customers find valuable about your products or services. You are basically bringing what is working for you offline to an online environment to promote more engagement and convenience of shopping for your customer and to gain a new market share of potential customers.

I want to describe the four structures your website can take on to give your visitors the confidence they have landed on the right website.

Brochure Site – You can compare this to handing out a flyer, magazine, brochure, or pamphlet about what you do, what you have to offer, and the benefits of doing business with you. This site has plenty of colorful and high-definition pictures that exemplify you and your company. A brochure site would be great for someone who was a singer, a media mogul, a graphic artist, a photographer, or just someone wanting to give information about their company as a presentation. This allows people to see samples of your work, and you can choose which display works best for their need.

Sales (Opt-in and Sales Page) Site – If you have decided to sell one product or a product package, then this type of website would be just the fit. This page is filled with any of the following: video with product demonstrations, testimonials, and any written content that describes the product in great detail. This website is to address *any* questions or concerns that you think your ideal customer would have so that they won't have a reason to not make the purchase. Throughout the sales page, which is also considered a sales letter, you will sprinkle in a *Buy Now* button to enable them to purchase at specific points throughout the page, without having to read all the way to the bottom. In order to see one in action, just go to Google and search for *"sample sales page template."*

Blog Site – I want you to realize that in today's technology, you can build this website with less than $150 if you decide to do it yourself with research, such as through the vastness of videos on YouTube, books, or business training. Most of the costs will come from your hosting company and domain name purchase. A blog is a website that allows you to be personal and make your own updates to keep your content fresh without the hassles of paying a web developer for updates. You can build your brand and business all on this one platform.

Even though I love using WordPress, I will still introduce you to the other blogging platforms so that you can decide for yourself. Here I will go into more detail about what I consider the top three blogging platforms that can serve you best.

> ➤ *Tumblr* was bought by Yahoo back in 2013. This is for the casual blogger and the person that wants something between Twitter and WordPress. Here you are encouraged to not write complete posts but upload and share more pictures, comics, infographics, links, and videos. It's great for the socialite, artist, or videographer. These are large, visually stunning themes for your site. It's very user-friendly and easy to set up.
> ➤ *Blogger* is also known as BlogSpot. This is a blogging platform that is owned by Google. It was the first of its type and paved the way for the other blogging platforms. Monetization of your blog is easier through Google's AdSense. There is limited community support though and limited designs and themes. Some have said it can be hard to set up on your own domain as a newbie. I can say that anything of Google's that you use will most likely get you a higher ranking in the search engines since they own the largest search engine, but great content will also be in play.
> ➤ *WordPress* is the most popular blogging platform in the world. It can be used by the casual blogger and the full-fledged business

owner, such as the *Wall Street Journal* blogs and *People* magazine. There are hundreds and hundreds of themes you can choose from to express the heart of your business. Since WordPress is a free blogging platform, people in the community are constantly offering additional features that make your site as fit as the top organizations. You can have the feel and look of a larger company when you may be only a one-person show. It's flexible enough to run your ecommerce store or even your video blog, which can connect your social media channels.

Let's dig a little deeper into the WordPress platform. There is a WordPress.com and a WordPress.org, so I want to explain the difference between the two to avoid confusion. *WordPress.com* is a publishing platform that allows you to obtain a website that is set up and hosted (maintained) by a group of skilled developers. As of the writing of this book, you will be given a website domain name of www.whatevernameyouchoose.wordpress.com for the *free* service. You will not be given the option to choose your own business name unless you upgrade to a paid package. There are three packages: the beginner, which is free; premium, and business, both for a specified cost. You will be given the option to basically purchase whatever you need in an á la carte manner, meaning picking single services and combining them into a customized package. The cost can get a little pricey if you are on a budget or not careful about all the additional features you decide to add to your cart.

Under the *free* or *Beginner* structure, you will be at the mercy of the site's developers with the content you provide because there are certain restrictions to the content you can place on your site. If you do not read the restrictions and you violate one of them, you can wake up one morning to find out that your website and all its content are gone! You may also agree to having advertisements, not of your choice, displayed somewhere on your site unless you pay to opt out. If you would like to test drive a trial version, visit www.wordpress.com and choose "*Start Trial*," as of the writing of this book. Please make sure you read their

"Terms of Service" to understand what the specific expectations are for you and your content.

WordPress.org is the software platform that puts you in the driver's seat to control your website's feel, content, usability, and ownership of it all. WordPress.org is not free like WordPress.com. You will not have the freebies, such as the technical support or the domain name link to your new website. You will have to pay for a domain name or website address and for the hosting and maintenance of your website. If you are afraid of the techie stuff, then you may have a problem with setting this all up on your own. But the great part is that if you purchase your domain name from a great hosting company, their technical representatives will walk you through the process or even install your WordPress software on your new site for you. I will give you the names of great hosting companies that can help you in just a moment. I have tried both WordPress.com and WordPress.org and found it better to have total control of my websites. I would definitely suggest that you get more acquainted with the self-hosted version of WordPress by visiting www.wordpress.org. This will help you to better understand the steps we will discuss in just a moment.

E-commerce Site – This can be composed of an auction website, or it can be a manufacturer's website that sells various items that consumers can purchase. If you decide to sell your products wholesale, such as in a B2B (business-to-business) environment, then this is a great site to display your products. This type of site can also include private login information given to clients for easy and undisclosed access. Here are a few sites that you are already familiar with and may have even used to purchase a recent item. You can visit these sites to see how you might set up your own site. Also, Google *"ecommerce or wholesale sites"* to get a better understanding of what models would be best for you. Some great examples would be www.amazon.com, www.ebay.com and www.barnesandnobles.com.

Setting Up and Maintaining Your Website

There is so much that can be discussed about maintaining your website. It is most important that you understand how your website can be cared for to make your downtime minimal due to lack of experience or dedicated time. Making sure your website is always available for your customers will keep you from ever losing a possible sale. *Always remember, it is your website visitors that generate the income for your website and not the website itself, so it needs to be available 24/7.* You definitely want the channel open whenever God places a thought on someone's heart to go to your website at 3:00 a.m. to purchase exactly what they were looking for, right?

If you have decided to brave it out and set up your own website, then continue to follow along with me. If you have decided to hire someone, then I would still suggest following along because I want you to be fully aware of what you will be paying for so that you will not be taken advantage of unknowingly. God's word says, "My people perish for the lack of knowledge." Never shun an opportunity to learn although you may not want to always be the doer of it.

Here are some important things I want you to keep in mind *before* deciding to setup or possibly reinvent your website.

Decide what name you want for your website – Because of all the work you have done in the previous chapters defining your business, you should know exactly what name you want to use to describe your company. It could be your business name or your personal name if promoting yourself as the brand. It could be the name of your product. For example, "*wesellusedhondaaccords.com*" is a better way of saying *exactly* what you are all about. We will discuss *search engine optimization (SEO)* later in this chapter to explain how your website name can be used to gain traffic. The more descriptive you can be, if using your product, the better your customer can find you when using Google. Write down about three to five phrases or words that you think would best describe your business or product. Also, you want to buy the .com, .net, .org, or .uk and .co if you plan to do business internationally. If there is a domain name that you really feel you have to have and it is already taken then visit www.sedo.com to see if you can buy that particular website name.

Choose a hosting company for your domain name – An effective way of selecting a reliable and trustworthy web-hosting company is to do some research. Two premier sites to find their reviews are www.webhostingtalk.com and www.findmyhosting.com. You want to compare at least three hosting companies that can serve your needs based on price, technical support, and customer service. The reason I say this is that some companies have a lower price, but you cannot get through to anyone to get your questions answered or they have a history of complaints about their servers going down throughout the day. You can Google "top 10 hosting companies" and get a really good list. I have had the pleasure of working with these three companies. I am currently using Hostgator.com because I have several websites and the cost is more economical, but I also use GoDaddy.com because I can find special coupons and deals at certain times. That brings me to another point. Whichever hosting company you choose to use, always Google the words *coupon codes* along with the name of the *hosting company* to get awesome special pricing and other great deals.

Choose which hosting package is best for you – Be careful about choosing web hosting company that offers "free hosting." If you are looking to grow on a large scale or are building an ecommerce site, then you will be limited in your control over your site and subject to unwanted advertisements that can annoy you and your customers. As you will see, the pricing is discounted based on coupons or the longer period hosting packages. If you are established with customers and they know, like, and trust you, then I would buy a longer hosting package. As a new entrepreneur, after testing, you may find after six months you want a new name or to change your business industry. If this is true for you, then you are not stuck with that hosting package for five years. The good part is that if you choose to go with another website name, some hosting companies will allow you to switch another website name to that package. Check before purchasing your hosting company.

Set up WordPress on a Server – It's time to go live! Don't be afraid at this point if you feel you are not technically savvy enough to do this. You will have the option to have someone hold your hand through the process. With most hosting companies once you purchase the hosting package, you can call their technical support team, and they will load the software package for you on to your new site. If they won't, then I would suggest finding one that will because you may need their help again. I know for sure that GoDaddy.com and Hostgator.com will do it for you as a part of your purchase. If you are technically savvy, then there is an option once you purchase the hosting package to install WordPress yourself with the click of a button. From that point, you would fill in all the necessary information to bring your new website online.

This is a good place to decide if you want to hire someone to complete the process of changing the theme and adding your content to your site. If you choose to have someone else do it, then I would Google *"technical virtual assistant"* or *"webmaster"* to get some help. Remember we talked about outsourcing certain parts of your business that you didn't want to do or would save you time or money? Well, a technical virtual assistant can do so many things that you haven't realized you need done yet. You can hire them on an as-needed or a per-hour basis. You may want to write down exactly what you are looking for in a virtual assistant based on at least three Google searches. Then interview each to see how they can serve your needs and build a lasting relationship that will work out for you both, especially if you are still working full-time.

Let me let you in on another one of my secrets that helps me save time and energy. If you have not figured it out already, whenever there is something that you are not sure how to do, then take a quick leap on over to YouTube.com. This is one of the first places I go whenever I need a quick "how to" about anything because I don't have the time to read through a book or manual.

If you decide to go with a company that has told you they will take care of everything and you're comfortable with them then great! But make sure you ask these three most important questions before hiring them.

- Will I be the sole owner of the domain name you are giving me for *free* or does your company own it? (If you accept the domain for free, you will be at their mercy and have to pay whatever cost they charge to renew it under them. If you buy yours from your chosen hosting company you can get discounts through online coupons for renewals.)
- Will I have to pay for maintenance or updates that go over a certain number per day, week, or month? (If you are just setting up your site, then there will definitely be changes as you see things you would like to change often.)
- If I decide to leave and go with another company, will I be able to take my site with me? Will I have to pay a fee for transferring my database over to my new provider? (Some customers have lost their site because it costs them thousands of dollars to transfer their database. This is one of the unknowns that most emerging entrepreneurs fall prey to.)

There are more questions that you can ask, but these are the ones that I have seen catch most entrepreneurs off guard. Now, take the time to digest this information and go do some diligent seeking to make sure before you send traffic to your website. You don't want to lose any potential customers because you were in a hurry to get your website online.

Getting Traffic to Your Site-List Building

Honestly, you will gain greater visibility and profitability from the relationships that you build offline and bring online. Letting people know what you do is the highest form of customer attraction ever. What sense does it make to have a beautiful website with valuable products or services if no one knows you are even open for business? What I am going to focus on in this chapter is what I consider the most important strategies to building an effective and profitable website whether you are a home-based business or whether you are bringing your offline business online. I want to take you through the process of some simple optimizing strategies to get traffic to your site. In a later chapter, I will be discussing social media strategies you can apply once your website is up and running.

Here are a few ways that you can get traffic to your website and get them to signup for your special offers. Always remember, when building your business online, the money is in your email list!

Word of Mouth – There will never be a replacement for those magical words that come out of the mouths of your loyal customers. If you have ever done the very best you could for each and every one of those that have sought your products or services, your marketing budget has just decreased tremendously. These magical words translate into potential dollars from others through testimonials. Testimonials from past and present customers can bring in continued business and traffic to those who share them with others—especially through social media. Never underestimate a chance to "get it in writing" from a happy customer.

Opt-In Box – This is where your goldmine begins online! In order to have a list of raving fans, offer them something *free* and of *value* to make them want to know more about you and how you can help resolve their problem or need. Once you have a list of 100 or more people, you can make offers that will sell a lot faster than having to go out and solicit to others. Getting a person's name and email address is the first step to building a lasting relationship with them. You want to be the first person or company they go to when they have a specific need for your product or service. You can also use your list to partner with another expert that complements what you already have to sell. You've heard the saying that *your net worth is tied to your network.*

Keep Your Content Fresh – It is most important, especially for repeat visitors, to know that they will find the latest and greatest information, products, or services on your website. The best way is to prepare your website content a week or two in advance to make sure you stay ahead of the game. The best way to accomplish this is to research your topics online, and once you find something valuable, use Evernote® to bookmark all you see as references. Download the software at www.evernote.com. If you need further help due to time constraints, then outsource your article writing to keep your content top-notch.

Newsletters via email – One of the best ways to get your customers to know, like, and trust you is to offer them "exclusive" content they can get only by being on your email list. With your expertise, place your knowledge in blocks of 100 to 200 words within a branded newsletter representing your company. This is a great way to introduce your customers to a behind-the-scenes look at you and your company. Here are some great sites to check out, such as getresponse.com, constantcontact.com, mailchimp.com, and verticalresponse.com.

Email Advertisement – Send targeted emails that contain specific offers on your products. (If you don't have any, then you need to create one or two to start off with for sale.) Since you already have a captive audience, you may as well give them what they need to solve the problem that caused them to connect with you. This type of email can be incorporated into your weekly or monthly email newsletter, or you can send this out only when there is a sale going on or during the holidays.

Banner Ads – Now this is something that I have found that many newbie entrepreneurs and some seasoned ones do not utilize. Exchanging banner links with other like businesses (that aren't in your same niche) will increase the number of visitors to your site. For instance, if you help entrepreneurs with branding themselves, then you may exchange links with a graphic company because you both are attracting the same customers. Be careful about placing too many banners out there. You must always track them for their efficiency. Check the Internet for the various types of *ad tracking software* to help you.

Hold A Free Webinar – Never underestimate the power of the knowledge you have in your niche. Because you have stepped forward, it will really maximize your profits and notoriety to put together some PowerPoint slides on your favorite topic. This can be a one-hour webinar with one of your products or services being offered for a price at the end so that they can continue to find value in your business. All you will need is a forty-five-minute presentation with fifteen minutes left for Q & A. With today's technology, you can record the webinar as you are giving it and sell it for $27, $47 or even $97 as an educational product on your site. You can send it as a CD/DVD because some people love receiving a physical product, or you can make it available via a digital download for the "I want it now" customer. Most webinar companies will offer the first thirty days for free.

Ask for Emails at Live Events – This is something that I find can be very easily done. Once you collect cards from those that you feel are pertinent to your business, such as potentially needing your product or service, offer them a sample or free session to get to know exactly what you do to help them. Let them know in advance that you will add them to your email list so that they will be aware and not consider your emails SPAM.

Pay-Per-Click – Most of the social media channels and major search engines have ways you can pay for traffic to be sent to your website. You can use Facebook PPC, YouTube PPC, LinkedIn PPC, Twitter PPC, and Google PPC. I would suggest you choose one and test it until you find the one you like and stick with it until you master it and get the results you find profitable. PPC is a wonderful way to speed up the process by spending a set amount of money monthly to drive quick traffic to your website. The key here is to offer an excellent product or service, normally for *free,* through the use of very enticing and engaging words. Most of these PPC channels offer some great educational training through their representatives or information under this section on their website.

Add Video – This is one of the fastest ways to get traffic to your site. Create a YouTube channel where you can create public, private, and unlisted videos that can support private trainings and public videos showing demonstrations plus information about what you sell. Having this on the front page of your website is the best way to keep them on your site. And if the video is quality, your ideal customer will start to move to others parts of your page and then to do business with you. Online users and shoppers tend to go to YouTube first to get product reviews and instructional "how to" videos on just about anything *before* they take out their wallet to buy most products online. Your ideal customer may even Google you to find any and all information that pertains to you *before* they will work with you. So make sure you have enough information for them to make a well-supported decision to work with you.

If you always offer free quality and original content, this will build a great online presence that is most effective for having a long online life. If you continue to check out other ways to bring great value, you can build a healthy list in no time. The more qualified your leads, the faster your website-selling machine will become profitable for you.

SEO (Search Engine Optimization)

I conducted a workshop called *"SEO Unlocked – Understanding SEO for Beginners."* This is an area that can sometimes be gray to those who are just bringing their business online and even to you who may already have a website. You could pay upwards of $3,000 to $5,000 or more a month to hire an SEO webmaster to complete this task for you. Search engine optimization is a process that takes time; it is not an overnight success. Users' keywords and searches change, so you will have to continuously monitor your website on a weekly, bi-weekly, or monthly basis to make sure that you are ranking high enough for your keywords to be seen on the first page of the Google search engine. This section is not intended to give you advanced knowledge of what SEO is all about, but to *expose* you to a task that has to be done by you or by a hired professional in order to maximize your presence online. The way I want to approach this topic is by answering some basic questions that will help you understand the *what, why,* and *how* search engine optimization needs to be a part of your online business success.

What is SEO?

SEO is the process of making improvements off and on your website in order to gain more exposure in search engine results. It begins with a website and a website strategy, which we have already gone through together in the previous chapters and sections. Many large companies today rely heavily on ranking in the top category in their marketplace. It has been proven time and time again that the data on search marketing and organic traffic (unpaid traffic) is even more relevant because of new-customer buying habits. If you have not begun or completed your website set up then you may have to revisit this section when your website is up and running.

Why Do You Need SEO?

I would compare implementing SEO to all the people that help make up the total package of a Broadway show that became a hit. Everyone that applauds and gives you raving reviews for a great show do not understand what took place behind the scenes to make your play as spectacular as it was. Your careful designing of your website will be rewarded by the structure of what you have working behind the scenes. A mindfully crafted show will indeed be rewarded by a front-page article in its rightful section of the newspaper, just as the search engines will boldly display your website for its details as a top feature on their front pages.

Search engines need to be able to read your website content, pages, images, and links when they come to your site. Whenever people go to a search engine, such as Google, Bing, or Yahoo, they type in certain words that describe what they are looking for on a website. These words are called *keywords* (e.g., "*dentist in Texas*"). Keywords can be compared to the major characters in your play. If people don't remember the name of the play or your website, they may type in the name of one of your characters or keywords to find your site. And if you have chosen your keywords correctly, you will show up as the top search result.

What are some SEO requirements?

There are certain areas that you want to concentrate on to get your website in tip-top shape for search engines before they start scouring your site with their automated robots to rank your website. We will get into more details about this in just a moment, but first let's discuss the two types of SEO methods for effectiveness.

Off-page optimization is probably more important than on-page optimization because the majority of your results will come from offline techniques, such as blogging, social bookmarks, press releases, RSS feeds, social media sites, directory submissions, forum marketing, and automated SEO-helping tools. (*See Appendix B for a listing of SEO Tools.*)

On-page optimization is critical to understanding your online research and web strategy. Always start your optimization with the online techniques. This is what you do on your website, such as understanding your niche and the keyword research you did in order to entice search engines to constantly visit your site for ranking. I want to show you some quick tips that can get you going much faster.

How to implement some SEO strategies?

Execute a strategy – What information do you want your customer to know and understand about you or your company—your specialty? Consider this example: what can a visitor to my website learn from me or our team? What does a visitor want to learn from me or my team?

These questions may sound the same, but this isn't quite the case. You can give a customer what you "think" they want, but you will have to discover what it is they "need" from you to improve their lives. You have to know what makes you better than your neighboring vendor or competitor for your customer.

Keyword Research – is a practice used by search engines to find and research actual search terms people enter into the "search box" when conducting their online search. And then people like you and I use keyword research in order to achieve better rankings for our desired keywords.

In Figure 13.1, if you were to type in the keywords *"car Camry,"* you will find that there are a higher number of returns in your chosen search engine because these words are more vague than they are specific. Keywords themselves are the search terms people type or enter into the search engines. If you use what is called *long tail* keywords, you are defining your product or service to its deepest level. A long tail keyword is quite simply a keyword that is really specific to what the Internet searcher is looking for. If your potential customer searches for *"used blue 2013 Toyota Camry,"* this will get them to your site quicker if these are the keywords you have identified on your website. By detailing your keywords, you see that there will be a lower volume of returned searches, a higher relevance, and lower competition.

The rule is you are not to stack or overuse your keywords because the search engines will frown upon this. This is why you should take the time to come up with as many keywords as you can and sprinkle some of them into long tail keywords. Finding the right keywords or keyword phrases for your website or blog should be a priority because this is most essential to your optimization campaign for your website. A strategic suggestion is to add your keywords to your domain name or website name. The rule is that you should not use more than seven words because the name may not show up completely in the search engines. It could be cut off and show dots for the rest of your website's name.

This can cause your site to be overlooked because your three seconds of introduction could be lost forever. If you're truly interested in knowing more about keywords, you can get a free trial at www.spyfu.com to look at the keywords of your competitors.

Figure 13.1 - Keywords vs Long tail Keywords

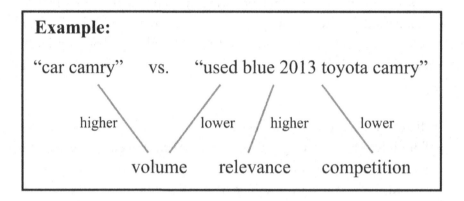

Create Content – Clearly defining what you will display or educate your customers about will gain you more leads, sales, and long-term customers. Customers want valuable content written on a regular basis, so creating content that shows your key audience that you understand them is vital. Content management must be handled properly by you or your hired assistants to enhance your online reputation. Define what can and cannot be posted because it should be in alignment with your website strategy and keywords. Search engines are highly based off being able to read the website code behind the scenes, which includes your images, links, videos, and text—including pdf's, Microsoft office products, or other visual data.

Hint: Having flash on your site can cause it to load very slowly in some browsers and can make it hard to read by search engines. It could cause the search engines and potential customers to leave your site instantly!

Build Links – You can do this in a number of ways, such as having internal and external links on your site. Internal linking is one of the most important on-page optimization opportunities to implement. It provides direct access to your web pages in order of importance. The *Category Pages* will be drop-down menu items that should be listed under the tab called "Cars" on your blog or website. Below is an example of basic link structuring. This is called *internal* linking, and we'll talk in just a moment about *external* linking for better results.

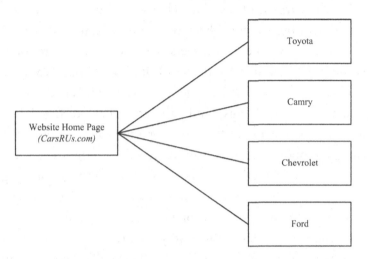

Resolve Technical Issues – You want to resolve any technical issues that you may have with your website or blog by checking your web links to make sure they are working properly, even if you have outsourced your website maintenance to someone else. As we discussed previously, you do not want to have a potential customer land on your website only to discover that your link is broken to a product or information that they want or need. Check your website categories and pages to make sure they are displaying correctly. The last thing you want is for your visitors to leave your site because it is not optimized for performance.

What are search engines looking for on my site?

In a nutshell, Google is looking for relevant and authoritative information from websites, preferably yours, that pertain to what a person is searching for when they type certain words into the Google search box. This is based on how your website page ranks amongst all others in your chosen niche. Remember our earlier example about the "*dentist in Texas*" keywords? Google is looking for keywords or relevant links that prove your content is valuable.

Maybe you've heard the term "Googlebot," which is the software that is run on many Google computers to crawl through all websites. It's safe to say that the purpose of the Googlebot software is to act as a Google robot, spider, or bot to report back information that will later be used or not used to serve their customers. Google sends the robot out to take account of, for indexing, the words it sees and the location of the words on each of your website pages. This is why it is most important that you use the "title tags" and "alt tags" that are listed for your website pictures, videos, or links to represent your content. It is said that Google's robots read your website from left to right and then your content. It is a best practice to make sure that your pages or categories are situated across the top portion of your website, horizontally, instead of listing them down the left side of your page, vertically, which would make the robots work harder to read your site or to index it properly. As a side note, if you are using a blog, then uploading a sitemap to Google webmaster tools is one of the best ways to help Google find all the content on your website. If you have a WordPress blog, you only have to do a search for the plug-in name "*google xml sitemap.*" It is said that the Googlebot can scan your website every two to three days or sooner if you make an update. Also, Google finds it hard to read rich media, such as Flash or HTML5 technology that has multiple levels of content in one place, such as video with landing pages, scrolling real-time social media responses, or even interactive games. There are ways around this, but you would need to visit *schema.org* for more backend coding or ask your website administrator to do it for you. (*See Appendix B for listing of SEO References*)

Search engines such as Bing, Yahoo! Search, Google, and Ask are looking for sites that have an expertise in that particular keyword and/or content validity. One way they find this is by scanning your site for any links that come back from other expert sites to your site, such as government or educational institutions. This is called external linking. These links can also come from an authority person or persons in the industry. Search engines consider this a "vote" from your site as being credible in what you do for others. Here's a quick way to see who is linking to your competition: go to Google and type in the search box (for example) "*link:www.amazon.com*" or whatever website you want. Beware of people that tell you if you pay them a certain fee they will create thousands of backlinks for you from other sites to raise your ranking. If you do use their service, you have to test the links to make sure they are real and that they are not broken because it will hurt your search engine rankings and could get you blocked by the major search engines. I tried using this kind of service. I paid pennies on the dollar for it, and that is what it was worth. I decided to check the links, and most of them were broken and going to fake websites. You live and learn! Although it's time consuming, you can write guest blog posts to get credible backlinks to your site. There are many other ways to accomplish this, but the best way is to Google the keyword "*backlinks*" to learn all about how it can be done.

According to Google, whenever they give a website a high ranking because of keywords, it's because they have "algorithmically determined that its content is more relevant to the user's query." No one but Google knows what algorithms they use. From my experience, it changes just like any other software technology has proven over the years. Just when you think you figured things out, they change the rules of the game. So having links that contain relevant and high-ranking keywords can help your site show higher on the search results and get picked up by other sites as they validate the authenticity of your content.

Chapter 13 - God-made Millionaire Exercise

This is an exploratory exercise to evaluate and test the validity of your keywords for better optimization. You or your hired professional will have to test them for the life of your business online.

1. Go to www.googlekeywordtool.com and become familiar with all the tools available to help you optimize your website. (Google the term *"keyword tool"*)

2. Start a brainstorming session, with others if necessary, where you come up with at least five to seven keywords to identify your brand.

3. Evaluate the search volume to get the numbers as low as possible by comprising several long tail keywords to use for your site.

Social Networking - Creating Relationships

"One of the greatest challenges companies face in adjusting to the impact of social media is knowing where to start." ~ Simon Mainwaring, CEO, Advertising Creative Director, Branding Consultant

Almost everyone knows that social networking is the greatest form of adverting and marketing ever known, especially for the emerging entrepreneur. There is so much out there to be discovered, but where does one start? Let's get into a little background knowledge on social networking and how it ties into God's master plan for your entrepreneurial life.

In God's word He mentions not to *forsake the assembling of yourselves.* He knew that networking and communicating with each other were very important to our existence and success in life and business. The greatest form of human assembly is through social technology. As you look around the world today, you can see how technology is responsible for a large percentage of our communication and buying capabilities. Technology is connecting the majority of our affairs to people and companies everywhere. As a result of this, social networking is growing exponentially and will for years to come. Social networking includes platforms such as LinkedIn, Facebook, Twitter, Instagram, Tumblr, and YouTube. Did you know that one in four people have said they use social media sites to *inform* their purchasing decisions? In business, the latest developments in technology have opened up a vast new world, which can be coined as "The Era of Social Mobile Computing." It's being used for shareable, relevant, value-driven content that people can access from anywhere in the world. Large companies and small businesses alike are realizing that social networking includes mobile networking to help create the greatest brand awareness ever.

According to MediaBistro.com, *"65% of traditional media reporters and editors use sites like Facebook and LinkedIn for story research and 52% use Twitter."* As of 2014, there are more than 645 million actively registered users on Twitter and 1.2 billion active Facebook users of which 680 million are mobile users, according to Statisticsbrain.com. As of 2013, LinkedIn is coming in with over 250 million users. The greatest way that people are staying connected to the world today is through their mobile devices and no longer their PCs.

Companies big and small are recognizing that a great way to stay connected to their loyal customers is through an app. Apps are the driving forces behind The Era of Social Mobile Computing. Apps account for at least one-third of the ways that consumers access social content. Nowhere in history has the means for communication been as widely available as it is today. With these kinds of statistics, can you imagine how much more your marketing and advertising efforts can grow? Using social networking along with mobile networking to grow your business through social media is becoming one of the most profitable ways to gain a long-term piece of the market share. (*If you are interested in creating your own app, even if you are not a developer, you can visit any of the following sites: GENWI.com, Mippin.com/web, Mobi-Cart. com or ShoutEm.com, as of the writing of this book.*)

If you've been using Facebook, then you've seen how many people have found loved ones and connected with past colleagues and friends. Social networking has opened new doors of opportunities for emerging entrepreneurs to do business across the globe with minimal costs. Social networking is the wave of the future as people are moving away from the more traditional marketing and advertising mediums of newspapers, business cards, and radio. It's not that they are obsolete, but it is necessary to make them available online where most people are hanging out. People today are carrying more electronic devices than ever before in history. Through the social networking tools available today, you can get the attention of a potential customer in a matter of seconds and get them to communicate with you and others to spread your brand message all across the globe.

Why Should I Use Social Networking?

Social networking is all about using the Internet *to find* and *be found* by people with similar interests, personally and in business. There are many people on opposite sides of the world that are being connected in minutes to help support a social cause that can change the world. Social networking is even responsible for assisting Obama's message for CHANGE in the winning of his last two terms in office. Law enforcement agencies are using social networking sites to help people find many lost family members and wanted criminals. People, churches, and other religious organizations are using social networking to spread the gospel to people all around the world with real-time responses. School systems account a large percentage of their growth in learning awareness to the incorporation of social media programs into their educational curriculum. Even the entertainment and media industries are using it for *coming soon* movies and are making strides in getting their targeted audiences out to the opening weekend shows months in advance by creating an anticipation and desire to attend and bring others along with them.

The entertainment's media department uses YouTube for movie trailers and to advertise the main characters special appearances and whereabouts through Facebook, Twitter, and their websites. This same marketing method should be used by any emerging entrepreneur that is trying to break into the marketplace as a leader. If people don't know you exist, then how can you ever expect to be a well- known hitter in your niche! So you must agree that social networking in your business can be very beneficial for the growth you seek through longevity of customer relationships and your business life. It's a chance to show your customer through *value* and *trust* that you are worth talking about.

While social networking can take place online and offline, its effectiveness is being highly used online. Some believe that there will never be a replacement for meeting people one on one, and I agree, but using social networking as a follow-up to a personal meeting is even better. It opens the door to your life for possible business ventures that can save you time and money for the trust-building factor. You can never tell everything about yourself in one meeting, so social networking is an extension of your personality, company, and expertise. Of course, this is assuming you are practicing strategic steps with your social networking efforts.

I know as an entrepreneur you may still be working as a full-time employee or even working full-time in your business and thinking that you don't have time to do another thing that will take time away from your family. Social networking is not intended to be another burden or mundane task on your list. It is meant to allow you to give "sneak peeks" (as they used in the entertainment industry) and spend about thirty minutes a day, at first, until you gradually increase your familiarity with the strategies you set for yourself. As time goes on, I would recommend spending about one hour per day in the social areas that bring you the best results. This means, for example, you can spend thirty minutes on Facebook, twenty minutes on Twitter, and ten minutes on YouTube or Google Plus. Of course, you will have to test the social networking tools you use over time, but monitoring it will show you where your customers are mostly hanging out. Google has some analytical tools that you can use to monitor your social networking efforts through your website and mobile apps. You can expand your knowledge by going to www.google.com/analytics/. Lastly, having social media accounts are crucial for your brand ability and credibility in the marketplace, which we will discuss later in this chapter.

How Are Social Networking Tools Going to Help My Business?

I want to explain the advantages of using social media as your catalyst. Many emerging entrepreneurs are not quite sure "how" to use social networking to maximize their exposure in the marketplace. You may be asking the question, "What is the difference between social networking and social media?" Basically, social networking is the "act" of using social media, apps, or other forms of communication and tools to connect you with people, preferably the *right* people. In this section, I may go back and forth and use the two terms interchangeably because they lie within the same category. Let me say, if you haven't figured it out already, a truly successful business is about building lasting relationships, and social media is the greatest way to do it.

To get the most out of social networking, as with anything in which you desire to be successful, it takes time and requires creative storytelling, artwork, heart, hustle, sincerity, and constant engagement on a consistent basis. This is why you must test your social networking tools and strategies to see which your customers prefer over the other. Your customers will show you with the online interactions and responses you receive from them. So it's important to not take on someone else's social success as your own unless they have already captured the audience you're going after.

There are several social networking tools you can use to help advance your online efforts. Some people may not feel comfortable using social media because they do not like sharing their personal experiences, publicly, especially if you are a baby boomer or have introverted tendencies—which was me! If this is you, then relax because you don't have to share your whole life—just a select few strategic pictures, your expertise, and up-to-date information to add value to your customer. Basically, most emerging entrepreneurs just want to know, "How do *I* get started for success?"

Before I get into the various social networking tools that are most widely used, let's discuss ways to identify yourself online so that you can establish your presence properly. As an emerging entrepreneur, the best place to start is with branding. You can find great brands in products, people, or services. Just like the great movie stars and entertainers of the world, you can find a place of awareness in the social media world, which can help you stand out in a very crowded place.

Online Branding for the Ultimate Experience

"Failing to get every single piece of a consistently mind-blowing experience right is where many small businesses fail when it comes to branding."
– Sarah Petty & Erin Verbeck, Marketing Experts

In a world where there is nothing new under the sun, there has to be something new or innovative about how your company does an old thing better. This is what sets all businesses apart in the marketplace. It's called "branding." If you are an entrepreneur and you want to be represented in the offline and online world, you need to decide what you want to be known for in your industry. So, what is the "brand" of your company? And what exactly is a brand? A brand is a name, term, design, symbol, or other feature that identifies you distinctly. When it comes to "service provider" branding, it is what promise, slogan, or results you want to be known for by your clients. If you don't want to be just another company or service professional, then you need to stand out!

Let's go over some strategies to help clarify and make your business stand out from the crowded online world. If any one of these is missing, your customer could become confused and not buy from you nor spread the word about your new business.

Identity – What exactly do people see or think when they look at your web page or your advertisement and marketing? Is it evident when they look at it that you are known for "excellent customer service," "you deliver in five minutes or less," or "delivery is guaranteed overnight"? So, what is your main specialty? When you hear "Just do it," you naturally think about Nike. Also, when you want a creative and innovative computing device, you may instantly think of Apple. When you hear "Like a good neighbor ...," you instantly think about State Farm. Adding a jingle can enhance their brand even more in your mind. These are the promises that your customers will come to think of whenever they hear the name of your company or you, as the brand. Your slogan can be summed up in a short sentence or a couple words, which is called a tagline or a motto. Remember when we spoke about knowing your *personal identity* back in Chapter 2? Now it's time to define your *business identity*. Once you know what your business brand is, your marketing efforts will be clearer, and you will make fewer mistakes in your presentation to your targeted audience. So what words define what you are all about—within fifteen seconds?

Attributes – This describes your business. These are what help others to definitively associate you with a brand name—logo, brand voice, brand story, and even brand colors. You've seen websites and social media tools that the experts use, and they all have the same colors, look, and feel to them. They even have the same picture, on occasions, so there will be no doubt in your mind that you are dealing with the same person or group. If you look at your business, can you say that all of these attributes are consistent in sending the message you want your company or yourself to be known for? If there is not a consistency throughout all your channels of communication, your customer won't understand your specialty of product/service or may not even recognize that they are one and the same. It is often said that it takes seven to ten contacts or impressions to turn a prospect into a customer.

Vision – The vision of your company is most important when it comes to keeping it moving forward in the right direction. Vision is something that must be emphasized and checked on a frequent basis. Being an emerging entrepreneur can be very challenging because your initial vision is still a work in progress. You normally start with one vision and it gets clearer over time. But as you start out in the marketplace, it is important for you to stay true to your vision until it is time to make the change. Always examine your daily activities to make sure they are in alignment with your current vision; if they are not, reexamine things and see if it is time to change the statement. Your vision statement, sometimes called a mission statement, is what drives the company (in my opinion)! So make sure your employees or contractors are aware of your vision as they are creating and devising intricate parts of your business development.

Value – Of course, if your customers are not getting any value out of what you offer, then there is no business profitability. As entrepreneurs, we often see things through rose-colored glasses and do not stop to think if this wonderful product or service is actually benefiting the customer. Oftentimes, it is necessary to ask questions and send surveys to see if your company is performing in a way that is giving your customers the benefits and results they seek. A good indication that your customers are receiving "value" for what you offer is by the "thank you dollars," as Gary Vaynerchuk calls them, the revenue you collect from the sales of your product or service. Your value will also be indicated by the number of interactions you receive through social media.

Trust – With your business, it is very important to establish trust with your customers because it is what sustains your brand and company through the years. Most of us have come to trust Coca-Cola for continuing to give us that great taste that has been their secret since 1892. We have come to trust the brand of car we continue to drive from year to year, whether it is Toyota, Chevrolet, or Ford. While growing up, your mom or dad had some product or service that they could not do without, and they spread the word to everyone they knew. Think back for a moment or call them and ask why they trusted that brand the way they did. Nine times out of ten, it will be because of the product's quality, and it will be evident in how many other people are still using that brand today. What are you building upon from day to day to cause your customers to trust you? Is it your attention to detail, customer service, or your ability to supply their needs on a continuous basis as you promised in your identity, attributes, vision, and value? Find out what part of your business gives the greatest value to your customers and stick with it. After your customer experiences you on a regular basis, you will become their brand of choice.

Another great way to build your brand is by sharing your customers' success stories on your website, brochures, business card, or social media. There is no quicker way to be known than by sharing the testimonials of happy customers! Better yet, why not get people to subscribe to your social media channels and reward them for their time to write about you? As an emerging brand, why not share your company's history about how you got started to provide motivation to others? In order to validate your expertise, why not write reviews of similar products or services and honestly let people know why your products are better on YouTube.

Remember, especially as an emerging entrepreneur, that your brand is established over time, so don't rush it. Be patient. Your long-term efforts will not go unnoticed as you practice consistency at all costs. You want to make sure that you or your company is always remembered for a specific promise of product or service for years to come! This is how you become known as a major brand.

Storytelling – Content That Sells

Another way to stand out and get known is by storytelling. Stories dominate the social world today for companies who understand how to implement it strategically. Storytelling has always been a way to capture the attention and hearts of children and people all across the world. It is something that has fascinated our minds about the possibilities of what could be. We all grew up believing and relating to at least one character in a childhood story. As a little girl, maybe you wanted to be a fairy princess with a beautiful dress and wings, or as a little boy, Superman with the power to fly and the strength to defeat any bad guy. As an adult, things have not changed much, except life has robbed us of our abilities to dream and believe we could ever be more than we are today. Do you find yourself thinking you're not strong enough to make it through something? Maybe you feel hopeless about a situation where no one seems to be able to help you to solve it?

Well, I am here to tell you that the stories in our adult lives today may not be about Peter Pan, fairy godmothers, or superheroes that can save us, but stories are here to show us the possibilities and strengths that lie within us. As a Christian, like me, I am sure you have been amazed by the great things that Jesus accomplished throughout his three-year reign on Earth through his miracles and his exceptional abilities to explain life. Throughout the Bible are wonderful stories that have captivated our hearts and minds and made us feel as though we can take on the world through God's mind and power. At times, the stories brought about sadness, joy, pain, and anger at the people and events that took place in that time.

A good storyteller will always captivate their audience's emotions in order to reveal the hidden treasures deep down inside of them. All the great speakers in the world can validate that! The way you come out of this emotional stagnation is by hearing someone tell you about how they made it through their dilemma. Something begins to rise up in you, and you now believe you *too* can overcome a situation.

In social networking through social media, you can take an idea or information, mash it up, share it, curate it, create a meme, take it for your own, and do something new and interesting with it. World news and events are the greatest way to get the attention of your followers or customers! People are always interested in the latest gossip, entertainer, newest product or political event that is presently rockin' the world. Just talking about your product or service or maybe even something that's happening in your company will get old after a while if it's not relevant. You will need to learn how to use your storytelling skills to relay news, entertainment, information, and even your product or services to gain the interaction and long-lasting relationships your business needs.

In an issue of *Psychological Science* published in 2011, they stated how through storytelling, you can get your content shared almost instantly.

*"The sharing of stories or information may be driven in part by arousal. When people are physiologically aroused, whether due to **emotional stimuli** or otherwise, the autonomic nervous is activated, which then **boosts social transmission**."*

Nike sends messages to its audience that inform and excite them. Have you ever sat and watched a Nike commercial or YouTube video? Wow, all sorts of emotions start to well up inside because of their impeccable way of communicating their message. Whenever I watch some of their advertisements, I feel like I am not doing what I should be doing, which is living a healthier life by exercising—and possibly in their gear, of course! Nike can be political in their messages all while fitting it into their international brand. I remember watching a Nike commercial or YouTube ad that displayed a woman running, in Nike gear, with an axe in her hand. They showed visuals of people marching and behaving in a communistic way. This part was displayed in black-and-white film footage. As the lady got closer, the men were all sitting down and watching a movie screen. She threw the axe at the screen they were watching and it exploded. This was Nike's way of staying engaged with the interest of the people and showing the *change* that was going on in America. It was a great and insightful integration of Obama's presidential campaign message of CHANGE and their ability to engage their audience into changing the way they think about this world event. And this created a huge awareness for their brand. They were staying relevant in the minds of their customers and getting possible social sharing to other potential customers.

In a simpler and less expensive way, you can take a newsworthy event, put it in your own words, and make it relevant to your product or service in a WordPress blog post and appeal to your customers' emotions through a short storyline. You can take that website link, from that story, and write an appealing headline in the 140-character-or-less Twitter box and start an instant conversation. You can take the actual video or photo image of the newsworthy event and write a story relevant to your product or service to gain the attention of your Facebook followers. You can also go to LinkedIn and post the video or image showing how you are engaged in world events and an expert on why this particular topic is relevant to your market industry. If you want to take it even further, you can do the LinkedIn expertise post as a short and to-the-point YouTube video for your visual customers for added trust.

The greatest takeaway here is to know that mixing a relevant current event with your product or service is going to keep you at the top of your industry. You are to appeal to the positive and negative emotions of your audience, but be strategic. Appealing to their positive emotions will *empower your brand* while appealing to their negative emotions will show your customer their inadequacies, which can help to *alert* and *educate them* in a specific area of their lives.

For more information for an emerging entrepreneur, I would suggest following some of the top storytelling brands on social media to become more skilled and brand-able, such as Oreo (*makes life better, friendlier and more fun*), Allstate (*prevent mayhem*), Kellogg's (*better life with right breakfast*) and, of course, Nike (*Just Do It – get off your tush*). Don't forget to follow the most impactful and influential people in your industry for educational purposes. Lastly, for content purposes, make sure you subscribe to or bookmark the websites that bring you the most eventful news and information to stay abreast of current events. Happy storytelling!

Social Media Domination Tactics

Your interaction on social media is like needing oxygen to breathe; without it, you are dead to the online world. Just like breathing and maintaining your health, it is going to take some cardiovascular work, in social media, to keep the heart of your interactions going with your followers until success arrives with a constant flow. We know that storytelling is one great way to do this, but let's examine some of the top social media platforms and strategies that will have you dominating your industry!

The first thing you want to do if you have not already is set up your social media accounts. You can start with one or two of the major social media platforms, such as Facebook, Twitter, LinkedIn, or YouTube. I am not going to spend time here showing you *how* to set up these accounts because there are numerous online tutorials that can have you up and running in no time. But once you have your social media accounts established, here are some strategies that I consider the top implementers that will have you building your online community in no time!

LinkedIn Business Strategies – Business-Oriented Networking

One might describe LinkedIn as a place where business professionals go to network online. LinkedIn is most useful for those in the B2B (business-to-business) sector because it allows you to connect to specific decision makers in any business who utilize this platform. It's also a great way to connect with your former bosses, friends, colleagues, and people you meet. But it is *not* a great place to sell all your products or services. LinkedIn is like your resume on steroids, and it's actually a great way to brand yourself for offline and online recognition. It's used mostly to sell you and help you connect with top people and companies that can use your service to accelerate their business goals! Here you can tell all about the great things that make you or your company the best choice for the job.

Top Strategies:

#1 – Customize Your LinkedIn Profile

- Your *photo image* is the first thing that any person sees who comes across your profile. You can bet that a visitor's subconscious mind goes into the mode of deciding whether or not they want to do business with you based on your photo. They will start to judge you by your attire or whether or not you have a friendly or professional outlook. This decision can take them approximately 2.5 seconds to make. Now, if you decided not to have a photo at all, this can really hurt your chances that much more of attracting a vendor that would love to hire you. I have seen colleagues of mine who have decided for one reason or another to *not* use their photo because they felt this could kill the deal for them. To me, if I can't represent myself as I am, then why would I even be in sales or any other business? Just think, if you were out there looking for a partner or addition to your team, would you choose to connect with someone who has no photo? Remember, the most important reason you are on LinkedIn is to display the business side of yourself, so why not show your business face?

A bit of advice: You should take the time to take a professional photo of yourself—preferably by a professional. Please don't take a selfie or use your webcam to snap your LinkedIn photo! Photos do not cost that much these days because Target, Sears, JCPenney and other portrait studios run specials all the time. You want to make your first impression count. I would suggest using a photo of you smiling and wearing professional attire. This displays that you are approachable—unless you are an Ultimate Fighter for hire. It can be a different photo or the same photo you used on your other social media profiles. Honestly, I keep my photo the same across all social media platforms to help impress my appearance upon their consciousness to remember me. You can choose to switch your photos from time to time. But just like any marketing campaign, it takes about seven to nine impressions before a consumer will take notice of your product. This would be the same for your consistent photo. Be careful and choose your photo wisely.

- Your **headline** is a most important piece of real estate on your profile. This area is for creating bold statements through the use of strategic *keywords* that describe what you do best and in what industry. But remember, you have only 140 characters. This will help others find you as they search for a specific skill or service in your niche. As you have worked in previous chapters to define who you or your business is as a brand, you should have come up with keywords that allow others to recognize exactly what you offer.

When creating your headline, make sure to use adjectives that your target audience recognizes as industry terms. There are two ways that you can do this: (1) Check out keywords people are searching for in your industry through the *Google AdWords Keyword Tool* online, and/or (2) You can look at the profiles of others in your industry and compile a list of the key words that are similar amongst them all. This will allow you to zone in on those terms that can move you to the top of the search within LinkedIn, Google, and other search engines.

- In your **Summary** this is where you can toot your horn as loud as you want, but remember you have only about 2,000 characters. This section basically highlights your experience for those areas in which you are looking to find work. You can use bullets to declare your experience, or you can write it in paragraph form. I would suggest using words that speak directly to a person that could be sitting right in front of you. Picture the perfect company you would present your service to in order to land the opportunity. Some people say you should talk about yourself in the third person, as if you are representing yourself to a person or company, such as "Letitia provides excellent service to ...." I think it would be best to just demonstrate *how* you are making an impact in the marketplace and *how* you would be an asset to their project or company. You are basically selling yourself!

My LinkedIn Summary example:

Emerging Entrepreneurs – I work with individuals that are looking for training and coaching in order to transition from employee to employer by owning and operating their own small or home-based business.

I help emerging entrepreneurs who struggle with fear, failure, and the frustrations of starting a business and would like to be more confident in their ability to succeed. What makes me different is that I take them by the hand and lead them step-by-step through the process, and because of this, my clients get so much more confidence in their abilities that they catapult themselves and their business to greater growth and profits in less time.

I provide assistance to emerging entrepreneurs through coaching, consulting, and classroom trainings.

I speak at Women's Events concerning social media, financial empowerment, and steps to starting your own business, which empowers one to take charge of their lives and business.

If you would like to take this section even further, you can add a short video of yourself, a product demo from YouTube, or your website blog's URL. Make sure the title and description of either URL (web link) contains your keywords, as you learned in the previous chapter with SEO, if possible.

- The **Experience** section is pretty self-explanatory. You will complete this section with the information that is listed on your resume sprinkled with keywords throughout for search purposes. You can take a quick look at mine at www.linkedin.com/in/letitiaharris. You will find that I changed careers midstream in my life to do more of what brings out the passion in me. But here, you are basically entering as much detailed information as possible about your past positions and experience gained while working for a previous company. Some people get afraid to list past jobs they have had that do not relate to what they are looking to do today. I believe that everything you have done in your past work life can be used as an asset in the direction you are moving toward. The fact is, you've gained some type of experience that was positive and can be translated into an asset that can serve others.

- Don't be afraid to list any *volunteer positions*, no matter if it was only for one week or one month. This shows that you care about others and about giving back to empower others to succeed. The fact that you are willing to do this position without pay shows that you will go up and beyond the call of duty and that life is not just all about the money. Here's a great suggestion: if you have not been able to work in a field that provided fulfillment, then find ways to volunteer in that area to gain the necessary skills to transition into the desired occupation.

- As for the *Specialties* area, there really isn't one. This is optional, but I add it at the bottom of my Summary Section as a highlighted area. If you have any room left after writing your summary, then you can use the space accordingly. Technically, the Specialties section can be used with one-word descriptors. I use it as a sneaky way to include my keywords again to stand out. This is called "tagging" yourself. The best advice I can give you here is to look at your top three people or companies that are in your industry and grab their keywords. If they are at the top of their game, then these keywords have got to be worth a try. You may notice that some people do not use keywords in their profile, but this is a big mistake! Anytime you have an open opportunity to use keywords in such a broad or specialty way, this allows you to be found among the best! I can't emphasize enough the importance of using Google's Online Keyword Search Tool for keyword search to stay abreast of the changing trends in your particular niche or industry.

My LinkedIn *Specialties* example:

> **Specialties:**
> Entrepreneur, Coaching, Training, Mentoring, Starting a Business, Instructor, Speaker, Trainer, Texas, Christian, Technology, Social Media

#2 – Build Your LinkedIn Connections. First, start inviting and connecting with people you already know. This is the best way to get your momentum going. While setting up your profile, LinkedIn will give you the ability to bring in contacts from other sources, such as your various email accounts. Whenever you go to networking events or meet people who compliment what you do, then immediately add them to your LinkedIn contact list. You never know who they know that can get you one step closer to the referral you need!

You can also use the "People You May Know" feature in LinkedIn to connect with those that are being suggested to you. Search for your keyword terms in the "Search" box and see whom you can connect with, either with your free or paid account. Look for bloggers, vendors, distributors, and key industry leaders that you can offer your services or product to for free as a way of showing off your stuff. You can even send products via mail as a direct marketing tactic to gain faster attention.

#3 – Use LinkedIn Skills/Endorsements. This feature allows others to validate your skills from all your experience. Make sure you add skills that your target audience will care about. All the people you know on a more personal level, which are called your "first-degree connections," are able to endorse your skills. So each person that worked with you on a job or project should be asked to endorse you. The more endorsements you can receive the better. You have the option to add skills that you want others to rate by those who have witnessed your expertise in these areas. It's a great idea to find those you know and endorse their skills and then ask them to reciprocate the favor. This allows you to build great credibility when companies are out looking online for their next speaker, coach, organization, or partner to bring into their projects. Please do not have others validate everything about you if they have not truly been *exposed* to your expertise or if they don't work in an area. If using your childhood friends and college mates, make sure they have been exposed to your blog, website, speaking engagements, or literary works so that it can be an authentic endorsement.

#4 – Join LinkedIn Groups. This is an awesome way to connect to people with similar interests. This is a great way to send InMail to people without having to upgrade (more about this in a moment). If you are a speaker, coach, or consultant, this is a great way to connect and find seminars, other coaches, or speaking-engagement opportunities. If there is a person you really want to connect with, then find the groups they are a part of and join them. However, it is not a great idea to join and spam the person with all kinds of nonsense. This is a quick way to build a bad reputation in the online networking community. Look at the discussions that are taking place and display your expertise to those in need of answers. Just think—if you are part of a well-known group, you can be picked for a job because they searched for that group's keywords.

#5 – Leave LinkedIn Recommendations. Are you proud of the products or services that you offer the public or other businesses? Do you hear them talking about what great value they gain from working with you? If you have taken pride in your company and its delivery in the marketplace, then you have something worth talking about. This is the only place on LinkedIn that you do not write about yourself. You may think that it is hard to get recommendations, but it takes only a moment to get some of your best customers to write one for you. I would even take my testimonials that I have received from past satisfied customers and ask them to incorporate those into letters of recommendation. In exchange for what you give them, this is something that most clients or customers are happy to help with. You do not need many, but see if you can get two or three letters; this should suffice. The best time to ask for recommendations is right after you have worked on a project, given a speech, or provided a service for someone.

Lastly, I want to talk to you about a part of LinkedIn that is completely optional on your part. As of the writing of this book, you can use LinkedIn as a *paid versus non-paid account*. A paid account is not necessary in order to be successful on LinkedIn. But using the paid account is a great way to get more results, advanced filters, and search alerts. With a paid account, you can see who is searching for you and get priority customer service from LinkedIn. Currently, most people are using the free version and getting great results. Also, by paying, you have the privilege of using the "InMail Message" feature with which you can send a direct message to *anyone* on LinkedIn (although a response is not guaranteed). LinkedIn supposedly gives you a credit if the person never answers your request. InMail will allow you to connect directly to those you would otherwise not have access to unless someone in your network introduced you to them.

Twitter Business Strategies – *Your Quickie Notes of "Aha" Moments*

Twitter has always been called *The Superhighway* because tweets/bits of information flow up your screen like a Maserati on the German Audubon. The majority of people feel as though Twitter is pointless because of the quality of information that seems to flow through it. But don't let the unskilled Twitter users deter you from doing what is very beneficial for your business. It's really a tool to communicate instantaneous news and information that is relevant to a segment of people across the world. Twitter becomes irrelevant when you use it ONLY to talk about what you have to SELL to anyone who wants it. Everything you offer to your followers should be something that they can use or need, even if it is just a word of encouragement and power to move them forward in life.

Top Strategies:

- **Choosing a strong username and creating a strong profile** – Deciding what name to use to represent your brand or company takes some thought. In business, your Twitter name should be a combination of words that explain your specialty or mimic your company name, especially if you are setting up a business account. Setting up a username like "handsomejimmycan" might work for a particular person, but it won't work for a potential customer looking to buy from a trustworthy business. People are constantly online searching for products and services they would like to purchase, so creating a strong username and profile can lead them directly to you. This is where having a well-thought-out, short-and-sweet profile can raise your rankings amongst others. If you haven't noticed already, anything having to do with the web requires strategic marketing and keyword advertising to get seen amongst the many businesses online vying for the same customer's attention. So why not make sure you are quite direct with your description of what you have to offer those who are looking to buy online.

- **Following the people who matter most** – I have found that most people who are majorly involved in the media such as entertainers, pastors, motivators, speakers, and major corporations can be found on Twitter. Their schedules are so busy they rarely have time to post to a blog or even interact consistently on Facebook. But you best believe they will tell you where they will be next, and they will post their thoughts and opinions about various topics of life. Those people whom you might not ever meet under certain circumstances can be spoken to in hopes of being noticed and responded to virtually. This is a great way to get to know your greatest heroes and potential mentors on your way to gain success in your business endeavors. Once you find great leaders in your industry, latch on to their coattails and follow them virtually and to various other places they are appearing in the world.

- **Providing support to customers and prospects** – Whether you know it or not, Twitter can be a great place for your customers to ask you questions and find out more about your company. Invite your Twitter followers to participate in questionnaires to rate your company in order to improve in particular areas. You can actually hire someone to monitor Twitter if you drive your customers from your blog or other social media channel to post testimonials and responses to offers online. If you are promoting a new product or service, then by all means offer trials or freebies as a gift for becoming a new Twitter follower.

- **Using hashtags and retweets** – Hashtags can be used to keep your customers up-to-date and engaged with you. For example, having a hashtag that says *#livelifenow* speaks volume to someone who is in need of an overhaul in life to spice it up today and not tomorrow. This hashtag suggests, "Preparing for a better life starts now!" You want to keep your hashtag as short as possible to make it easy for your followers to remember. Before creating or using a relevant hashtag for your business, do your research. There is nothing worse than having a hashtag with derogatory threads (streaming comments) that do not line up with your company's culture. As for retweets, find people that are well known in the industry that you would like to connect with and follow them. Whenever they tweet great information, retweet it to your followers. This shows them your Twitter name as the one who re-tweeted their message. As you come to re-tweet their messages often, they will begin to take notice of you and respond back. This will be additional credibility for you; your followers will notice and so will theirs, therefore creating possible new followers. Earnestly look at the information they provide and agree or disagree with valid reasons to keep conversations flowing with others.

- **Mini video links from YouTube** – Taking any videos that you have found to be motivating and inspiring to your followers can be used to show the personal and caring side of your company. Videos have been known to touch many hearts across the world through YouTube. Whenever you create product demonstrations on your video channel, post a quick link to display your goods. If you have a long YouTube web link, think about using the Twitter link shortener at http://t.co that works only on Twitter. You can also use the link shortener called www.bitly.com that enables you to track how many clicks you had to study your metrics. This will be beneficial in allowing you to add other pertinent information within the 140 characters in the main tweet area. You will find yourself trying to rephrase tweets many times to get it all in with one tweet.

- **Tweeting from your live events or an event you are attending** – If you follow those who are making a difference in the marketplace, you know they are providing conferences, teleseminars, and events that promote themselves and their products and services to their customer base. When attending any of their live or virtual events, you can be sure they are posting photos, profound words, and testimonials from the room. This is a great way to get potential customers involved in the culture of the room through social media. Just in case one of your clients could not make it, they can get real-time conversations going with those at the event and even follow links to get the products from the live event they missed by not being there. If you have an event or an event you are speaking at, let your Twitter followers know where to find you and engage them in the experience by tweeting what the others are saying to provide value to them from afar.

Facebook Business Strategies – *Expressing, Motivating, Educating & Providing*

This is one of the largest and fastest-growing social networking platforms created! Zuckerberg is constantly testing the waters to see what will work best for its users, which includes businesses and the Facebook Company. Although there are mixed emotions about the people who are now using Facebook, it does serve the emerging entrepreneur and business community wisely, for the most part. It seems the teenage community sees no need for Facebook because they can communicate with their friends in person, plus who wants to get a friend request from your mom? That's not cool! So that leaves the tweens and the more mature audience as its target.

I recall reading somewhere in a magazine that over the past years, Mark Zuckerberg has been snatching up all sorts of start-ups to enhance the Facebook experience for its users. He attempted to buy some potential enhancers, such as Snapchat (a photo messaging app), Tinder (online dating app), Whisper (anonymous postings of insecurities), WhatsApp (ad-free message and photo sharing app through your data plan), and Oculus VR (virtual-reality headset company) for an all-out attempt to dominate the industry like Coca-Cola, which has been in business for over 125 years. I, for one, am not upset at Zuckerberg's high aspirations for his company. There is always a desire to be bigger and better than you were the day before, despite the critics. Facebook has had some failures along the way, such as with Gifts, Beacon, Graph Search, Camera and Facebook email—most of which you may never have heard of, which explains their life span. But there is an area in which Facebook is kicking butt! And that's in the area of advertising.

It's been all over social media and in the news about how Facebook would never find a way to make money with its users because of its initial intention for people to just connect to one another. But by George, I think he's got it! According to a July/August 2014 article titled "Facebook Everywhere" in *Fast Company*, Facebook earns 59 percent of its revenue from mobile. Their first quarter revenue of 2014 was $2.5 billion, of which $642 million was profit. This makes a huge difference to the emerging entrepreneur who wants to get their message out quickly to the masses within their chosen market. We'll discuss, in a moment, what to look for when creating your first Facebook Ad. Of course, your advertising efforts are going to take some time and testing to be perfected, but this is a great place to start—assuming you have a marketing plan and strategy in place.

Facebook for business is about motivating, educating, (some) selling, and providing valuable content about your product or service. As an emerging entrepreneur, this is the perfect place to introduce your customers to you and your business. You can accomplish this by pouring positive words, visual education, and updates into your customers, and by providing a place of support for them to get their questions answered. The sole purpose of your Facebook business page is to build up your customer base, keep interaction consistent and high, plus drive traffic and leads to your website! I want to introduce you to some *initial strategies* and steps to build your Facebook pages. I believe this will move you forward faster toward your social media goals. If you want to know more about how to set up your Facebook page, visit https://www.facebook.com/about/pages.

Top Strategies:

- ***Facebook Profile vs. Facebook Page*** – A Facebook profile is meant for an individual. Your Facebook profile is simply used to express yourself to those you know and love. If you are using your Facebook profile to represent your business, this is a no-no. Facebook can shut you down if they find out you are doing this. They are advocating that you set up a Facebook page for business in order to communicate your brand to your customers. Although your friends, family and co-workers like you as a person, this does not mean that they want to be *sold* to. Some people may argue that there is no separation between you personally and your business. I think differently, but there should be a mesh between the two to show people both sides of your life. You can easily display pictures of yourself, your employees, and events that you want right on your Facebook business page to peel back the layers to humanize your brand. Just like on your personal Facebook profile, let your personality shine. Also, make sure your icon is your face if you have a personable brand, and a logo/symbol if you're presenting yourself as a company.
- ***"About" Section*** – This is the area where you want to stand out the most. This is your opportunity to let your potential fan base know just why they should be clicking the "like" button on your page. This section will attract people to your page—or detract them if not worded properly. So take some time and view other similar profiles in order to get this right. Use this section to, once again, include keywords to describe your products and services and how your company is able to help others. You can include a web link that leads to your website, a landing page, or a YouTube channel that can allow people to get a great first

impression of you and your company. This area is normally static and changes only when you change something major about your brand.

- *Facebook Groups* – This is a great way to create a community that is free! It's a great way to provide value and increase your visibility. You do not want to sell products and services here; instead, offer a place for a certain level of customers you serve to have access to you as a part of a paid program. You can use this as a place for your group or team members to congregate while everyone works on a specific project. You can upload photos, videos, or documents if necessary to keep from having to meet in an office. Any groups you create can be *open to the public* or *closed* to only the group members you choose. People must request your permission to be part of the group, and you must approve them by granting them access. You can access chat and even create events right within your group for attendance. You can ask your group questions by clicking the "Ask Question" button at the top of the group. This includes multiple-choice questions. Visit www.facebook.com/help.

- *Keeping Content Interactions High* – The quickest way to get your followers to engage and interact with you is to be relevant in your content and be consistent. Because Facebook is constantly changing their algorithms, just as Google does, one strategy may work today and be obsolete tomorrow. But as of now, you can use promoted posts to reach more of a target audience and even your current audience. The cost starts at $5 and goes up, so you'll have to test to see how much is enough to see great results. Certain posts get more views than others. According to Socialbakers.com, photos are shared at 93 percent, status updates at 3 percent, links at 2 percent, and videos at 2 percent. So this means that any post you put in the newsfeed needs to have a picture attached to its description. If you post a web link, Facebook automatically offers an option to choose from a group of photos it found on that page. Here are a few ways to generate some great content for your followers:

- ○ WordPress/Blog posts
- ○ Videos and photos
- ○ Exciting company news
- ○ Upcoming events
- ○ Quotes (people love positive words!)
- ○ Information about celebrities and entertainment
- ○ Shout-outs to those you partner with in the community
- ○ Other posts and articles related to your industry/niche

In addition to having great content, you want to make sure that you are ready to respond when a fan/customer comments on a post. The best way to do this is by downloading the Facebook app to your mobile phone. If a customer asks you a question about a post you wrote, you want them to know they matter by responding! I have noticed when I respond to someone many others join right into the conversation. When someone comments on your posts, it will show on their newsfeed and to those who choose to receive notification of your responses. This gives you possible free followers without having to pay for Facebook Ads to grow your fan base.

- *Using Facebook Ads*– You can use Facebook Ads to grow your fan base or to bring about brand awareness. When you start Facebook for your business, you will be asked if you would like to invite those that are on your personal page to join you. This will automatically send out notifications to your list that you have a new page and would like for them to join you. To gain more followers, start to ask those you meet in various places to "like" your page for further growth. At some point, you will come to a slow-churn with the number of Facebook likes that come in each week, so you should consider using Facebook Ads to grow your fan base even more! Your ads can appear in the newsfeed, the right column, or on the logout page of your friends or targeted audience. Facebook will even pair your ad with other social interactions that your friends have been involved in recently. For example, when you like

Walmart, Facebook will let your friends know that you just "liked" them. When you create your first paid advertisement, once anyone likes your ad, it can be shown in the right-side column of Facebook that they just liked your page. This will then give their friends the choice to learn more about you and to possibly "like" your page as well. Here are some tips I want you to consider when placing your Facebook Ad:

- ○ ***Identify your goal*** – Know the reason why you are placing this ad. Is it to promote an event, product, or service?

- ○ ***Be specific in segment targeting*** – This goes back to finding out who your target market is—kids, teens, tweens, adults between the ages of twenty-five and forty-five? Take your time when going through the ad setup because you could spend money unnecessarily on overlooked choices. You will be able to choose from the following categories.
  - Age
  - Gender
  - Location
  - Interest
  - Workplace
  - Education

Note: You can even choose specific entertainers, speakers, or companies and target their audience by selecting their name, such as Joel Osteen under the "Interest" category. (Whomever you choose must have a Facebook Page already established.)

- ○ ***Use keyword targeting*** – You can choose specific keywords or phrases that may be listed in your target audience's Facebook profile, such as Internet marketing, online sales, making money, and affiliate marketing. While setting up your targets, you will be given an estimated audience that your ad will have the potential to reach. Make sure to keep your audience between one to two million (1-2M) if possible. You want it to be as tightly targeted as possible to get the best results.

○ ***Make the ad clear, concise, and simple*** – Your headline has to be bold and captivating and only twenty-five characters in length. If it doesn't grab their attention, they will NEVER click on your ad to find out more. Since photos get the most attention from Facebook users, you must use a person, preferably a smiling person, or an interesting piece of artwork tailored to your brand or message to grab their attention! Your description is approximately ninety characters in length, so you must write this out several ways to see which ad pulls in the most likes or views.

○ ***Use a call to action*** – Most users don't know what you want them to do with your ad if you don't tell them, so make sure you incorporate words such as "Click Here," "Like Us," or "To Learn More, Go Here." In order to get the results you want, it may be necessary to guide your potential customer through the process to completion.

○ ***Give away something for free!*** – Who doesn't like receiving a free and valuable gift that helps you and saves you money? This is the whole reason for the creation of your Facebook Ad. Your ad should be offering a free video, free download, or free information that can be mailed out to allow a sampling of your product or service by the potential customer. This will not only serve the customer well, but it will also allow you to capture their name, email, or mailing address to add to your list for future product sales.

I would suggest testing your keywords by running two different ads to see which one does the best. This is called split-testing, and it allows you to run one ad with the same photo but two different descriptions and for two different timeframes. Maybe you will have one ad run for thirty days and the other run for sixty days. You will have to monitor the ads because you may need to adjust them due to cost or not enough interest, to expand your targeted audience. If you are not well known in the industry, this process will serve you well.

To find out more information about setting up your Facebook business page and using Facebook advertising to grow your business, visit https://www.facebook.com/advertising/ as of the writing of this book.

YouTube Business Strategies – *Displaying your world visually*

There are over 1 billion visitors to YouTube each month with over 6 billion videos being watched by the masses. YouTube is centralized in more than sixty countries and across sixty-one languages. There are over 100 hours of video uploaded every hour, and the Nielsen ratings say that YouTube reaches more people between the ages of eighteen and thirty-four than *any* cable network. Now how is that for the validity of a social networking platform! YouTube has been around since 2005 and was bought out by Google for $1.65 billion worth of stock in 2006 because the world adapted to it so quickly. People are using their mobile devices more and more for accessing videos from their family, friends, favorite companies, and those that seem to entertain them the most. The world will gain quicker access to your video from their phone than from their computer. This is a great option because if they are following you on your YouTube Channel, they can get your updates from wherever they are in the world.

YouTube can be one of the most intricate parts of your business because it allows people to actually see you or your product in action. This is the greatest way to prove your credibility in the marketplace without betting the farm to find airtime during primetime for viewership. You sell more of what you promote when people come to know, like, and trust you. One of the most effective ways of attracting customers is by creating short videos that promote your brand and validate your existence in your industry. The world of having *only* a website is over. This world is filled with reality TV segments, which are growing by leaps and bounds. People want to *see* who you truly are—your authentic self.

Today, many emerging entrepreneurs are afraid to get on video because they feel they are unattractive, they will be too nervous to be taken seriously, or that they will plainly look foolish. These are not the right reasons to avoid recording a video for your company's product or service. People will feel more comfortable if they can see a video that shows you are a real person behind the brand. It will be up to you to use someone else to represent your brand if you feel this would be better.

To get started, I would suggest if you are selling a service to create a short video of no more than three minutes that explains the problem you are solving for your customer. If you are selling a product, then find people who love your product and have gotten results to be a testament to how great it is. Remember, the greatest part of it all is you do not have to be a professional videographer. Actually, any flaws and bloopers you have in your videos will serve to show you are human, so don't trash your mess-ups. If you prefer not to keep the bloopers, then add them to the end of your videos to show how much time and fun you had in putting the video together for them. It's a great personal touch.

Top Strategies:

- *Optimize Your YouTube username/channel title* – Choose a YouTube username that reflects your brand as a person or product. Make sure it is not too long because you want prospects to remember it and possibly its spelling. This makes it easier when you meet someone to give them a memorable link. By default, your username will become your YouTube Channel name. You want your channel name to be something that is more of a phrase. For example, your username may be "500SkateboardTricks," which alludes to what your expertise is, but your channel name could be "Skateboarding Tutorials & Tricks" to show what you will be teaching them.

- ***Record Product Demos/Reviews*** – If you have a product that you know solves a problem better than a competing product, then do a demonstration of its use. Brands do it all the time. They find another similar product and compare how their product is superior in quality, features, or ease of use. This video can take you only one to two minutes or so to present while someone records you or while someone else performs the demonstration. Go on YouTube and search out a product that you use often to see if there are videos demonstrating its features and get pointers from that. If you have a service-based business, then shoot a short video of you or an employee performing the task. I once had a guy that came to me because he wasn't getting enough leads per day. He was utilizing social media but really didn't have time to update it. Since he was an appliance repair technician, I advised him to create short videos that showed customers how to better care for their appliances by implementing the tips he was providing on a daily basis. This way, customers would see that he was indeed an expert, and he would, without cost, provide them with valuable information that could save them time and money. Isn't that what most consumers are looking for, a better product and ideas, for less? This is just enough to keep your company first place in their minds when they need your type of service.

- ***Answer questions in video*** – This was one of my favorites, and it's one of the easiest ways to show off your expertise and gain quick credibility. I would have a place on my website/ blog where I would ask customers to leave their name, which was optional, and a question that they needed answered. On a weekly basis, I would pull one of the questions and answer it through a podcast. I would record the question and answer on Soundcloud.com and upload it to my website. This way people could subscribe to my website and get the weekly updates and possibly find their question being answered.

- A quick way to get questions that you can answer is by taking the questions that have been asked of you while out working on a project or the questions asked through your "Contact Us" tab on your website. These are considered FAQs that you see on some sites. This is a great tactic used by many well-known gurus because the questions were asked by their many followers. I believe that having people hear and see more of you and your company will help to brand your name in their minds like a jingle that won't go away. You, as an expert, can get someone to video record you answering the questions you collected from your FAQs as though you were in the "hot seat."

- *Interview Experts at Tradeshows/Events/Conferences* – There has never been a greater way to gain credibility than from someone who is already an expert in your field. When the opportunity presents itself to take a picture or a video snapshot, or to interview a guru for advice, then capture this moment immediately because it may never come again. Experts love the opportunity to commune with those that support them. It is part of the law of reciprocity because they know that giving is a part of receiving. Once you're done, quickly upload it to YouTube for all to see!

- *Spread the Word* – As start to create more videos for your customers and potential customers, spread them to other social networking channels to gain more exposure. Your Facebook business page is a great place to start because Facebook says pictures rank high. You would take a snapshot of the video's main screen using SnagIt, Jing, Camtasia, or Tiny Take and add a link to your YouTube video in your Facebook post. Do not put the whole video in your post because videos, currently, are not ranked as high. I wouldn't necessarily take the link and put it on every channel either because all information is not great for all social platforms unless you change up the wording. If you want to place the same information on many channels, just make sure that you present it in a way that the audience understands. For example, those on Twitter will want short and to-the-point details about a topic. Facebook fans will want to see and hear some worthwhile details and be asked to share their comments.

You might also want to look into adding your video(s) to other video-sharing sites, such as Vimeo, Tumblr, and Daily Motion. You can always Google "video-sharing sites" to get more education. Some of these do require paid subscriptions, but they can be free for a short period of time for testing purposes.

Putting It All Together

By now you have several techniques and strategies that you can use for social networking on social media. Depending on the amount of time you have to dedicate to this task, it is best to have a plan to carry out your actions. If it hasn't registered with you yet, having a plan and setting goals is a must for any successful business to thrive! You should have a plan of action for anything and everything that has the potential to grow your business. You can schedule time for your daily online social activities by outsourcing it, or you can do it yourself. I set up a scheduled plan to help me monitor my time more effectively to include social media. As I stated earlier, find out through testing which social media platform works best with your target market. Once you find out where they are hanging out, then add this platform to your schedule. You don't have to be involved in them all from the beginning, but gradually choose one to two in order to get familiar with the process. In Figure 14.1, I am including a snapshot of what my schedule looks like. Of course, it changes according to what strategy I have set for my business, and so will yours. But use this template as an outline for how you can better control your time when it comes to communicating with your audience. If you would like to get a copy of this template, you can find it in the Entrepreneur Toolkit at

www.godmademillionairethebook.com/toolkit.

Figure 14.1 – Sample Social Media

Social Media Time Management Schedule								
Time	Social Media	Monday	Tuesday	Wednesday	Thursday	Friday	Saturday	Sunday
1hr	Facebook	Graphic Art/ Quotes	Graphic Art/ Quotes	Media Art/ Quotes	Media Art/ Quotes	Media Art/ Quotes	off	off
20 min	Twitter	quote/info/ product promo	quote/info/ product promo	quote/info/ product promo	quote/info/ product promo	quote/info/ product promo		off
30 min	WordPress - Blog		Blog Post		Blog Post		pre-write 3 articles	off
20 min	LinkedIn	Share New Post from Blog	Connect w/3 people			Search for needed experts		off
15 min	Pinterest		Share others pins!	Update Board(s)		Update Board(s)		off
varies	YouTube	Motivational Video	Tutorial Video		Shared partner video			off
1 day	Monthly Newsletter			24th day of month				off
2 days	Bi-weekly Newsletter				Twice a month			off

Chapter 14 – God-made Millionaire Exercise

We have gone over much information in this chapter, and this is only a small portion of social networking. Take some time and devise a plan around these questions so that you can be more focused and profitable in your social networking efforts.

1. Which one or two social networking platforms will you use first and why?

2. How will you define your unique value in each of your profiles?

3. Whom will you influence?

4. What topics will you cover when communicating with your followers? (Have at least four or five topics to pull from, such as motivation, inspiration, new product or service, your thoughts on a topic, in the news, etc.)

5. Do you have any testimonials or product demonstrations you can use to create a one- to three-minute video?

6. Create a schedule where you can dedicate at least five hours a week to preferably two social media platforms to become accustomed to interacting with your followers.

Chapter 15

Sharing Your Wealth –
The Great Responsibility

"Give, and it shall be given unto you; good measure, pressed down, and shaken together, and running over, shall men give into your bosom. For with the same measure that ye mete withal it shall be measured to you again." ~Lk 6:38 KJV

You don't have to be a millionaire to share what God has placed in your hands. My definition of wealth is any asset, whether material, spiritual, or a God-given talent, that can be utilized to benefit and enhance another's well-being in life. God has given treasures to you, and your great responsibility is to share them with as many people as possible. You might be thinking, "But I don't have *enough* to share. I have been waiting for my *Day in the Lord*, but it has not yet arrived." That's okay because though it seems to be taking a long time, it will surely come as you continue to wait in faith. Nothing of any value comes without a price. Jesus paid a price that NO other human being would dare to sacrifice for others they do not know. God's only begotten Son, Jesus, took on the cost for our sins and *shared* His blessings with the rest of the world.

There are only two costs we have to pay in life—our time and our money. Your cost may be waiting on the Lord to purge erroneous beliefs about certain people and perceptions in your life. It could be giving you principles and changing your habits with money to make sure it doesn't slip through your fingers. Your cost might be monetary due to some financial losses while you learn the discipline of better money management. This can also be an example of time because it may take weeks, months, or years to perfect your God-given gift depending on your willingness to be patient about the process. A good thing to remember while you are allowing God's process to take place in you is to be grateful for everything he is transforming for your good and the good of those you will impact.

Having Gratitude Is an Asset

I would be in the wrong if I did not mention the biggest ingredient behind what really makes sharing so spectacular. It's the attitude of gratitude! Being grateful is one of the best seeds that can be sown in the Kingdom of God. This seed is one that is tended directly by God. Once this emotion gets deep down into the heart of any matter, it can change your whole world around you. It's almost like finally seeing the world through rose-colored glasses because it's beautiful and healthy to the soul. Even if you feel you are not happy with where you are today, there is still plenty to be grateful for. Just think for a moment.

Gratitude … we have so much in our lives to be grateful for. Millions of people around the world are merely surviving, hoping to see a day to have life, liberty, and the pursuit of happiness. If you're sitting here reading this book, then you have a roof over your head, you have food in your stomach, and you probably have at least one of these items—your health, someone who loves you, and maybe even an abundance of material comforts.

What else do you have? You have a wealth of strengths, skills, knowledge, and gifts too, whether they have been discovered yet or not.

Now here's a question only you can answer: are you grateful for the things and people you have in your life, right now?

Gratitude is such a powerful emotion. Gratitude has the power to transform your life beyond measure and even extend your health. There is no bigger smile than the one that comes with being thankful in any moment. There is a surge that goes through your body that seems to heal or fill any pain in your body. It's even greater when you share it with others.

When you give back as a result of being grateful, it becomes contagious, and you can't wait to do it again. You become aware of the needs of others, and you seek others in order to serve as many as possible.

When you give back, this opens the floodgates of heaven to allow God to bring blessings into your life. This shows Him that you understand that it is not from you that makes things possible but from Him in which all blessings flow.

When you give back, you leave small legacies that can lead to bigger ones that get passed down from generation to generation.

Gratitude with the spirit of God opens your heart up so wide that those in your presence can do nothing but be blessed. Being grateful is a precursor to having the ability to be an extension of God's hand. You, no matter what level you're on, have the mind-blowing opportunity to improve the lives of others in a number of ways, whether personally or through your product or service, and it is *the* most rewarding success of all!

Let me take just a moment to profile some great people as an example of their philanthropic acts that are revolutionizing and impacting certain parts of the world. Your wealth can afford you to fight for new laws and laws that need to be changed to make your country a better place. You can become the powerhouse behind causes that support your highest beliefs.

A good example is Oprah Winfrey who used her wealth and power to get the *PROTECT Our Children Act, U.S. Senate Bill 1738* passed into law in 2008. She was also instrumental in yet another bill being passed called the National Child Protection Act of 1991 which was signed on December 20, 1993. Could she have done all of this if God had not built up her reputation, following, and wealth to sustain her during her rallying? She also has a school located in Africa for girls that she is raising up as future leaders to combat the poverty and lack that is taking place in certain areas there. Although she does not have children of her own, God gave her many daughters to care for and made her a mother-of-many! It took her time and money to make this all possible. Wealthy people understand that giving back is one of THE greatest responsibilities that make life worth what they've endured to get where they are today.

Winston Churchill said, *"We make a living by what we get; we make a life by what we give."*

The whole point of desiring to become a God-made millionaire should be to further God's kingdom. Out of your love for Him and to do His will, he pours out His love for you by giving you the things you've only dreamed about as your reward. Although He gave you the desire to gain wealth, He already knew whether or not He could trust you because He knows your end from your beginning. The habit of giving is how all the great men and women in the world are reaping great harvests!

Another example of a great giver, once again, would be the Cathy Truett organization, owner of Chick-fil-A, which has done some amazing things as well. He was quoted as saying in an article on the Philanthropy Roundtable website: *"My wife and I were brought up to believe that the more you give, the more you have. Few people actually believe in this, but we do."* In the past, it has also been mentioned that Cathy's WinShape Foundation spent millions on foster homes, college scholarships, a summer camp, and marriage-counseling programs. It is said the company has provided more than $23 million in scholarship assistance to more than 23,000 employees.

When I see efforts like this and the impact they make on people, it makes me press even harder for the prize and high calling the Lord has made on my life! I have never been addicted to drugs, but if it feels anything like the satisfaction of seeing another person's tears of joy, I can understand the insatiableness it causes in those who dare to try it. There are so many more people and organizations that are doing magnificent things in the marketplace in the name of the Lord. Most of them are unknown to the world as a whole. They are diligently serving goodwill to others to bring about the change that God has intended for His people.

As an emerging entrepreneur, I remember when I was at a meeting and the speaker said, "My advice to you all is to give away the house and keep the backyard." This would give the paranoid business owner a heart attack. *Giving away 95 percent of what you know, nowadays, is the new normal. People can find most answers to any questions they have on the Internet.* So don't be afraid to distribute your best up front because the rewards are far greater than having a fire sale. And if you think about it, you probably got a large portion of what you know from the Internet or an expert in your field anyway. Now, the profit comes from your unique delivery and distribution of this same information. Your gifts, skills and talents coupled with this information are what give you the market advantage. In this day and time, in order to get more you have to deliver more! Your customers have come to expect this, from you *and* your competitor.

Charitable Giving

Giving begins right where you are today! If you can give out of your little, then God can trust you with more. The true key to making a million dollars is to serve a million people. Since this book is to help you with your business, then sharing your gifts with as many people as possible will create a momentum and harvest that will eventually overtake you. This is the secret to Oprah Winfrey, Cathy Truett, and many other amazing people or organizations of wealth!

I remember one time in church at The Potter's House, Bishop Jakes announced we were going to have a new building for the children of tomorrow to have a place to grow and worship. Dr. Jazz, the pastor of The Daughter of Thunder church in York, PA, was preaching that day and announced there were people in the room who could commit a large sum of money that would come from their harvest. She announced that someone in that room had the ability to sow $1 million toward the building fund. None other than Tyler Perry was in the congregation and pledged the million dollars. Could he have done that if he had not been obedient to the voice of the Lord and operated in his God-given purpose? No, he would still be searching and listening to those that are living an average life. You best believe he will see that money multiplied in many ways to give him what he needs to complete his mission in God. I am sure this was not the first time he had given a charitable contribution of this size. It is an amazing act to be able to give out of your abundance and still have enough left over to live the life you could only dream of. If you ever get the opportunity to meet Tyler Perry, ask him how he's living! He'll probably tell you a God-favored life.

Volunteering for Goodness' Sake

I have found this to be an amazing way to get exposure for a particular gift, skill, or talent you would love to exercise. I remember when I was changing careers and going from the information technology field to work more in the financial market. I didn't have any history, education, or training in this area. I knew my time was up in my current career, but I didn't know how to safely make the switch. I want you to know that I use the word "safely" loosely because it is a gamble and a risk, but you know deep down inside that no matter what it takes, it has to be done. So I embarked on a journey to step into my new future that God was leading me into. First of all, I started applying for careers that dealt with coaching, teaching, and money management, but because I had no experience, my chances looked very slim. I started doing my research to see how I could serve and get the experience and exposure for where I wanted to go. Over time, I found that volunteering might be the way to go. Volunteering is a great way to know if you are operating out of passion because if you can do this and not get paid but feel awesome until you see your checking account, then you best believe this career path is the one!

I kept searching and meeting with people until one day I met with a representative from an organization that offered financial empowerment to women and some brave men. I felt what they were doing was right in alignment with what I wanted to do. I was initially meeting with her to promote their program to a group of women I would bring together for money-management lessons. So I decided I would take the class to see what it had to offer before getting a group of women together. To my surprise, I ended up loving the class and could see myself facilitating a class of my own. Eventually, I became one of their volunteer teachers because I saw the growth and experience I would gain from helping others in this area. I felt inside this was my next step toward purpose! I was working and teaching in their organization and loving every minute of it. Was I scared initially? Yes, but I kept moving through the fear. Did I do everything right in the beginning? No, but I got better over time based on the participants' hunger and feedback. God made it possible for me to try on my purpose to see if it fit. I ended up being the first volunteer who ever had a 100 percent participant graduation. I loved them and they loved me according to their feedback and hunger for more. I grew in so many ways and got rid of my fear of speaking in front of others (although I still get nervous). I don't think the nervousness ever goes away when you are consistently thinking about how to become an even better person, especially if you are serious about serving others and making a difference.

The more seeds of giving you plant in others, the greater your harvest. There is something called "The Law of Reciprocity." This basically means that whatever you sow, you will reap and in a greater measure. A better example of this would be the opening scripture of this chapter as according to Luke 6:38, "*Give and it shall be given to you, pressed down, shaken together and running over.*" There is no way you can sow kindness, wisdom, finances, mercy, and so forth into anyone and not reap the benefits of it in time. You may not receive it back from the same person, but this law requires that it will come back to you.

Tithing – A Privilege

God has made a way for us to learn more about what giving means by allowing us to give out of our finances to a people or organization. Now, you might be thinking, "But I don't go to church. I just read my Bible and live a godly life all on my own." Okay, this is all well and good, but everyone needs to be poured into by someone, whether paid or not paid, but most spiritual counsel comes from a shepherd of God. If you are being spiritually fed from a pastor, minister, teacher, or organization, then you should be sharing at least 10 percent of your monies amongst them. If you don't have any money, then you are probably sleeping under a bridge. There is no better way to increase your income than to share it with others. I can't guarantee *when* the increase will come, but it will come!

I am indeed a recipient of tithing. I believe tithing is the umbrella that protects our family through any times of financial lack or hardship. When I lost my job due to a massive layoff from a company I worked for in my previous career, I had become an avid tither and couldn't be persuaded it was not the right thing to do to honor and thank God for all I had. We were saving for a down payment on a home, and I had $1,000 I was about to use to pay down a debt. Then God asked me to give to this particular church to help them in their endeavors. It wasn't even a church I attended, but their pastor was speaking on that day. I tried to reason with God, but my reasoning didn't sit well with my spirit, so I sowed it in faith. Was it easy? Not at all! But it was a learning process about the ways of God.

About two months later, and about one week before the closing on our newly built home in Texas, I got laid off from my job. I didn't know what to do. I needed that next paycheck to complete the money we needed for closing. I kept rolling the thought over in my mind as to how this could happen to me after trusting God to show me the way, but a peace came over me that said, "God knew this was going to happen, and because of your obedience in tithing to take care of his house, He will take care of yours." As they were packing up all my belongings and told me goodbye after the team meeting, the consequences this could have on our family hadn't hit me yet.

While I was driving home, it finally hit me that I had just lost my source of income. I had to pull over because I started crying as if a dam had broken. I cried for what seemed like hours. All of a sudden, the sun came out so brightly it was as though someone was trying to get my attention. I felt like a dark cloud was hovering over me, but this light was so bright I couldn't do anything but start to dry my eyes in peace. The scriptures and the love of God started to overwhelm any feelings of fear and discouragement that were trying to wage a war against me. I sat a little longer, thinking back over all the times I trusted God and how every situation had turned out for my good. The closing attorney never asked if I still had a job, and I had received a severance package with four months' pay as a result of the layoff. I later realized that the $1,000 I let go of was the catalyst for the finances God would put in my hands for a future season. God is so good! He knows what we need before we ever ask. Who wouldn't want to serve a God like this!

If you sow love, you reap love. If you sow mercy, you reap mercy. If you sow money, you reap money. If the farmer plants corn, he gets corn back. Can you sow time? Yes, you can. If you sow time with others, this will come back to you when you need it. The Old and the New Testaments talk about tithing and giving of your income to keep God's house and business operating in its fullness, such as in Malachi 3:10-12 and Proverbs 3:9-10, which speak of giving and testing His word and giving out of your wealth. By contributing, you are helping God's Kingdom to grow the number of souls being saved and finding help when you need it. As in Chapter 10, the scripture says, "Money answereth all things." So if you are not keen on sowing the 10 percent, then sow what you have, but just remember, "Whoever sows sparingly will also reap sparingly, and whoever sows generously will also reap generously." Because of your giving and willingness, God will set you up to be a display and distribution center for His Kingdom and glory!

God's Distribution Centers

God has a need for dedicated and committed people to carry out his will. He needs people He can trust to give to others—including organizations— the financial assistance they need. Followers of Christ are the hands, eyes, ears, and touch of God, which makes up the Body of Christ as Christ is the universal head of us all. Some people have a problem with letting go of their money to someone or to a cause they are unfamiliar with. It's not so much about having money from God only to give it all away and not spend any on your desires. Giving financial assistance to charities is more of a grateful and fulfilling part of becoming complete in the fullness of God. As depicted in **Figure 15.1**, you can see how God uses many vessels to complete caring for the mind, body, and soul of those who need Him. These distribution centers are set up to save those in need and the lost. Without these methods of distribution, the world would be in utter chaos and decay. Each center of giving distributes the love of God as they are told who's behind the giving. Never let the praise be upon you, but give it to our amazing God to glorify Him. This allows those who are on the receiving end to have their thanksgiving go to the rightful place to gain the recognition of God. This is to help facilitate their own willingness to find sufficiency in Christ.

As you can see, there is an opportunity for you to become one of God's distribution centers too. Starting off by giving from what you have paves the way for God to deliver more material and financial possessions into your hands. It is indeed an honor to be chosen by God to be His ambassador and center of hope. People will come to know you, and your influence will grow in the community, therefore giving God a voice through you to make a major impact in a strategic area.

Let me clue you in on how God will prove if you are ready to distribute for Him. He may ask you to give to someone you have never met before. He will send them to you in their time of need, which is appointed. You may have just received a bit of money and are now ready to allocate it to something you want or think you need. Although God made a way for you to receive that money; He wants to see where your heart is. This proves that you are attached to His will and not the money. This has happened to me on many occasions, and I tried to tell Him I needed the money for something important. But each time I surrendered and trusted the voice of God to do what was asked or expected of me, it made my future worth every bit of discomfort I experienced. I think back on those situations and see God was allowing me to release what was in my hand so that He could release what was in His hand—but multiplied. One thing you can count on is that God will never ask you for anything He hasn't already given you. So don't get bent out of shape if someone asks for something you don't have because you just may not have it. You will know when it's God because when He gives it to you, He will call for it soon after. I like to say He is a God who knows His creation. He knows that if He doesn't call for it right away, we will spend it on something.

The whole point of God giving you the ability to get wealth is simply that He wants you to share and distribute it possibly on a grander scale with those who are less fortunate so that He can show them the life they were meant to live. If and when you decide that no matter what, you will follow God to the ends of the Earth and not focus on your own agenda, you will see the miracle workings of God in your life. Allow God to transform your heart, mind, and soul so that He can share His wealth with you so that you can live like never before!

God's Distribution Centers

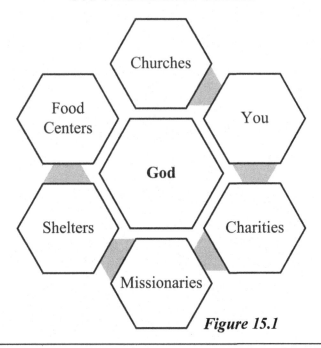

Figure 15.1

Exercise 15 – God-made Millionaire Exercise

1. What is your vision for giving back as a result of your success and wealth?

2. If you are not operating in a profession that is rewarding for you, then look to volunteer at an organization that is doing what you know to be your passion. Google non-profit or entry-level employers that can get you started in the right direction.

Conclusion

By the grace God has given me, I laid a foundation as a wise builder, and someone else is building on it. But each one should build with care.[11] For no one can lay any foundation other than the one already laid, which is Jesus Christ.[12] If anyone builds on this foundation using gold, silver, costly stones, wood, hay or straw,[13] their work will be shown for what it is, because the Day will bring it to light. It will be revealed with fire, and the fire will test the quality of each person's work.[14] If what has been built survives, the builder will receive a reward.[15] If it is burned up, the builder will suffer loss but yet will be saved—even though only as one escaping through the flames. ~ I Corin 3:10-15

Everything that has been written in this book is for your benefit to help you reach the point in life that brings you fulfillment through entrepreneurship. I can bring you the strategies, principles, and even resources, but ultimately the choice to succeed is up to you. I gave you the foundation for *all* success, and that is to learn to trust and follow our Lord and Savior Jesus Christ. If you decide to skip this step and go for the personal glory of doing business by any means necessary, the scripture above states that in time your efforts will be tried by fire. So when trouble comes and there is nothing for you to fall back on but yourself, everyone will see what you were made of, which could have been to earn a buck through any means necessary. The scripture says you will make it through—you may suffer some losses—but you will survive to try it again.

Being a God-made millionaire is not just about the money. It's about having access to all that is His! If you have a desire to put new computers in elementary schools that lack funding for kids in the city of Newark, New Jersey, then God can help you get the $200,000 funding it will take to help them. If you decide you want to assemble a team to build a village of homes in an underprivileged area in Africa, then God can help you with the $1.5 million funding through your business or investors. He knows where it all is and can point it, at His word, in your direction. So having a concern to be only *financially* wealthy is just a small request to a God who has unlimited access to all resources, such as people, places, materials, cash, ideas, and power, to make it all happen. So don't ever fret about getting what you need from God as long as it includes the lives of others!

It's all about being transformed into the image of Christ. This is when you can partake in the riches that God has given us through Jesus. You will now have everything you need to accomplish your destiny. This in turn makes you valuable and influential in your designated area of business. You will then attract others that will help you achieve success.

God is doing a new thing that is promoting and pushing people all over the world to become the emerging entrepreneurs He created you to be. God is pouring out His spirit in the Earth like never before, and it is time for each and every person to start the change they desire to see. The change brings about the security and financial needs that Jesus died and rose to give us all. Every person possesses the creative ability to devise something that can change the world around them. But whatever that *something* is, it is unique to you. As I said before, is entrepreneurship for everyone? No, it is not. But for those that know it, **now is the time** to put action behind those thoughts.

God has set you apart so that you can do that which He created you to do. He has been knocking at your door for quite some time, and you may not have decided to follow Him yet. Finding your purpose is the end of being lost; it's the end of doing things your way and getting nowhere. God continues to show Himself in various ways to His people, but it is up to you to accept the call. Slowly but surely you will find the world cannot help you, but God's signs and wonders will come to show you the way.

I would like to close and share a dream with you concerning your decision to trust Jesus for your change. This is very indicative to your journey to purpose in God.

God-made Millionaire Moment:

In this dream, the sun was starting to go down. I was standing on a porch in front of what looked to be an end apartment unit with a screen door. I knew it was a familiar place because there were adults and kids in the house with whom I felt comfortable; as they peeked out the door, I was not alarmed. The porch was elevated above the ground about three feet or so with about four steps leading out. I was standing on the concrete porch in shorts and a shirt with no shoes on. I knew that I was supposed to step off the porch to go somewhere, but I had reasons for not wanting to go.

Number one, I looked at my feet and saw I was wearing no shoes. I was concerned that my feet would hurt or get cut. It was apparent to me that I did not have any shoes in my possession to put on; therefore, I would have to go barefoot if I was going to go at all. While I was contemplating, it was getting darker. The second reason I did not want to go was that I was becoming afraid because I did not know what lay beyond the porch. I felt comfortable staying right where I was, but something inside me kept telling me I had to make the step. It was what I was supposed to do at that time.

The path from the porch looked so dark and unfamiliar, especially with this narrow path running between the porch and this wooded area of tall trees. As I decided to make the journey, I kept arguing with myself that I couldn't step on the ground with no shoes because I would get stuck by sticks and rocks. All of a sudden, I began to see this black wolf in the darkness as I started down the steps. I decided to back up and get back onto the porch. As I backed up, I lost sight of the wolf. I couldn't see where he went because it was so dark. Something within me said, "Go ahead. He won't hurt you."

At that thought, I decided to step off the porch, and there appeared the wolf growling at me. Fear raged in me so rampantly that I was paralyzed! But for some reason, I knew I couldn't go back, so I kept walking forward and the wolf disappeared. I walked quickly through the tall trees down the narrow path, which turned into a trail.

I followed the trail until I began to see a light beyond the trees at the end of the path. I walked even faster to quickly get where I was going. As I got closer, I heard people talking. Once I was able to see a bit better, I saw people wearing bright yellowish-gold colored shorts and shirts. People were standing all around in this open stadium, some of them on a concrete platform with railings as though they were spectators, and others were on a running track. Everyone had on the same clothing. As I continued to examine my surroundings, I realized they were dressed in athletic gear. One of them standing on the platform watching the race turned around and saw me coming. He said, "Where have you been? We have been waiting for you." To my surprise, he gave me my own athletic gear to put on that matched everyone else's in order to join them. This is where I woke up.

Lesson Learned:

The moral of the dream is that when deciding to trust God, you will feel as though you don't want to leave the comfort zone of your present life, family, or friends. But you have to understand that to follow God is to leave everyone else behind—for good or maybe for a season—to see what He has in store for you. After choosing to trust God, there will be a fear that may come over you that tries to prevent you from venturing into the unknown. We often like to stay where we feel we will be safe or comfortable. You will have to take the initial journey with God alone because you are the *sole* decision maker to accept your destiny—not those around you. Deciding to continue to follow God's calling will lead you through dark places, but the path He puts you on is holy ground. It has been spiritually crafted by God! If you follow the voice of God, as in the dream, he will continue to move you forward, and you will not be hurt to the point of destruction. Just know He has already prepared the way. He will lead you out of a place of fear and into a place of courage. You will realize that you are not the only person to take this journey. That's what the path represented as it turned into a trail that had been travelled by others. All those in the stadium had also made the decision to trust and follow God. All of them can be considered the decision makers and mighty athletes of God that were waiting for their instructions to discover purpose. And once you say *yes* to God's calling on your life, there will be a suit of glory waiting for you on your journey as well!

Become determined to never give up on your dream!. You must sacrifice whatever it takes to honor God in your life. If, indeed, you are called to be a God-made millionaire then the time is now for you to rise up creation and take your rightful place in the Kingdom.

My Prayer for You ...

"Heavenly Father, I pray that those reading this book will find the answers that they are seeking to have a successful life. I pray that each one that is willing to take the leap of faith to believe that you are the one and only God of this universe will enter into your space and time and learn of your mighty ways. I pray that as they surrender their heart, mind, and soul, they will experience a life of blessings that have long awaited their acceptance. May their dreams, goals, desires, and prayers to become an emerging and successful entrepreneur not go unanswered. May they find strength and peace in you when they are weak and feel they cannot go on. Let the angels of heaven come to their bidding to carry out your will according to the scriptures they believe to be true. I pray that they not be allowed to leave this Earth until purpose has been discovered, in their lives and for your glory. In Jesus' name I pray. Amen.

Appendix A – Funding For Women

As of the writing of this book, here are ten places that have lending programs for women in business and that make microloans to women business owners, minorities, and small businesses.

1. **ACCION USA**
2. **The Delaware Access Program**
3. **Grameen Bank** - New York
4. **Illinois Minority, Women, and Disabled Participation Loan Program**
5. **Mississippi Development Authority**
6. **Key Bank**
7. **Massachusetts Capital Access Program**
8. **The Loan Fund – Alternative Lending for New Mexico Women Entrepreneurs**
9. **Wisconsin Women's Business Initiative Corporation** (WBIC)
10. **Women's Economic Ventures**

Appendix B – SEO Tools Resources

➢ **Google Webmaster Tools** – mainly for webmasters but allow you to be diligent about checking the indexing and visibility of your website

➢ **Google AdWords** – allows you to place text ads that appear when potential customers type certain keywords into the Google Search Engine

➢ **Google Analytics** – provides website statistics about traffic that you receive or drive to your website with text ads, blogs, banners, or links

➢ **OpensiteExplorer.org** – daily report, limited to five if using FREE version

➢ **Moz** (www.moz.com) – receive data about your social media, rankings, links, and traffic that is organic vs. paid

➢ **Schema.org & Schema.org/localbusiness** – for business contact information

➢ **Magesticseo.org** – show backlink history for comparison, keyword checker included

➢ **Google.com/placesforbusiness** – if you have a physical location

➢ **Getlisted.org** – allows you to know how your local business looks across the web for local recognition of name, address, and phone number

➢ – Check to see if your website is mobile device effective

Appendix C – Did you know the following are Christian businesses?

Forever 21 – http://www.forever21.com/
Tyson Foods – http://www.tysonfoods.com/
Chick-fil-A – http://www.chick-fil-a.com/
Mary Kay – http://www.marykay.com/
In-N-Out Burger – http://www.in-n-out.com/
Timberland – http://www.timberland.com/
Alaska Air – http://www.alaskaair.com/
Marriott – http://www.marriott.com/
Curves – http://www.curves.com/
Jet Blue – http://www.jetblue.com/
Interstate Batteries – http://www.interstatebatteries.com/
Hobby Lobby – http://www.hobbylobby.com/
Toms of Maine – http://www.tomsofmainestore.com/
ServiceMaster (includes Merry Maids, Terminix, and American Home Shield) – http://www.servicemaster.com/
H.E.B. (a grocery-store chain with hundreds of stores in Texas and Mexico) – http://www.heb.com/

Appendix D – Business Affirmations

Affirmations help bring your mind and body into alignment to move in unison with a focused purpose. Here are a few affirmations I use on any given day to keep me on track in business. You may need these only for a season, but they can be used to move you strategically forward to achieve your goals.

1. _____ *(Your Company)* is a multimillion-dollar business.

2. _____ *(Your Workshop)* is growing in participant attendance by leaps and bounds.

3. _____ *(Your Coaching Program)* are sought after for the value I give and the results people are achieving and receiving.

4. I am constantly creating products and services that benefit my client/customer.

5. I wake up daily to see sales receipts and orders in my business and on my website.

6. _____ *(Your Company)* is getting rave reviews for its value in the marketplace.

7. I deserve to be followed by those who need my help because I am passionate about their well-being.

8. I am a leader that can bring people along with me to help them realize their dreams.

9. People are following me because I am talking, acting, and coming across as a leader in my community/business.

10. My marketing efforts are effectively bringing people into my business.

11. I now know what my target market is thinking and needing. I know what their biggest pains, problems, challenges, dreams, and desires are.

12. I am a God-made millionaire.

References

Introduction

1. Bhasin, Kim. Meet S. Truett Cathy, The 91-Year-Old Billionaire Behind Chick-fil-A. 23 July 2012. <http://www.businessinsider.com/meet-chick-fil-a-founder-s-truett-cathy-2012-7?op=1#ixzz2oQlyonT1>.

Chapter 1

1. Bhasin, Kim. Meet S. Truett Cathy, The 91-Year-Old Billionaire Behind Chick-fil-A. 23 July 2012. <http://www.businessinsider.com/meet-chick-fil-a-founder-s-truett-cathy-2012-7?op=1#ixzz2oQlyonT1>.

2. Fry, Richard and Kochhar, Rakesh. America's wealth gap between middle-income and upper-income families is widest on record. 17 December 2014. 15 January 2015 <http://www.pewresearch.org/fact-tank/2014/12/17/wealth-gap-upper-middle-income/>.

3. Nepo, Mark. Oprah and Mark Nepo, Parts 1 and 2 Oprah Winfrey. 10 November 2013.

Chapter 4

1. http://www.biography.com/people/walt-disney-9275533

2. http://www.biography.com/people/mary-kay-ash-197044#early-career

Chapter 7

1. http://www.inc.com/sara-blakely/how-sara-blakley-started-spanx.html

Chapter 8

1. Creating A Successful Marketing Strategy for your small new business by Stanley F. Stasch, Loyola University Chicago, 2010, Praeger, an imprint of ABC-CLIO, LLC

Chapter 9

1. http://www.oprah.com/pressroom/
   Oprah-Calls-for-Action-Against-Child-Predators#ixzz2p1puSY7e

2. Do You Need An EIN? http://www.irs.gov/Businesses/
   Small-Businesses-&-Self-Employed/Do-You-Need-an-EIN?

Chapter 10

1. http://www.irs.gov/Businesses/Small-Businesses-&-Self-Employed/
   Do-You-Need-an-EIN

Chapter 11

1. *A Popular History of American Invention.* (Waldemar Kaempffert, ed.) Vol II, New York Scribner's Sons, 1924, pg. 385-386.

2. http://www.madamcjwalker.com/bios/madam-c-j-walker/

3. http://www.mylifetime.com/movies/the-gabby-douglas-story/video/beyond-the-headlines-the-gabby-douglas-story Movie TV

Chapter 14

1. http://www.socialbakers.com/blog/1749-photos-make-up-93-of-the-most-engaging-posts-on-facebook

2. *"Why Do We Share Stories, News, and Information With Others?"* Psychological Science- Journal of Association for Psychological Science, June 28, 2011, http://www.psychologicalscience.org/index.php/news/releases/why-do-we-share-our-feelings-with-others.html

Chapter 15

1. http://www.oprah.com/pressroom/Oprah-Calls-for-Action-Against-Child-Predators

2. http://www.oprah.com/entertainment/Building-a-Dream

About the Author

Letitia Harris' passion for business began in her youth. In elementary school, she bought candy at a low price and resold it to classmates for a premium. She created bracelets and necklaces from her mom's bamboo curtains and sold them to friends. She remembers how it felt as a kid to be able to exchange goods for money. It was a wonderful feeling to know she had something others wanted to buy! In both cases, though, the doors closed. The candy shop closed because the kids got wise to her profit margins, and the bamboo jewelry shop closed because her mom found out she was deliberately destroying her bamboo curtain for its material.

Letitia is an author, speaker, coach, trainer, and advocate for spiritual, entrepreneurial, and financial empowerment. It is her passion to help others use these three traits to gain mastery in a weakened world. From her own desires to understand *why* she was created, she embarked on a journey to discover profound spiritual and intellectual answers that would be the catalyst to lead others to personal and financial freedom.

She graduated magna cum laude from DeVry University. She has a background that includes over ten years in the information technology industry, over fifteen years in customer service, and over seven years in real estate and investing. She has owned several businesses, whose successes and failures are a shining light to her clients and students.

She has set out to help emerging entrepreneurs overcome life's obstacles that stand in the way of being spiritually led and financially free. She believes that with the right help, tools, and resources, anyone can live their dream of being a successful entrepreneur all while living a life they've only dreamed of.

Letitia also volunteers and teaches students for a nationally known non-profit organization on how to be debt-free by understanding the basic principles and practices of having better money-management skills. She teaches students how to transform their financial fears and inadequacies into powerful strategies and disciplines that increase their income and confidence. She believes that mastering your money in your personal life is a precursor to having a successful business that actually earns profits.

Letitia is the founder of ***Rise Up Creation Intl.***™ She moved from Atlanta, Georgia, to Frisco, Texas, where she now lives with her husband, two children, and their cocker spaniel.

For More Information

Letitia Harris wants to hear from you! For more information about Letitia Harris' trainings, programs, products, and seminars, or to find out how to book Letitia for your next event, contact:

Rise Up Creation Intl
8811 Teel Pkwy, Ste #5023
Frisco, Texas 75035
Phone: (877) 406-4636
www.letitiaharris.com

TRUE DIRECTIONS
An affiliate of Tarcher Books

OUR MISSION

Tarcher's mission has always been to publish books
that contain great ideas. Why? Because:

GREAT LIVES BEGIN WITH GREAT IDEAS

At Tarcher, we recognize that many talented authors, speakers,
educators, and thought-leaders share this mission and deserve to be
published – many more than Tarcher can reasonably publish ourselves.
True Directions is ideal for authors and books that increase awareness,
raise consciousness, and inspire others to live their ideals and passions.

Like Tarcher, True Directions books are designed to do three things:
inspire, inform, and motivate.

Thus, True Directions is an ideal way for these important voices to
bring their messages of hope, healing, and help to the world.

Every book published by True Directions– whether it is non-fiction, memoir,
novel, poetry or children's book – continues Tarcher's mission to publish works
that bring positive change in the world. We invite you to join our mission.

For more information, see the True Directions website:
www.iUniverse.com/TrueDirections/SignUp

Be a part of Tarcher's community to bring positive change in this world!
See exclusive author videos, discover new and exciting books, learn about
upcoming events, connect with author blogs and websites, and more!
www.tarcherbooks.com

TRUE DIRECTIONS
AN AFFILIATE OF TARCHER BOOKS

Printed in the United States
By Bookmasters